Automatic Cyberbullying Detection:

Emerging Research and Opportunities

Michal E. Ptaszynski
Kitami Institute of Technology, Japan

Fumito Masui
Kitami Institute of Technology, Japan

A volume in the Advances in Human and Social Aspects of Technology (AHSAT) Book Series

IGI Global
DISSEMINATOR OF KNOWLEDGE

Published in the United States of America by
IGI Global
Information Science Reference (an imprint of IGI Global)
701 E. Chocolate Avenue
Hershey PA, USA 17033
Tel: 717-533-8845
Fax: 717-533-8661
E-mail: cust@igi-global.com
Web site: http://www.igi-global.com

Library of Congress Cataloging-in-Publication Data

Names: Ptaszynski, Michal E., 1981- author. | Masui, Fumito, 1966- author.
Title: Automatic cyberbullying detection : emerging research and opportunities / by Michal E. Ptaszynski and Fumito Masui.
Description: Hershey : Information Science Reference, [2018]
Identifiers: LCCN 2017037450| ISBN 9781522552499 (hardcover) | ISBN 9781522552505 (ebook)
Subjects: LCSH: Cyberbullying--Research--Methodology. | Data mining.
Classification: LCC HV6773.15.C92 P83 2018 | DDC 302.34/30285--dc23 LC record available at https://lccn.loc.gov/2017037450

This book is published in the IGI Global book series Advances in Human and Social Aspects of Technology (AHSAT) (ISSN: 2328-1316; eISSN: 2328-1324)

British Cataloguing in Publication Data
A Cataloguing in Publication record for this book is available from the British Library.

Advances in Human and Social Aspects of Technology (AHSAT) Book Series

ISSN:2328-1316
EISSN:2328-1324

Editor-in-Chief: Ashish Dwivedi, The University of Hull, UK

MISSION

In recent years, the societal impact of technology has been noted as we become increasingly more connected and are presented with more digital tools and devices. With the popularity of digital devices such as cell phones and tablets, it is crucial to consider the implications of our digital dependence and the presence of technology in our everyday lives.

The **Advances in Human and Social Aspects of Technology (AHSAT) Book Series** seeks to explore the ways in which society and human beings have been affected by technology and how the technological revolution has changed the way we conduct our lives as well as our behavior. The AHSAT book series aims to publish the most cutting-edge research on human behavior and interaction with technology and the ways in which the digital age is changing society.

COVERAGE

- Technoself
- ICTs and social change
- Information ethics
- Activism and ICTs
- Technology Dependence
- Cyber Bullying
- Philosophy of technology
- Human-Computer Interaction
- Computer-Mediated Communication
- ICTs and human empowerment

IGI Global is currently accepting manuscripts for publication within this series. To submit a proposal for a volume in this series, please contact our Acquisition Editors at Acquisitions@igi-global.com or visit: http://www.igi-global.com/publish/.

The Advances in Human and Social Aspects of Technology (AHSAT) Book Series (ISSN 2328-1316) is published by IGI Global, 701 E. Chocolate Avenue, Hershey, PA 17033-1240, USA, www.igi-global.com. This series is composed of titles available for purchase individually; each title is edited to be contextually exclusive from any other title within the series. For pricing and ordering information please visit http://www.igi-global.com/book-series/advances-human-social-aspects-technology/37145. Postmaster: Send all address changes to above address.

Titles in this Series

For a list of additional titles in this series, please visit:
https://www.igi-global.com/book-series/advances-human-social-aspects-technology/37145

Handbook of Research on Technology Integration in the Global World
Efosa C. Idemudia (Arkansas Tech University, USA)
Information Science Reference • ©2019 • 535pp • H/C (ISBN: 9781522563679) • US $195.00

Returning to Interpersonal Dialogue and Understanding Human Communication in the ...
Michael A. Brown Sr. (Florida International University, USA) and Leigh Hersey (University of Louisiana at Monroe, USA)
Information Science Reference • ©2019 • 299pp • H/C (ISBN: 9781522541684) • US $180.00

Intimacy and Developing Personal Relationships in the Virtual World
Rejani Thudalikunnil Gopalan (Gujarat Forensic Sciences University, India)
Information Science Reference • ©2019 • 355pp • H/C (ISBN: 9781522540472) • US $175.00

Handbook of Research on Children's Consumption of Digital Media
Gülşah Sarı (Abant Izzet Baysal University, Turkey)
Information Science Reference • ©2019 • 423pp • H/C (ISBN: 9781522557333) • US $225.00

Handbook of Research on Multicultural Perspectives on Gender and Aging
Rekha Pande (University of Hyderabad, India) and Theo van der Weide (Radboud University Nijmegen, The Netherlands)
Information Science Reference • ©2018 • 361pp • H/C (ISBN: 9781522547723) • US $225.00

Narratives and the Role of Philosophy in Cross-Disciplinary Studies Emerging Research ...
Ana-Maria Pascal (Regent's University London, UK)
Information Science Reference • ©2018 • 198pp • H/C (ISBN: 9781522555728) • US $135.00

Information Visualization Techniques in the Social Sciences and Humanities
Veslava Osinska (Nicolaus Copernicus University, Poland) and Grzegorz Osinski (College of Social and Media Culture, Poland)
Information Science Reference • ©2018 • 356pp • H/C (ISBN: 9781522549901) • US $195.00

For an entire list of titles in this series, please visit:
https://www.igi-global.com/book-series/advances-human-social-aspects-technology/37145

IGI Global
DISSEMINATOR OF KNOWLEDGE

701 East Chocolate Avenue, Hershey, PA 17033, USA
Tel: 717-533-8845 x100 • Fax: 717-533-8661
E-Mail: cust@igi-global.com • www.igi-global.com

Table of Contents

Foreword

Interest of scholars and researchers in hostile behaviours among school children and teenagers started in mid-seventies of 20th century. It began with a series of suicides of teenage boys in Norwegian schools. Many of those tragic cases originated with unpleasant and aggressive treatment of the victims by school peers. It is obvious that in a group of people quarrels or other unpleasant situations sometimes happen. Normally they do not lead to serious problems and consequences such as the ones described above or similar (e.g. mental health problems, refusal to go to school, etc.). However, in some cases – to use the metaphor – on the sea of this "normal" situations we may come across a rock that can break a ship. This rock is bullying understood as a serious peer violence. The concept of bullying has been established after Norwegian cases by a psychologist Dan Olweus who defined it giving three characteristics: repetition (aggression is introduced multiple times against the same victim), imbalance of power (perpetrators are stronger or perceived as stronger by a victim) and intention (perpetrators are willing to harm a victim). Traditionally the concept included physical and verbal aggression followed by relational aggression (e.g. exclusion from the group). The concept has been adopted by many researchers and during over forty years a large knowledge base has been gathered about it. The most important finding based on analysis has proved links between bullying involvement and mental health outcomes in victims. Those include serious problems such as depression, psychosomatic problems, social anxiety, etc. Many of those, as longitudinal research show, may also have negative impact after many years also in adulthood. This makes bullying a serious educational and social problem. There were also a lot of research looking for characteristics of bullying actors – perpetrators, victims and those who witness bullying – bystanders. The research results have been translated in some widely known anti-bullying initiatives such as Bullying Prevention Program, Kiva or Zero. Those programs have proved to be effective but still new solutions are sought, particularly to some specific issues (e.g. bullying against young people with special needs).

Beginning of 21st century brought new kind of bullying perpetrated by means of Web 2.0. Some young people started to use computer devices and Internet instruments to extend the "school yard" or face-to-face bullying. The public and scientific interest started again with some serious cases widely presented in the media. They brought attention but also raised some moral panic at the beginning.

Under the large umbrella of *cyberbullying* many different kinds of aggressive acts are included, such as publishing visual material presenting a victim in an unpleasant or uncomfortable situation, bad comments in social networking sites, revealing secrets online, etc. After over a decade of research we can say that cyberbullying should not be treated separately from traditional bullying. There is an overlap – those being cyber perpetrators are almost always also face-to-face perpetrators. The same mechanism refers to victims – most of them experience both kinds of victimization that makes their situation even worse. However, cyberbullying brings also some characteristics that are perceived as new, although they have been present in traditional bullying as well, though to smaller extent. Due to features of online communication that is ongoing and permanent (materials may be available for a long time) a victim suffers from ongoing attacks. In the past he or she was relatively safe when not in the presence of perpetrators. Additionally, the compromising materials may as well be seen far outside the peer group making the situation even more intimidating. It is also easier to feel more anonymous on the Internet (very rarely being fully anonymous in technical sense). This feeling of anonymity can cause disinhibition in perpetrators (they do more than they would do face-to-face) and further helplessness on victims' site (as they are sometimes not sure who is attacking).

As society we are now at the stage when, based on research results, we need to find effective measures to prevent cyberbullying. As a researcher of cyberbullying for almost ten years, who conducted numerous international and national research I am also at this stage of my work. I look for tailored educational solutions for students and teachers that should provide them knowledge and competences to deal with the issue. But this is from the social science perspective. Cyberbullying as such can also be viewed from a technical perspective – so inclusion of researchers from technical and informatics areas should be very rewarding.

Three years ago I was very glad to be invited for cooperation by the team of Michal Ptaszynski and Professor Fumito Masui from Kitami Institute of Technology. They were involved in the research on automatic detection of cyberbullying incidents in online communication and needed some social science insight that would be helpful for their work. I have been invited to Kitami and gave some lectures and had some fruitful scientific discussions with the Kitami research team members. This proved that such multidisciplinary cooperation is always rewarding. It opened the new door for cyberbullying prevention – the software and methods prepared by the team may be used in different ways – as detection software for school administrators but also as the tool for young people to help them become more reflective of the quality of their own online communication and its impact on other users.

Surely, this can be achieved only when carefully planned and implemented, and used as a part of holistic approach including also other solutions (e.g. educational ones).

I am very grateful for the invitation to cooperate by Professor Fumito Masui and Michal Ptaszynski and at the same time very happy that the book presenting their valuable work is now available for readers.

Jacek Pyzalski
Adam Mickiewicz University in Poznan, Poland & Nofer Institute of Occupational Medicine, Poland

Jacek Pyzalski *is a Doctor of Humanities in the field of Pedagogy (UAM, 2012, PhD in Humanities in the Field of Pedagogy – University of Lodz, 2002). He is a professor of the Adam Mickiewicz University in Poznan. He works at the Department of Educational Studies at the University (UAM in Poznań) and is an adjunct at the Institute of Occupational Medicine in Łódź at the National Center for Health Promotion at Work. He is also a court mediator, author of numerous publications, trainer in the area of communication and difficult behaviors, and an expert in the field of media education. He is a member of the Polish Society of Media Education, and his research interests relate to the issues of electronic aggression, new media, school communication, health promotion, cyberbullying among young people. He is also the author of the first monograph on the Polish market concerning electronic aggression, Electronic Aggression Among Children and Adolescents (GWP, Sopot 2011).*

Preface

It was evening of September the 3rd, 2009. The banquet of PACLING 2009, the 9th Conference of the Pacific Association for Computational Linguistics, held on the 13th floor of Hotel Monterey Edelhof in Sapporo, Japan. It is sometimes said that conference banquets rarely result in actual further research cooperation. This banquet was different. At least for us – Fumito Masui and Michal E. Ptaszynski – two researchers, who accidentally sat next to each other. Michal was a young researcher in the fields of Natural Language Processing and Affective Computing, trying to find new areas to apply his newly developed affect analysis techniques. Fumito, Associate Professor of Kitami Institute of Technology, was looking for someone to push forward his project on automatic detection and mitigation of cyberbullying.

The story this research begins two years before our first meeting. The so called Takigawa High School Incident, which happened in July of 2007, spurred a country-wide discussion about cyberbullying in Japan. In the incident a 17-year-old boy, after being bullied by four of his classmates on an informal school Website, committed a suicide, by jumping from the school roof during classes. One of the results of the social discussion which began after the incident was creating a national program for prevention of bullying and cyberbullying in schools, founded by the Ministry of Education, Culture, Sports, Science and Technology (later: MEXT) in Japan. However, no matter how well designed, a policy or a social program on its own would not be effective if not supported by specific practical solutions. We, Fumito Masui, Michal E. Ptaszynski and other team members became the first to tackle the problem of cyberbullying with the use of practical technological solutions based on Artificial Intelligence, Natural Language Processing and Affective Computing.

We began the challenge by discussing the problem with the staff of Human Right Center in Mie Prefecture, Japan – a nonprofit organization concerned with human rights and mental health of citizens. The discussions revealed that the main ways cyberbullying is realized are harmful entries appearing on informal school Websites and electronic bulletin boards (BBS). The BBS in themselves were not a problem *per se*. Such informal school Websites have been widely used by school pupils for a number of purposes, such as exchanging information, helping each other with homework, or chatting with classmates. Unfortunately, sometimes the conversations, usually in the form of written entries, drifted away from mere information exchange and took the form of bullying directed at a particular person, usually one of the students. Because even one set of such online bullying conversations could lead to a tragedy, it became clear that prompt and precise detection of such unwanted entries would be the main task. In those days, Japanese society was still in shock after the Takigawa tragedy, and at the same time puzzled by other cyberbullying cases happening among students, taking place on multiple Websites and BBS of various schools. Members of Parent-Teacher Associations (PTA) had made significant efforts to watch the BBS. Parents, teachers and school personnel, began a voluntary work to patrol unofficial school Websites in search for harmful and suspicious entries. Unfortunately, it was difficult to keep the continuous surveillance due to the large number of such Websites, with new ones appearing daily. Our discussion with the NPO resulted in a conclusion that the most useful support technology could provide would be a method for automatic detection of harmful entries on informal school Websites and BBS. Therefore helping PTA members in their Internet patrol became the main motivation for us to start this research, and lead us to the point we are today.

Due to the spread of social network services (SNS), like Facebook or Twitter, in many countries the problem of cyberbullying became a major social issue during the last decade. Therefore, since we began our study, many other research teams around the world undertook the same task – of automatically detecting and mitigating cyberbullying. Ten years after the Takigawa Incident, and nearly ten years since the beginning of our research, we present the readers the following book – a milestone in the research on cyberbullying detection. The book summarizes the story of our research in a step-by-step manner. By addressing also other discoveries, we explain our own results, and present the knowledge we gained during the research. Today we know which methods were successful, and which eventually did not meet the initial expectations. In this book the reader will find explanations and reasoning for each of the applied method, their pros and cons when applied to the language of online bullying, together with some generalizations about the cyberbullying as a phenomenon and how to approach the problem from practical technology-backed point of view.

Internet hate, harassment, cyberstalking, cyberbullying – these terms, which were almost unknown ten years ago, today are in the everyday lexicon of all Internet users. Cyberbullying happens in many languages, in many cultures. We strongly believe and hope, that the presented book will become a useful knowledge base for all researchers starting their research in cyberbullying detection and related topics. May our efforts effect in better, safer Internet, and in more aware and empathic global society.

Michal E. Ptaszynski
Kitami Institute of Technology, Japan

Fumito Masui
Kitami Institute of Technology, Japan

Acknowledgment

This book could not come to life without our closest research colleagues who have been supporting us in the study on automatic cyberbullying detection for nearly a decade, and in other research for much longer time. In particular, we would like to thank (in alphabetical order): Kenji Araki of Hokkaido University in Sapporo/Japan, for his many wise advices; Pawel Dybala, of Jagiellonian University in Cracow/Poland, for his help with developing the affect analysis tools applied in the initial study; Juuso Kalevi Kristian Eronen of Tampere University of Technology in Tampere/Finland, for his invaluable help with setting up the machine learning and neural network environments; Suzuha Hatakeyama, graduated from Kitami Institute of Technology, Kitami/Japan, for her laborious work in optimizing the Web mining method; Yasutomo Kimura, of Otaru University of Commerce, Otaru/Japan, for his invaluable insight in data and real-life approach; Pawel Lempa, of Cracow University of Technology, Cracow/Poland, graduated from Kitami Institute of Technology, Kitami/Japan, for his help with developing the Android application. Tatsuaki Matsuba and Naohiro Satomi, graduated from Mie University, Tsu/Japan, for their original research in developing machine learning and ranking method; Motoki Matsumura from Human Rights Research Institute Against All Forms for Discrimination and Racism in Mie Prefecture, Japan, for giving us the chance to consider the problem and providing of cyberbullying data obtained with his great efforts; Taisei Nitta, graduated from Kitami Institute of Technology, Kitami/Japan, for his tedious work on category maximized method for cyberbullying entry ranking; Jacek Pyżalski, of Adam Mickiewicz University in Poznan/Poland and Nofer Institute of Occupational Medicine, Lodz, Poland, for his time invested in long discussions with us on the problem of cyberbullying and methods to mitigate it in real life, also for helping us keep our heads above purely information technology-based thinking, and, above all, for the beautiful and strong foreword to this book; Rafal Rzepka, of Hokkaido University in Sapporo/Japan, for his common-sense approach, both in the developed solutions, and to life in general; Kazuhide Yamamoto, of Nagaoka University of Technology, Nagaoka/Japan, for his great help with developing the method for automatic optimization of seed word sets.

The research was supported for the many years by the following research grants: KAKENHI Grant-in-Aid for Scientific Research (C) (Project Number: 20500833) (years 2008–2011), KAKENHI Grant-in-Aid for Scientific Research (Project Number: 24600001) (years 2012–2015), KAKENHI Grant-in-Aid for Research Activity Start-up (Project Number: 25880003) (years 2013–2015), KAKENHI Grant-in-Aid for Encouragement of Young Scientists (B) (Project Number: 15K16044) (years 2016-2018)

Finally, we would like to thank our families for having supported us through all these years.

Chapter 1
Introduction

ABSTRACT

In this chapter, the authors present an introduction to this book. They explain the motivation that drove them in the research and draft an outline of the whole book.

MOTIVATION

Contributions of Information Technology (IT) to preservation, support and development of generally perceived public health are numerous. Some of the recent ones include analysis and prediction of the spread of epidemics (Aramaki, Maskawa & Morita, 2011), analysis of health data (Buntin et al., 2011; Kitajima, Rzepka & Araki, 2014) or construction of biomedical ontologies (Smith et al., 2005). However, most of these contributions address physical sphere of public health. The mental or psychological part, although equally important, has been mostly disregarded.

On the other hand, the recent decade has brought to light a problem of unethical behaviors in Internet environments, which has been greatly impairing public mental health in adults and, for the most, in younger users and children. It is the problem of *cyberbullying (CB)*, defined as exploitation of open online means of communication, such as Internet forum boards, or Social Networking Services (SNS) to convey harmful and disturbing information about private individuals, often children and students.

DOI: 10.4018/978-1-5225-5249-9.ch001

Although the problem of humiliating and slandering people through the Internet has existed almost as long as communication via Internet between people, the appearance of new devices, such as smartphones and tablet computers, which allow using this medium not only at home, work or school but also in motion, sometimes with different access points and simplified anonymity, has further exacerbated that problem.

Messages classifiable as cyberbullying, include ridiculing someone's personality, body type, or appearance, slandering or spreading rumors and insinuations. Some cases of cyberbullying lead the victims to self-mutilation or suicides, or on the other hand, attacking their offenders. In USA, a great focus on this issue began in 2006 after a 13-year-old girl from Missouri committed suicide after receiving bullying messages on Myspace (https://myspace.com/). Her story was a beginning of a wide debate over the use of and the influence the Internet has on young people (Megan Meier Foundation, n.d.). Similar cases have been noticed in other countries, including Japan, on which this research is focused. Growing number of cyberbullying cases around the world opened an ongoing public debate on whether such messages could be spotted earlier to prevent the tragedies from happening and on the freedom of speech on the Internet in general (Leets, 2001).

One of the countries in which the problem is considered as more severe in comparison with other countries is Japan (Ministry of Education, Culture, Sports, Science, and Technology, 2008), where bullying in general (including cyberbullying) has been considered as one of the most common cause of suicides among school pupils for many years (Ministry of Education, Culture, Sports, Science, and Technology, 2011, 2013).

The problem of cyberbullying in particular has become widely discussed in Japan after the so called Takigawa High School Incident, which happened in July 2007. In the incident, a 17 year old boy, after being bullied on an informal school Website by four of his classmates, committed a suicide, by jumping from the school roof during classes. The Takigawa High School Incident became a starting point for a country-wide discussion about cyberbullying, and gave birth to a national program for prevention of bullying and cyberbullying in schools, founded by the Ministry of Education, Culture, Sports, Science, and Technology, (2008). Within the program, during the same year 2007, Japanese school personnel and members of Parent-Teacher Associations (PTA)[1] have started monitoring activities under the general name Internet Patrol (later: net-patrol) to spot Web sites containing such inappropriate contents. However, the net-patrol has been performed manually as a volunteer work, while countless amounts of data on the Internet make this an uphill task.

Figure 1. Indigo awareness ribbon (targeted individuals of bullying, harassment, stalking, etc.)
Source: Wikipedia (n.d.)

A second, more recent example of possible tragic consequences of cyberbullying was the Ootsu Junior High School Incident, which took place in 2011. In the incident a 13-year-old boy committed a suicide by jumping from the window of his apartment after being bullied and humiliated multiple times by his classmates. The incident became a strong push for creating the Bullying Prevention Act, implemented in 2013 in Japan.

Due to the severity of the problem, Japan has in recent years started a number of projects to increase the recognition of bullying in schools among both students and teachers. This caused a slow decrease in the number of reported bullying cases. However, it must be remembered that for cyberbullying, the actual number of cases is estimated as over three times larger as the number reported (Hinduja & Patchin, 2009). Unfortunately, the most disturbing is the fact that, although the number of cases reported in schools is dropping, the number of children claiming they have been bullied in fact remains the same (Ministry of Education, Culture, Sports, Science, and Technology, 2011, 2013; Weber & Dixon, 2016). This suggests that most of the bullying has moved online and gradually takes the form of cyberbullying.

To deal with the problem of cyberbullying, in Japan members of Parent-Teacher Association (PTA) perform the abovementioned web site monitoring activities called "Internet-patrol" (or shortly "net-patrol"). When a harmful entry is detected a net-patrol member who found it sends a request to the Internet provider or Web site administrator to remove the entry. Examples of such harmful CB entries that actually happened on informal school BBS, include ridiculing student's personality, body type or appearance, slandering students or insinuating they had performed deviate sexual intercourses. Some cases of cyberbullying lead the bullied students to self-mutilation, even suicide, or on the other hand, cause them to attack the students who put the harmful entries on the Internet. Some of the actual examples of harmful entries which were requested for deletion are represented in Table 1 (names, phone numbers and other personal information was changed).

Unfortunately, net-patrol has been carried out mostly manually. It takes much time and effort to find harmful entries (entries that contain information and expressions aimed to harm other users) in a large amount of contents appearing on countless number of electronic Bulletin Board (BBS) pages. Moreover, the task comes with a great psychological burden on mental health to the Internet Patrol members.

The research presented in this book was directly motivated and influenced by the abovementioned incidents. We started the research in 2008 after the Takigawa High School Incident, with a motivation to help PTA members

Table 1. Examples of harmful entries which were requested for deletion. Japanese (above), transliteration (middle), English translation (below). Mobage and Gree are online game service Web sites

- 調子乗りすぎいっぺん殺らなあかんで *(Chōshi nori sugi ippen yara na akan de)* "Don't get excited that much or I'll kill ya!"
- 新田キモイつかキショイほんま死んで *(Nitta kimoi tsuka kishoi honma shinde)* "Nitta [proper noun], you're ugly, or rather fugly, just die, man"
- ンな奴どつき回したれ *(N'na yatsu dotsuki mawashi tare)* "What an ass, slap him"
- 性格わるーい　ぶちゃいく一笑 *(Seikaku waru–i buchaiku– warai)* "Baaad personality, and an ugly hag, lol"
- >> 17あの女、昔、モバだったかグリに登録してたヤリマンじゃん。 *(Ano onna, mukashi, Moba dattaka Guri ni tōroku shiteta yariman jan)* ">>17 that woman is the same one who was bitching around before on Mobage or Gree."
- すぐにヤレる。01234567890。めっちゃカワイイで *(Sugu ni yareru. 01234567890. Meccha kawaii de.)* "You can take her out even now. 01234567890. She's a great lay."

engaged in Internet Patrol. We started the research as a long term project, in which we aim to contribute to detecting, preventing, and ultimately solving the problem of cyberbullying. The present book represents the first complete step in our research, in which we firstly aimed at developing a systematic approach to automatically detect and classify cyberbullying entries, which could help and ease the burden of the net-patrol members, and in effect prevent incidents such as the two mentioned above. One of the main goals of the project is to create a net-patrol support solution for automatic spotting of cyberbullying entries on the Web and reporting them to appropriate organs. In this part of research we developed a number of methods for the detection of Internet entries related to or directly classifiable as cyberbullying.

Another aim of the research was to contribute to the prevention of the cyberbullying problem by transferring and testing the developed cyberbullying detection methods on mobile devices. In this part we developed a test application for Android devices, to test whether it is possible to apply the detecting algorithms, previously developed on much more powerful machines, on mobile devices such as smartphones. First results of the long-term study and its possible implications were included in this book.

OUTLINE

The general outline of the rest of this book is as follows. In Chapter 1, we present an introduction to this book. We explain the motivations that drove us in the research and describe the outline of the whole book. In Chapter 2, we present the background for the research described in this book. We describe the problem of cyberbullying, and previous research done in the topic of cyberbullying detection. In Chapter 3, we describe the datasets used in cyberbullying detection research. We also perform an initial analysis of the dataset applied in this research to find its various characteristics, and on its basis we create an initial baseline method for cyberbullying classification and harmfulness ranking. In Chapter 4, we develop a method for detection and ranking of cyberbullying entries according to their harmfulness, based on an extended SO-PMI-IR method along with some additional improvements including automatic acquisition and filtering of seed words. In Chapter 5, we present a completely novel method for automatic detection of cyberbullying, based on a combinatorial approach to language modeling. By automatically extracting sophisticated patterns from sentences and applying them in classification the method grasps a wide scope of implicit information conveyed in cyberbullying messages. In Chapter 6, we present our closing study in cyberbullying detection with the use of various traditional classifiers, including a Deep Convolutional Neural Networks. In Chapter 7, we present an application for Android smartphones developed for testing previously created methods. Finally, in Chapter 8 we summarize the whole book, and discuss the potential and limitations of technology-based cyberbullying detection and mitigation tools. We provide general conclusions resulting from the research presented in the book, and sketch paths for future improvement and further development in the research on automatic cyberbullying detection.

REFERENCES

Aramaki, E., Maskawa, S., & Morita, M. (2011). Twitter catches the flu: detecting influenza epidemics using Twitter. *Proceedings of the Conference on Empirical Methods in Natural Language Processing (EMNLP)*, 1568-1576.

Buntin, M. B., Burke, M. F., Hoaglin, M. C., & Blumenthal, D. (2011). The benefits of health information technology: A review of the recent literature shows predominantly positive results. *Health Affairs*, *30*(3), 464–471. doi:10.1377/hlthaff.2011.0178 PMID:21383365

Kitajima, S., Rzepka, R., & Araki, K. (2014). Blog Snippets Based Drug Effects Extraction System Using Lexical and Grammatical Restrictions. *International Journal of Multimedia Data Engineering and Management*, *5*(2), 1–17. doi:10.4018/ijmdem.2014040101

Smith, B., Ceusters, W., Klagges, B., Köhler, J., & Kumar, A. (2005). Relations in biomedical ontologies. *Genome Biology*, *6*(5), R46. doi:10.1186/gb-2005-6-5-r46 PMID:15892874

Megan Meier Foundation. (n.d.). *Megan Meier Foundation.* Retrieved from: https://www.meganmeierfoundation.org/megans-story.html

Leets, L. (2001). Responses to Internet hate sites: Is speech too free in cyberspace? *Communication Law and Policy*, *6*(2), 287–317. doi:10.1207/S15326926CLP0602_2

Ministry of Education, Culture, Sports, Science, and Technology (MEXT). (2008). *'Netto-jō no ijime' ni kansuru taiō manyuaru jirei shū (gakkō, kyōin muke)* ["Bullying on the Net" Manual for handling and collection of cases (for schools and teachers)] (in Japanese). MEXT.

Ministry of Education, Culture, Sports, Science, and Technology. (2011). *2011-nendo jidō seito no mondai kōdo-to seito shidō jō shomondai ni kansuru chōsa* [Fiscal year 2011 Survey on Problematic Behavior Among Schoolchildren and Other Issues] (in Japanese). Author.

Ministry of Education. Culture, Sports, Science, and Technology. (2013). 2013-nendo jidō seito no mondai kōdo-to seito shidō jō shomondai ni kansuru chōsa [Fiscal year 2013 Survey on Problematic Behavior Among Schoolchildren and Other Issues] (in Japanese). Author.

Hinduja, S., & Patchin, J. W. (2009). *Bullying beyond the schoolyard: Preventing and responding to cyberbullying*. Corwin Press.

Weber, S., & Dixon, S. (Eds.). (2016). *Growing up online: young people and digital technologies*. Springer.

Wikipedia. (n.d.). Indigo awareness ribbon. In *Wikipedia*. Retrieved from: http://commons.wikimedia.org/wiki/File:Targeted_Individuals.png

ENDNOTE

1 Local school-dependent organizations composed of parents and school personnel, whose goal is to help managing and improving school experience for children.

Chapter 2
Background

ABSTRACT

In this chapter, the authors present the background for the research described in this book. They describe the problem of cyberbullying in general, with specific reference to its status quo in Japan. They also describe some of the most relevant previous research done on the topic of cyberbullying detection and point out research gaps that they aim to fill with this book.

CYBERBULLYING: A SOCIAL PROBLEM

The problem of harmful and offending messages on the Internet has existed for many years. One of the reasons such activities evolved was the anonymity of communication on the Internet, giving users the feeling that anything can go unpunished.

However, scientific conceptualization of the problem, officially defining it and labelling as cyberbullying is a recent step. As for the definitions, various organs and institutions define the problem in their own words, although all definitions represent a general consensus. For example, the National Crime Prevention Council of the US defines that CB happens "when the Internet, cell phones or other devices are used to send or post text or images intended to hurt or embarrass another person" (NCPC, n.d.). Another definition says that cyberbullying "involves the use of information and communication technologies to support deliberate, repeated, and hostile behavior by an individual or group, that is intended to harm others" (Belsey, n.d.).

DOI: 10.4018/978-1-5225-5249-9.ch002

Some of the first robust research on CB was done by Hinduja and Patchin, who performed numerous surveys about the subject in the U.S. (Patchin & Hinduja, 2006; Hinduja & Patchin, 2009). They found out that the harmful information may include threats, sexual remarks, pejorative labels, or false statements aimed to humiliate others. When posted on a social network, such as Facebook, Twitter, or an Internet forum, it may disclose humiliating personal data of the victim defaming and ridiculing them personally.

Around the years 2009-2011 a number of large scale questionnaire studies and social campaigns have been conducted to measure the degree of occurrence of cyberbullying and work out methods to mitigate the problem. For example, Cross et al. (2009) in Australia found out that cyberbullying in Australian schools happens for about five to eight percent of children depending on their school year (Cross et al. 2009). Comparable results have been noticed in United States (Kowalski & Limber, 2007), Finland (Sourander et al., 2010), and across Europe (Hasenbrink, 2011). Hasenbrink et al. (2009) present even larger estimates, that even one in five young people (not limited to school environment) have had experienced bullying or harassment through the Internet or mobile devices. These estimates are also confirmed in Qing (2007), Pyżalski (2012), and more recently by Kann et al. (2014).

Cyberbullying has also been thoroughly studied and analyzed by Dooley, Pyżalski, and Cross (2009), who performed an in-depth comparative analysis of traditional face-to-face bullying and cyberbullying, while Lazuras et al. (2012) discussed implications of cyberbullying for teachers in school environments.

Especially Dooley, Pyżalski, and Cross (2009) point out some of the similarities, between traditional face-to-face bullying, but also mention some of the differences making cyberbullying in some aspects a problem more difficult to contain. As for the similarities, which contribute to classifying the problem as a kind of bullying, there are such features as: *peer group*, such as classmates in face-to-face bullying and friends from groups on Social Networking portals (Facebook, Twitter, etc.), which in reality often overlap, and play a crucial role in victimization of bullying targets; *repetitiveness* of bullying acts, which especially with the use of Internet can occur more often than face-to-face bullying; or *imbalance of power*, meaning that usually one person, or a small group of people become bullied by an overwhelming number of bullies. This is also a feature distinguishing bullying from other types of cyber-aggression.

However, the environment (Internet, SNS) and the tools used also make cyberbullying even more humiliating experience, than its face-to-face counterpart. For example, with the use of Internet, cyberbullying can occur on much larger scale making it an overwhelming experience. Also with the popularity of Social Network Services, humiliating a person publicly, such as on their official Facebook homepage, makes the attack public not only for a limited number of viewers, but open to the general public, which in worst cases could even appear in search engine results, thus making a person exposed theoretically to the whole world. Additionally, the indirectness of the relationship caused by the limitations of the communication channel in the online environment, which causes emotional disconnection in some people, add to the higher possibility of becoming a bystander, or a person, who is a witness of a bullying act, but does not react. This in result increases the sense of impunity in potential bullies.

Another characteristic feature of cyberbullying is its typical victim age range. One of the most recent cross-cultural study summarizing the problem strongly highlighted that cyberbullying, although appearing in various age and social groups, is the most prevalent among young people, mostly school pupils and students (Smith, Kwak, & Toda, 2016). In particular, it is estimated that at least about 24% of pupils were bullied with the use of modern technology (computer, smart-phones, etc.) and Internet services (Facebook, Twitter), and about 17% participated actively in such online bullying activities.

As more children have easier access to modern technologies and Internet nearly every day (Weber & Dixon, 2016), this makes cyberbullying one of the most, if not the most crucial problem when it comes to children interacting with computers. Especially in Japan, on which this book focuses the most, the ratio of everyday use of mobile phones among schoolchildren is an astonishing 75.2% for primary school, 95.7% for junior high school, and 99.4% for senior high school (Ministry of Education, Culture, Sports, Science and Technology, 2012).

Cyberbullying and Internet Patrol in Japan

In Japan, where a person's belonging and the role played in the society is considered a major defining feature of the person in general, the problem of cyberbullying and traditional bullying, often realized in the form of gossip or ostracism, has profound implications on one's personality and mental health (Sugimori, 2012). Despite this fact, research on cyberbullying in Japan has gained on speed only recently (Aoyama, Utsumi & Hasegawa, 2012), after several cases of suicides of CB victims not being able to bear the humiliation. This has made MEXT to consider the problem as serious enough to start a movement against the problem. In a manual for spotting and handling the cases of cyberbullying (Ministry of Education, Culture, Sports, Science and Technology (MEXT), 2008), the Ministry puts a great importance on early spotting of the suspicious entries and messages, and distinguishes several types of cyberbullying noticed in Japan. These are:

1. Cyberbullying appearing on BBS forums, blogs and on private profile Web-sites;
   a. Entries containing libelous, slanderous or abusive contents;
   b. Disclosing personal data of natural persons without their authorization;
   c. Entries and humiliating online activities performed in the name of another person;
2. Cyberbullying appearing in electronic mail;
   a. E-mails directed to a certain person/child, containing libelous, slanderous or abusive contents;
   b. E-mails in the form of chain letters containing libelous, slanderous or abusive contents;
   c. E-mails send in the name of another person, containing humiliating contents;

Figure 1. Route of internet patrol

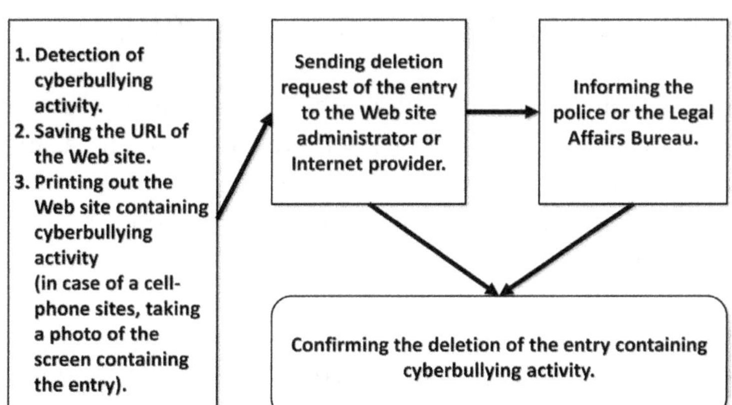

In this research we focused mostly on the cases of cyberbullying that appear on informal Web sites of Japanese schools. Informal school web sites are Web sites where school pupils gather to exchange information about school subjects or contents of tests, etc. However, as was noticed by Watanabe and Sunayama (2006), on such pages there have been a rapid increase of entries containing insulting or slandering information about other pupils or even teachers. Cases like that make other users uncomfortable using the Web sites and cause undesirable misunderstandings.

To deal with such malicious entries, a movement of Internet Patrol (later: net-patrol) was founded. Participants of this movement are usually teachers and PTA members. Based on the MEXT definition of cyberbullying, they read through all available entries, decide whether an entry is dangerous or not and, if necessary, send a deletion request to the Web page administrator. Finally, they send a report about the event to the police. The typical Internet Patrol route is presented on Figure 1.

Unfortunately, at present state of affairs, the school personnel and PTA members taking part in Internet Patrol perform all tasks manually as voluntary work, beginning from reading the countless numbers of entries and deciding about the appropriateness of their contents, through printing out or taking photos of the pages containing cyberbullying entries, and finally sending the reports and deletion requests to the appropriate organs. Moreover, since the number of entries rises by the day, surveillance of the whole Web becomes an uphill task for the small number of patrol members.

With this research we aim to create a Web crawler capable to perform this difficult task instead of humans, or at least to ease the burden of the Online Patrol volunteers.

PREVIOUS RESEARCH IN CYBERBULLYING DETECTION

Although the problem of cyberbullying has been studied in social sciences and child psychology for over ten years, there has been only a small number of attempts to detect and study the problem using methods from the field of artificial intelligence (AI) or natural language processing (NLP). Below we present the most relevant research to this day. The publications were also summarized in Table 1. We mostly focused on journal-level publications, since they represent the most mature state of research.

The first journal publication written in the topic of cyberbullying detection, cyberbullying analysis and mitigation with the use of methods from the fields

Table 1. Summary of previous research in cyberbullying detection

Authors, Year	Language of processing	Feature Extraction Method	Classification Method
Ptaszynski et al. (2010)	Japanese	unigrams (BoW)	SVM
Ishisaka and Yamamoto (2010)	Japanese	4-grams	n-gram language model matching
Ikeda et al. (2010)	Japanese	unigrams (harmful single words)	keyword matching
Fujii et al. (2010)	Japanese	unigrams co-occurring with sexting black and grey words	keyword matching
Hashimoto et al. (2010)	Japanese	separate words	surrounding word co-occurrence with harmful words
Matuba et al. (2011)	Japanese	9 seed words	SO-PMI-IR averaged for all seed words
Sood et al. (2012)	English	unigrams, bigrams, stems	SVM, various weighting (presence, freq, tf-idf)
Dinakar et al. (2012)	English	unigrams, hand-crafted word-lists (Ortony lexicon of negative words, profane words, frequently occurring stereotypical words), POS	SVM, JRip, Naïve Bayes, J48
Nitta et al. (2013)	Japanese	seed words grouped in 3 categories	SO-PMI-IR maximized for category
Cano et al. (2013)	English	violence-related words (derived from violence-related topics from Twitter and DBPedia)	VDM (weakly supervised Bayesian model)
Sarna et al. (2015)	English (?)	``bad words", positive and negative sentiment words, pronouns, proper nouns, links	Naïve Bayes, kNN, Decision Trees, SVM
Marathe et al. (2015)	English	BoW, video metadata (time stamp, popularity), character n-grams	Naïve Bayes
Ptaszynski et al. (2016)	Japanese	seed words grouped in 3 categories	SO-PMI-IR maximized for category with seed word optimization

of artificial intelligence, machine learning and natural language processing was the publication by Ptaszynski et al. (2010). They performed affect analysis of a small dataset of cyberbullying entries to find out that distinctive features for cyberbullying were vulgar words. They applied a lexicon of such words to train an SVM classifier. With a number of optimizations the system was able to detect cyberbullying with 88.2% of F-score. However, increasing the data caused a decrease in results, which made them abandon SVMs as not ideal to deal with frequent language ambiguities typical for cyberbullying.

Later, Ishisaka and Yamamoto (2010) developed a dictionary of abusive expressions based on a large Japanese BBS (electronic Bulletin Board

System, a form of an electronic forum) *2channel*. In their research they labeled words and paragraphs in which the speaker explicitly insults other people with words and phrases like *baka* ("stupid"), or *masugomi no kuzu* ("trash of mass-mudia"). Based on which words appeared most often with abusive vocabulary, they extracted abusive expressions from the surrounding context. Unfortunately, their method, based on 4-gram model did not extract sufficient number of abusive words, with both Precision and Recall scoring around or lower than 30%.

Ikeda et al. (2010) manually collected a set of harmful and non-harmful separate sentences. Based on word occurrence within the corpus they created a list of keywords for classification of harmful contents. In their method based on keyword matching in input documents the documents were selected as harmful, when the number of harmful words found in them was higher than a pre-set threshold. To deal with small Recall of the method they applied a semantic generalization of documents and based their matching on generalized dependency chunks within input sentences. Their highest Precision was around 60% with Recall around 35%. Unfortunately, they mostly struggled with variations of the same expressions differing with only one or two characters, such as *bakuha* "blow up" and *baku–ha* "blooow up". All variations of the same expression needed to be collected manually, which was a weakness of the method.

Fujii et al. (2010) proposed a system for detecting documents containing excessive sexual descriptions using a concept of distance between two words in a sentence. They defined as harmful "black words" those in close distance to words appearing only in harmful context, rather than in both harmful and non-harmful context ("grey words").

Hashimoto et al. (2010) proposed a method for detecting harmful meaning of separate words used in jargon. In their method they assumed that the non-standard meaning is determined by the words surrounding the word in question. They detected the harmful meaning based on calculating co-occurrence of a word with its surroundings.

In another research, Matsuba et al. (2011) proposed a method to automatically detect harmful entries online, in which they extended the SO-PMI-IR score to calculate the relevance of a document with harmful contents (Turney, 2002). With the use of a small number of seed words they were able to detect large numbers of candidates for harmful documents with an accuracy of 83% on test data.

Later, Nitta et al. (2013) proposed an improvement to Matsuba et al.'s method. They grouped the seed words into three categories (abusive, violent, obscene) to calculate SO-PMI-IR score and maximized the relevance of categories. Their method scored much better than the original method proposed by Matsuba et al.

Nitta et al. (2013), based their information retrieval (IR) procedure on Yahoo! search engine API. In a re-evaluation performed by Ptaszynski et al. (2016) two years after the original paper, the method showed a major drop in Precision (about 30 percentage-points) across two years. Later in the chapter, when comparing to previous methods, we discuss the possible reasons for such changes and hypothesize they could have been caused by a change in information available on the Internet (Web page re-ranking, changes in user policies, etc.). Ptaszynski et al. (2016) tried to further improve the method by automatically acquiring and filtering harmful new seed words, in which they achieved a considerable success.

All the above research was done for Japanese language. For English research, in the topics related to cyberbullying detection begun around 2012 with the research by Sood et al., (2012). They did not yet however recognize the full negative weight of harmful online contents. The major problem they focused on were personal insults, negative influence of which in their assumptions could at most cause the Internet community to stop growing or fall into recession. This means that at the year 2012 the problem of cyberbullying and its consequences were not yet fully recognized by the scientific society in the US. Despite that, Sood et al., (2012) focused on the detection of such personal insults on Internet fora recognizing it as a part of standard community management procedure. In their research they used as features single words and bigrams, weighted them using either presence (feature present in input or not 1/0), frequency or tf-idf, and used them to train an SVM classifier. As a dataset they used a corpus of six thousand entries they collected from various online fora. To prepare gold standard for their experiments they used a crowd-sourcing approach with untrained layperson annotators hired for a classification task through Mechanical Turk.

Later, Dinakar et al., (2012) proposed their approach to detection and mitigation of cyberbullying. An improvement of this research in comparison to previous research was its wider perspective. Dinakar et al., (2012) did not only focus on the detection of cyberbullying. They also proposed some methods for mitigation. A disadvantage of this research comparing to previous ones were the research and experiment settings. Dinakar et al. assumed they focus on cyberbullying, however they did not define the concept strictly enough, and in effect focused not on the detection of cyberbullying, but rather on detection of entries that contain sexual or racial harassment.

While these often overlap with cyberbullying, they do not reflect the whole picture of the problem. To prepare the dataset for experiments, entries and comments from YouTube and Formspring, Dinakar et al., similarly to Sood et al., (2012), applied Mechanical Turk, which formulates the problem as a task for layperson annotators, while the sophistication of the problem would require expert annotators. Despite the lacks in overall research settings, the classifiers they used scored up to 58-77% of F-score depending on the kind of harassment contents they detected. Their best proposed classifier was based on Support Vector Machines, which confirmed for English the research done by Ptaszynski et al. for Japanese in 2010.

An interesting work was done by Kontostathis, et al. (2013), who performed a thorough analysis of cyberbullying entries on Formspring.me. They were able to identify common cyberbullying terms, and applied them in classification with the use of a machine learning method based on Essential Dimensions of Latent Semantic Indexing (EDLSI).

At the same time, Nitta, et al. (2013) proposed their extended SO-PMI-IR method for cyberbullying detection, Nitta and Cano, (2013) proposed their Violence Detection Model (VDM), a weekly supervised Bayesian model. They did not however focus strictly on cyberbullying, but widened their scope to more generally understood "violence." This approach to problem formulation makes it more understandable, and thus feasible to annotate, by layperson annotators, which allowed them to study the problem without the need to ask expert annotators for help with annotating their datasets. The datasets for training were extracted from violence-related topics on Twitter and DBPedia and the model was tested on Twitter.

Sarna and Bhatia (2015) proposed categorization of cyberbullying messages into direct and indirect bullying. They based their method on a set of features like "bad words", as well as words indicating positive or negative sentiment, and other common features like pronouns and proper nouns, to estimate user credibility. They used a top-down approach to feature extraction meaning they assumed some features correlate with cyberbullying (e.g., "bad words", or emotion words). They applied those features to classify messages into direct bullying, indirect bullying and non-bullying with the use of four standard classifiers (Naive Bayes, kNN, Decision Trees, SVM). The results of the classification were further used in User Behavior Analysis model (BAU), which provided the output for analysis of user credibility (CAU). An interesting part in their research was recognizing from the start that cyberbullying can be performed directly in the form of insults, as well as indirectly, which would include both phenomena such as irony, but also rumors. Unfortunately, in practice, Sarna and Bhatia (2015) only focused on messages which contained "bad words" (which they also failed to specify in the paper), which undermined their primary assumption. The problem with their research was that they did not provide any detailed information about the dataset they used (except that it was crawled from Twitter), nor how they performed the annotation of the dataset (by expert or layperson annotators). Therefore, a direct comparison to their method, as well as its objective evaluation remains problematic.

Marathe and Shirsat (2015) applied a Naive Bayes classifier to detect cyberbullying comments on YouTube. They first searched for videos promoting cyberbullying (the search was done subjectively). Next, they extracted features related to those videos, such as video metadata (time stamp, duration, popularity), of Bag-of-Words extracted from video title, description, comments, and profiles of users who uploaded the videos. Next, they build a character n-gram model based on such features and trained the Naive Bayes classifier to detect whether a new input video (or its metadata) relates to cyberbullying. Although neither their data collection approach, nor their results could be considered as state-of-the-art, the idea to include a context wider than simple Bag-of-Words is noteworthy.

RESEARCH GAPS

Based on the above field survey we recognized the following research gaps, or areas for improvement in cyberbullying detection research.

1. **Dataset Preparation:** Most of the above-mentioned methods suffered from unprofessional, or subjective data preparation. In some research, such as Cano, et al. (2013) or Dinakar, et al. (2012), the datasets were indeed collected with sufficient scrutiny (e.g., using Mechanical Turk, or applying already existing available dataset), although did not define the problem properly. The problem of cyberbullying is a complex social phenomenon and data representing its samples need to be handled by expert annotators. Some researchers, like Ishisaka and Yamamoto (2010), Sood, et al. (2012), or Cano, et al. (2013) recognize this difficulty in defining the problem, and formulate it in other terms, so the use of experts is not needed, and focus on, e.g., detecting generally perceived violence, or aggression. Some researchers use the term cyberbullying, although what they actually focus on is overlapping, but not equivalent to cyberbullying, such as sexual or racial harassment. On the other

hand, in other research, such as Sarna and Bhatia (2015) or Marathe and Shirsat (2015) the datasets were collected ad hoc and with no specific standardization. From all of the research, the studies by Ptaszynski, et al. (2010), Matsuba, et al. (2011), Nitta, et al. (2013), and Ptaszynski, et al. (2016) were the only ones that defined the cyberbullying problem with proper depth and made the effort to collect datasets with sufficient scrutiny and standardization. They obtained their dataset from an official source, namely, one of Japanese branches of Human Right Center, which collected the data fully labeled by Internet Patrol members, who search for cyberbullying cases on the Internet as part of their job, based on an official government definition of cyberbullying (MEXT, 2008).

2. **Feature Extraction:** Almost all of the reviewed research included as features only words (unigrams), or n-grams at best. Some research, such as Matsuba, et al. (2011) or Nitta, et al. (2013) applied only a small number of features, while others, e.g., Dinakar, et al. (2012) or Marathe and Shirsat (2015) build up more complex models, however still not exceeding a Bag-of-Words model. Moreover, research, such as Matsuba, et al. (2011), Ishisaka and Yamamoto (2010), Nitta, et al. (2013), Sarna and Bhatia, (2015) used only a small top-down selected features. While it is to some extent reasonable to apply in cyberbullying detection, e.g., violent or obscene words, top-down feature selection requires time, human workload and background knowledge about the dataset, and is thus inefficient and limited. Moreover, interestingly, in some research significant findings of other previous research were disregarded. For example, Ptaszynski, et al. (2010) found out with sufficient certainty that emotion-related words are not effective in cyberbullying detection, but Sarna and Bhatia (2015) still put much weight on using positive and negative sentiment words in their classification. In our research, to allow full comparison to previous research, except proposing our original methods, we also allowed simple Bag-of-Words and n-grams models.
3. **Classification Methods:** Previous research tested many different classifiers, such as SVMs, Naive Bayes, or Decision Trees. However, in most cases, SVMs reached highest scores. Interestingly, despite Ptaszynski, et al. (2010) concludes that SVMs, especially trained on BoW, are not ideal to grasp the sophistication of language used in cyberbullying, in most of later research, when comparing various classifiers, other researchers report that they obtained their highest scores exactly for SVMs. Therefore, in this research we also used SVMs for comparison with our proposed methods. Moreover, one major disadvantage of

traditional machine learning is the fact that although one can set groups of specific features that influence the results, it is not possible to specify which exactly feature in which case influenced the acquired result. One of the methods presented in this book is capable of providing such information, which could be useful in further filtering and optimizing the features for other specific cyberbullying datasets.

4. **Human Effort Reduction:** In our research we aimed at the minimization of human effort. Most of the previous research assumed that using vulgar words as seeds will help detecting cyberbullying. However, all of them notice that vulgar words are only one kind of distinctive vocabulary and do not cover all cases. We assumed that this kind of vocabulary could be extracted automatically. Moreover, we did not restrict the scope to words (unigrams, tokens), or even phrases (ngrams). We extended the search to sophisticated patterns with disjointed elements. To achieve this we developed a pattern extraction method based on the idea of brute force search algorithm, which although being computationally heavy in the training phase, relieves most of the workload from the researchers and provides a method capable of relieving the Internet Patrol members in their search for cyberbullying entries on the Internet (see Chapter 5).

REFERENCES

Aoyama, I., Utsumi, S., & Hasegawa, M. (2012). Cyberbullying in Japan. In Cyberbullying in the Global Playground: Research from International Perspectives. John Wiley & Sons. doi:10.1002/9781119954484.ch9

Belsey, B. (n.d.). Cyberbullying: An Emerging Threat for the "Always On" Generation. *Cyberbullying*. Retrieved from: http://www.cyberbullying.ca/pdf Cyberbullying_Presentation_Description.pdf

Cano, A. E., He, Y., Liu, K., & Zhao, J. (2013). A Weakly Supervised Bayesian Model for Violence Detection in Social Media. *Proceedings of the 6th International Joint Conference on Natural Language Processing (IJCNLP 2013).*

Cross, D., Shaw, T., Hearn, L., Epstein, M., Monks, H., Lester, L., & Thomas, L. (2009). Australian Covert Bullying Prevalence Study (ACBPS). Child Health Promotion Research Centre, Edith Cowan University.

Dinakar, K., Jones, B., Havasi, C., Lieberman, H., & Picard, R. (2012). Commonsense Reasoning for Detection, Prevention and Mitigation of Cyberbullying. ACM Transactions on Intelligent Interactive Systems, 2(3).

Dooley, J. J., Pyżalski, J., & Cross, D. (2009). Cyberbullying Versus Face-to-Face Bullying: A Theoretical and Conceptual Review, Zeitschrift für Psychologie. *The Journal of Psychology, 217*(4), 182–188.

Fujii, Y., Ando, S., & Ito, T. (2010). Yūgai jōhō firutaringu no tame no 2-tangokan no kyori oyobi kyōki jōhō ni yoru bunshō bunrui shuhō no teian [Developing a method based on 2-word co-occurence information for filtering harmful information]. *Proceedings of The 24th Annual Conference of The Japanese Society for Artificial Intelligence (JSAI2010),* 1-4.

Hasebrink, U., Gorzig, A., Haddon, L., Kalmus, V., & Livingstone, S. (2011). Patterns of risk and safety online. In-depth analyses from the EU Kids Online survey of 9- to 16-year-olds and their parents in 25 European countries. *LSE Research Online*. Retrieved from: http://eprints.lse.ac.uk/39356/1/Patterns_of_risk_and_safety_online_%28LSERO%29.pdf

Hasebrink, U., Livingstone, S., Haddon, L., & Ólafsson, K. (2009). *Comparing children's online opportunities and risks across Europe: Cross-national comparisons for EU Kids Online. LSE.* London: EU Kids Online.

Hashimoto, H., Kinoshita, T. & Harada, M. (2010). *Firutaringu no tame no ingo no yūgai goi kenshutsu kinō no imi kaiseki shisutemu SAGE e no kumikomi* [Implementing a function for filtering harmful slang words into the semantic analysis system SAGE]. IPSJ SIG Notes, 2010-SLP-81(14), pp. 1-6.

Hinduja, S., & Patchin, J. W. (2009). *Bullying beyond the schoolyard: Preventing and responding to cyberbullying*. Corwin Press.

Ikeda, K., Yanagihara, T., Matsumoto, K., & Takishima, Y. (2010). Kakuyōso no chūshōka ni motozuku ihō-, yūgai-bunsho kenshutsu shuhō no teian to hyōka [Proposal and evaluation of a method for illegal and harmful document detection based on the abstraction of case elements]. *Proceedings of 72nd National Convention of Information Processing Society of Japan (IPSJ72),* 71-72.

Ishisaka, T., & Yamamoto, K. (2010). 2chaeru wo taishō to shita waruguchi hyōgen no chūshutsu [Extraction of abusive expressions from 2channel]. *Proceedings of The Sixteenth Annual Meeting of The Association for Natural Language Processing (NLP2010)*, 178-181.

Kann, L., & Kinchen, S. Shanklin, Shari L., Flint, Katherine H., Hawkins, J., Harris, William A., Lowry, R., OMalley-Olsen, E., McManus, T., Chyen, D., Whittle, L., Taylor, E., Demissie, Z., Brener, N., Thornton, J., Moore, J., & Zaza, S. (2013). Youth Risk Behavior Surveillance United States. Morbidity and Mortality Weekly Report (MMWR). Centers for Disease Control and Prevention, 63(4), 66.

Kontostathis, A., Reynolds, K., Garron, A., & Edwards, L. (2013). Detecting Cyberbullying: Query Terms and Techniques. *Proceedings of the 5th ACM WebScience Conference (WEBSCI2013)*, 195-204. 10.1145/2464464.2464499

Kowalski, R. M., & Limber, S. P. (2007). Electronic bullying among middle school students. *The Journal of Adolescent Health, 41*(6Suppl 1), S22S30. doi:10.1016/j.jadohealth.2007.08.017 PMID:18047942

Lazuras L., Pyżalski J., Barkoukis V., Tsorbazoudis H. (2012). Empathy and Moral Disengagement in Adolescent Cyberbullying: Implications for Educational Intervention and Pedagogical Practice. *Studia Edukacyjne, 23*, 57-69.

Marathe, S.S. & Shirsat, K.P. (2015). Contextual Features Based Nave Bayes Classifier for Cyberbullying Detection on YouTube. *International Journal of Scientific and Engineering Research, 6*(11), 1109-1114.

Matsuba, T., Masui, F., Kawai, A., & Isu, N. (2011). Gakkō hi-kōshiki saito ni okeru yūgai jōhō kenshutsu wo mokuteki to shita kyokusei hantei moderu ni kansuru kenkyū [A study on the polarity classification model for the purpose of detecting harmful information on informal school sites] (in Japanese). *Proceedings of The Seventeenth Annual Meeting of The Association for Natural Language Processing (NLP2011)*, 388-391.

Ministry of Education, Culture, Sports, Science, and Technology (MEXT). (2008). *'Netto-jō no ijime' ni kansuru taiō manyuaru jirei shū (gakkō, kyōin muke)* ["Bullying on the Net" Manual for handling and collection of cases (for schools and teachers)] (in Japanese). MEXT.

Ministry of Education, Culture, Sports, Science, and Technology. (2012). *Gakkō nettopatorōru ni kansuru torikumi jirei shiryōshū (kyōiku iinkai-tō-muke)* [A collection of examples of implementing Internet Patrol in schools (for PTA, etc.)] (in Japanese). Author.

NCPC. (n.d.). *Cyberbullying*. The National Crime Prevention Council of the US. Retrieved from: http://www.ncpc.org/topics/ cyberbullying/cyberbullying-faq-for-teens

Nitta, T., Masui, F., Ptaszynski, M., Kimura, Y., Rzepka, R., & Araki, K. (2013). Detecting Cyberbullying Entries on Informal School Websites Based on Category Relevance Maximization. *Proceedings of the 6th International Joint Conference on Natural Language Processing (IJCNLP 2013)*, 579-586.

Patchin, J. W., & Hinduja, S. (2006). Bullies move beyond the schoolyard: A preliminary look at cyberbullying. *Youth Violence and Juvenile Justice*, *4*(2), 148–169. doi:10.1177/1541204006286288

Ptaszynski, M., Dybala, P., Matsuba, T., Masui, F., Rzepka, R., Araki, K., & Momouchi, Y. (2010). In the Service of Online Order: Tackling cyberbullying with Machine Learning and Affect Analysis. *International Journal of Computational Linguistics Research*, *1*(3), 135–154.

Ptaszynski, M., Masui, F., Nitta, T., Hatakeyama, S., Kimura, Y., Rzepka, R., & Araki, K. (2016). Sustainable cyberbullying detection with category-maximized relevance of harmful phrases and double-filtered automatic optimization. *International Journal of Child-Computer Interaction*, *8*, 15–30. doi:10.1016/j.ijcci.2016.07.002

Pyżalski, J. (2012). From cyberbullying to electronic aggression: Typology of the phenomenon. *Emotional & Behavioural Difficulties*, *17*(3-4), 305–317. doi:10.1080/13632752.2012.704319

Qing, L. (2007). Bullying in the New Playground: Research into Cyberbullying and Cyber Victimisation. *Australasian Journal of Educational Technology*, *23*(4), 435454.

Sarna, G., & Bhatia, M. P. S. (2015). Content based approach to find the credibility of user in social networks: An application of cyberbullying. *International Journal of Machine Learning and Cybernetics*, 1–13.

Smith, P. K., Kwak, K., & Toda, Y. (Eds.). (2016). *School Bullying in Different Cultures*. Cambridge University Press. doi:10.1017/CBO9781139410878

Sood, S. O., Churchill, E. F., & Antin, J. (2012). Automatic identification of personal insults on social news sites. *Journal of the American Society for Information Science and Technology*, *63*(2), 270–285. doi:10.1002/asi.21690

Sourander, A., Brunstein Klomek, A., Ikonen, M., Lindroos, J., Luntamo, T., Koskelainen, M., ... Helenius, H. (2010). Psychosocial risk factors associated with cyberbullying among adolescents: A population-based study. *Archives of General Psychiatry*, *67*(7), 720728. doi:10.1001/archgenpsychiatry.2010.79 PMID:20603453

Sugimori, S. (2012). Anatomy of Japanese Bullying, https://www.nippon.com/en/currents/d00054/

Turney, P. D. (2002). Thumbs Up or Thumbs Down? Semantic Orientation Applied to Unsupervised Classification of Reviews. *Proc. of the 40th Annual Meeting of the Association for Computational Linguistics*, 417-424.

Watanabe, H. & Sunayama, W. (2006). *Denshi keijiban ni okeru yūza no seishitsu no hyōka* [User nature evalution on BBS] (in Japanese). IEICE Technical Report, 105(652), 2006-KBSE, pp. 25-30.

Weber, S., & Dixon, S. (Eds.). (2016). *Growing up online: young people and digital technologies*. Springer.

Chapter 3
Description and Initial Analysis of Cyberbullying Dataset

ABSTRACT

In this chapter, the authors focus on datasets used in cyberbullying detection research. They describe and compare several datasets applied in previous research and describe in detail the dataset that they decided to apply in their research. They also perform an initial analysis of the dataset to find various characteristics. They preprocess the dataset in several ways for further use and perform affect analysis to find out whether emotion-related features tend to be characteristic for cyberbullying. Based on the results of affect analysis, they also perform an initial attempt to classify cyberbullying data using a simple machine learning approach, which will be considered as a baseline in forthcoming chapters.

DESCRIPTION OF AVAILABLE CYBERBULLYING DATASETS

The research on cyberbullying detection started globally around the year 2009/2010. Since then a number of research teams attempted to tackle the problem. The general description of some of the research done previously has been presented in previous chapter. Here, we focus on datasets used in those research. There were several conditions we applied to choose the dataset for description in this chapter. Firstly, the dataset needed to be applied in more than one research paper. Moreover, we focused on datasets which were

DOI: 10.4018/978-1-5225-5249-9.ch003

significantly large, meaning, several thousands of samples or larger, desirably with balanced distribution of samples (cyberbullying to non-cyberbullying). All analyzed datasets were summarized in Table 1.

Historically the first dataset containing cyberbullying messages was the one created originally in 2008 and applied by Matsuba et al. (2009), and since then has been widely used by others (Matsuba et al., 2010, 2011; Ptaszynski et al., 2010; Nitta et al., 2013; Ptaszynski et al., 2015a, 2015b; Ptaszynski et al., 2016). It contains 1,490 harmful and 1,508 non-harmful entries in Japanese collected from unofficial school Web sites and fora, usually represented in the form of Electronic Bulletin Board Systems (BBS). The original data was provided by the Human Rights Research Institute Against All Forms for Discrimination and Racism in Mie Prefecture, Japan (http://www.pref.mie.lg.jp/jinkenc/hp/). The harmful and non-harmful sentences were collected and manually labeled by Internet Patrol members (expert annotators) according to instructions included in the governmental manual for dealing with cyberbullying (Ministry of Education, Culture, Sports, Science and Technology, 2008). More detailed descriptions of the instructions were explained in later sections of this chapter.

In 2009, Xu and Zhu (2010) collected a set of 11,670 comments in English from YouTube videos. They extracted the dataset half automatically, by using a set of offensive words. Because of the way the dataset was collected, it cannot be considered as fully cyberbullying-oriented, since offensive words can appear in a large variety of contexts. However, despite being largely imbalanced (harmful information was less than 15%), the authors later proved, that the corpus can be applied in a task related to cyberbullying detection with some success (Chen et al., 2012).

Also in 2009 a workshop called Content Analysis for the WEB 2.0 (CAW2.0) collocated with The 18th International World Wide Web Conference (WWW2009) released a dataset containing data from a number of SNS (Kongregate, Slashdot, MySpace, etc.) with application in a series of tasks (all data in English). One of the tasks was called "Misbehavior Detection" and considered detecting a generally defined malicious messages posted on such SNS. The dataset was applied in a number of studies on detection of Internet harassment (Yin et al., 2009; Bayzick, Kontostathis & Edwards, 2011).

In 2010, Ishisaka and colleagues automatically collected a dataset of, what they called "nasty comments" from a Japanese BBS forum 2channel (https://www.2ch.net/, recently renamed to 5channel, https://5ch.net/) (Ishisaka &

Table 1. Datasets containing cyberbullying labels

Dataset	Year	Contents	Developer/Provider	Language	No. of samples	No. of harmful samples	Ratio of harmful samples	Used by
BBS	2008	Messages from informal school BBS	Internet Patrol members / Human Right Center	Japanese	2,998	1,490	49.7%	(Matsuba et al, 2009, 2010, 2011; Ptaszynski et al., 2010; Nitta et al., 2013; Ptaszynski et al., 2015a, 2015b; Ptaszynski et al., 2016)
YouTube (1)	2009	Comments from YouTube videos containing offensive words	Researchers (subjective)	English	11,670	1,739	14.9%	(Xu & Zhu, 2010; Chen et al, 2012)
CAW 2.0	2009	Messages from Kongregate, Slashdot and MySpace	Fundacion Barcelona Media (FBM)	English	Kongregate: 4803	42	0.9%	(Yin et al., 2009; Bayzick, Kontostathis & Edwards, 2011)
					Slashdot: 1948	65	3.3%	
					MySpace: 4304	60	1.4%	
2channel	2010	Nasty comments on 2ch.net	Researchers (subjective)	Japanese	700,000	200,000	28.6%	(Ishisaka & Yamoto, 2010a, 2010b)
YouTube (2)	2011	Comments from YouTube videos	Researchers (subjective)	English	4,500	2,277	50.6%	(Dinakar et al, 2012; Dinakar, Reichart & Lieberman, 2011)
Viacom Data	2011	Comments collected from www.athinline.org	Viacom International Inc.	English	7,323	1197	16.3%	(Dinakar et al, 2012; Dinakar, Reichart & Lieberman, 2011)
PervertedJustice	2011	Chat transcripts with sexual predators	PervertedJustice	English	506 (chats)	506	100%	(Kontostathis, Edwards & Leatherman, 2010; McGhee et al., 2011)
Formspring	2013	Messages from Formspring.me	Researchers (subjective)	English	10,685	1,185	11.1%	(Reynolds, Kontostathis & Edwards, 2011; Kontostathis et al., 2013)
Instagram	2015	Instagram posts with comments (called ``media sessions")	Researchers (subjective)	English	1,954	567	29.0%	(Hosseinmardi et al., 2014; Hosseinmardi et al., 2015)

Yamamoto, 2010a, 2010b). The forum, famous for its anonymity, is often a place of verbal relief for stressed users, which in general results in many sarcastic and harmful entries. Ishisaka collected their dataset by downloading all entries containing one of the expressions they established as harmful in a psychological experiment. Although the dataset is not a cyberbullying dataset per se, its large size suggests that with a proper post-processing one could extract from it a large number of entries typical in cyberbullying.

In 2011 Dinakar et al. (2011, 2012) collected two datasets closely related to cyberbullying. First contained comments from YouTube, similarly to Xu and Zhu (2010), although had a more balanced ratio of harmful to non-harmful samples. The problem with this dataset was that in collecting it researchers applied their own subjective criteria, and did not focus directly on bullying, but rather on comments revealing sexual harassment, racial harassment or questioning intelligence of other users.

The second, larger dataset, was collected with the help of the Viacom company (http://www.viacom.com/), which helped creating and managing a Website for uploading comments that were "over the line" (that could hurt other users). This dataset contained over seven thousand samples, however, the ratio of harmful samples was about 16 percent.

Also in 2011 Kontostathis and colleagues applied a dataset of Internet chats with sexual predators, created by a Website called Perverted Justice (http://www.perverted-justice.com/) (Kontostathis, Edwards & Leatherman, 2010; McGhee et al., 2011). The managers behind the Website aim at hunting sexual predators by posing as victims, and later working together with the Police to convict the perpetrators, and additionally revealing their identities online together with the evidence (chat logs). Kontostathis et al. collected those chatlogs to build a general model of chat messages typical to sexual predators. The original set contained 506 conversations, each consisting of several to several thousand lines (chat turns). the time of writing this book (2018.08.28) the Website contains 623 chat transcripts, freely available for download.

Kontostathis et al. has also collected a dataset of harmful messages from the Formspring.me SNS (Reynolds, Kontostathis & Edwards, 2011; Kontostathis et al., 2013). The dataset contained over ten thousand messages and comments with about 11 percent of it being harmful.

A more recent dataset was created by Hosseinmardi et al. (2014, 2015) in 2014. It consists of nearly two thousand carefully selected Instagram posts together with their comments (called in general "media sessions"), with about one third accounting for being harmful.

In our research we aimed at applying as professionally created dataset as possible. We also aimed at using samples specifically related to cyberbullying, and not harmful in general, such as generally defined "nasty comments" or simply comments containing harmful expressions. Therefore in our research we focused on thorough analysis of the dataset created by Matsuba et al. (2009). The dataset has also been applied in a sufficiently large number of research, some of it being presented in this book. Below we describe the dataset in more detail.

DESCRIPTION AND DETAILED ANALYSIS OF APPLIED CYBERBULLYING DATASET

As mentioned above, in this research we applied the dataset created originally by Matsuba et al (2009) and developed further by Matsuba et al (2010, 2011). It contains 1,490 harmful and 1,508 non-harmful entries, 2998 entries in total. The harmful and non-harmful sentences were manually labeled by Internet Patrol members according to instructions included in the MEXT manual for dealing with cyberbullying (Ministry of Education, Culture, Sports, Science and Technology, 2008). Some of those instructions are explained shortly below.

The official governmental definition, created by Japan Ministry of Education, Culture, Sports, Science and Technology (MEXT) assumes that cyberbullying happens when a person is personally offended on the Web. This includes disclosing the person's name, personal information and other areas of privacy. Therefore, as the first feature distinguishable for cyberbullying MEXT defines private names. This includes such information as:

- Private names and surnames (e.g. "Michal Ptaszynski"),
    - When a person's name can be clearly distinguished
- Initials and nicknames (e.g. "Mr. P.", "Mi*al Ptasz*ski"),
    - When a person's identity can be clearly distinguished
    - When a person's identity cannot be clearly distinguished
- Names of institutions and affiliations (e.g. "That foreign professor from Kitami Institute of Technology").
    - When a person's identity can be clearly distinguished
    - When a person's identity cannot be clearly distinguished

As the second feature distinguishable for cyberbullying MEXT defines any other type of personal information. This includes:

- Address, phone numbers, etc. (e.g. "165 Koen-cho, Kitami, 090-8507, Japan", or "+81-157-26-9327"),
  - When the information refers to a private person
  - When the information is public or refers to a public entity
- Questions about private persons (e.g. "Who is that tall foreigner straying on Computer Science Dept. corridors?"),
  - Always considered as undesirable and harmful, including situations, in which the object is described in a positive way
- Entries revealing personal information (e.g. "I heard that guy is responsible for the new project.").
  - When a person's identity can be clearly distinguished
  - When a person's identity cannot be clearly distinguished

Literature on cyberbullying also indicates vulgarities as one of the most distinctive features of cyberbullying (Patchin & Hinduja, 2006, 2009; Ptaszynski et al., 2010). Also according to MEXT vulgar language is distinguishable for cyberbullying, due to its ability to convey offenses against particular persons. Examples of such words are, in English: *shit, fuck,* or *bitch*, in Japanese: *uzai* (freaking annoying), or *kimoi* (freaking ugly).

Table 2. Four examples of cyberbullying entries gathered during Internet Patrol. The upper three represent strong sarcasm despite of the use of positive expressions in the sentence. English translation below Japanese content. English translations were made to correspond as closely to Japanese as possible.

>>*104 Senzuri koi te shinu nante? sonna hageshii senzuri sugee naa. "Senzuri masutaa" toshite isshou agamete yaru yo.* >>104 Dying by 'flicking the bean'? Can't imagine how one could do it so fiercely. I'm gonna worship her as a 'master-bator', that's for sure.
2-nen no tsutsuji no onna meccha busu suki na hito barashimashoka? 1-nen no anoko desuyo ne? kimogatterunde yamete agete kudasai Wanna know who likes that awfully ugly 2nd-grade Azalea girl? It's that 1st-grader isn't it? He's disgusting, so let's leave him mercifully in peace.
Aitsu wa busakute sega takai dake no onna, busakute se takai dake ya noni yatara otoko-zuki meccha tarashide panko anna onna owatteru She's just tall and a part from that she's so freakin' ugly, and despite of that she's such a cock-loving slut, she's finished already.
Shinde kureeee, daibu kiraware-mono de yuumei, subete ga itaitashii... Please, dieeee, you're so famous for being disliked by everyone, everything in you is so pathetic

In the prepared dataset all entries containing any of the above information was classified as harmful. Some examples from the dataset are represented in Table 2.

AFFECT ANALYSIS OF CYBERBULLYING DATASET

As was shown by Chen and colleagues (Chen et al., 2004; Abbasi & Chen, 2007), analysis of affect intensity in various areas of the Internet, especially negatively infused Internet fora, such as Dark Web fora often helps specifying the character of the forum. Aiming to find any correlations between expressing emotions and cyberbullying activities we performed a study and analyzed affective level of the cyberbullying data.

The affect analysis was performed with ML-Ask system for affect analysis of textual input in Japanese and CAO system for analysis of emoticons, both developed previously by Ptaszynski and colleagues (Ptaszynski et al., 2017, 2010). Below we briefly describe both systems.

ML-Ask: Affect Analysis System

ML-Ask (eMotive eLements / Emotive Expressions Analysis System) (Ptaszynski et al., 2017) is a system developed for analyzing emotive contents of utterances. It provides information on emotions expressed in input, and specifies lexical elements representing emotive features and their grammatical categories.

The system uses a two-step procedure. Firstly, it analyzes general emotiveness of an utterance by detecting emotive elements, or *emotemes*, used by the speaker and classifies the utterance as emotive or non-emotive. Secondly, ML-Ask recognizes particular emotion types expressed in the input by extracting expressions of particular emotions from the utterance.

Emotive Elements or Emotemes

Emotemes represent elements conveyed in an utterance indicating that the speaker was emotionally involved in the utterance, but not detailing the specific emotion types. For example, interjections, like "ooh," "woow," or "aaah" are typical examples of emotemes. In Japanese language this group is linguistically realized by e.g., interjections, exclamations, mimetic expressions, or vulgar

Figure 1. Flow chart of ML-Ask system

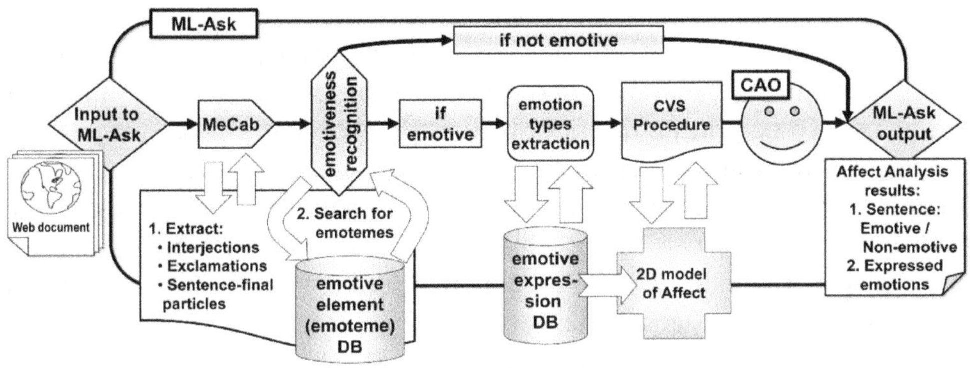

language. Examples are: *sugee* (great!), *wakuwaku* (heart pounding), *-yagaru* (a vulgarization of a verb); The manually-selected emotive element database of ML-Ask consists of interjections, mimetic expressions, endearments, vulgarities, and representations of non-verbal emotive elements, such as exclamation marks or ellipses, 907 elements in total.

Emotive Expressions

This group contains words used to describe emotional states. However, they function as expressions of the speaker's emotions only when used in emotionally involved utterances. In non-emotive sentences they fulfill a function of simple descriptive expressions. The group is realized by various parts of speech, like nouns, verbs, adjectives, etc. Examples are: *aijou* (love), *kanashimu* (to feel sad), *ureshii* (happy), respectively. The database of emotive expressions contains 2100 emotive expressions, each classified into one of ten emotion types they express.

A system for analysis of emoticons was also added, as emoticons are symbols commonly used in everyday text-based communication to convey emotions. The description of the system for emoticon analysis was presented in separate section below.

Short Description of Affect Analysis Procedure in ML-Ask

For textual input provided by the user, two features are computed in order: emotiveness of an utterance and specific type of emotion the utterance expresses. To determine the first feature, the system searches for emotive elements in the input to determine whether the input is emotive or non-emotive. In order to do this, the system at first uses MeCab for morphological analysis and separates every part of speech (Kudo, 2001). MeCab recognizes some parts of speech which belong to the group of emotemes, such as interjections, exclamations or emphatic sentence-final particles (*-zo*, *-yo*, or *-ne*). If these appear, they are extracted from the utterance as emotemes. Next, the system searches and extracts every emoteme based on the system's emoteme database (907 items).

Next, the input is processed by CAO (Ptaszynski et al., 2010), a system for analysis of emoticons (described in detail in later section). Emoticons belong to both emotemes, and emotive expressions, as their appearance in an input always indicates emotional attitude of the user and for most emoticons it is possible to specify the emotion type they convey. All of the extracted elements mentioned above (exclamations from MeCab, emotemes and emoticons) indicate the emotional level of the utterance. The emotional value of an input is calculated quantitatively; the more emotemes, the higher is the emotional value.

Figure 2. Grouping Nakamura's classification of emotions on Russell's space

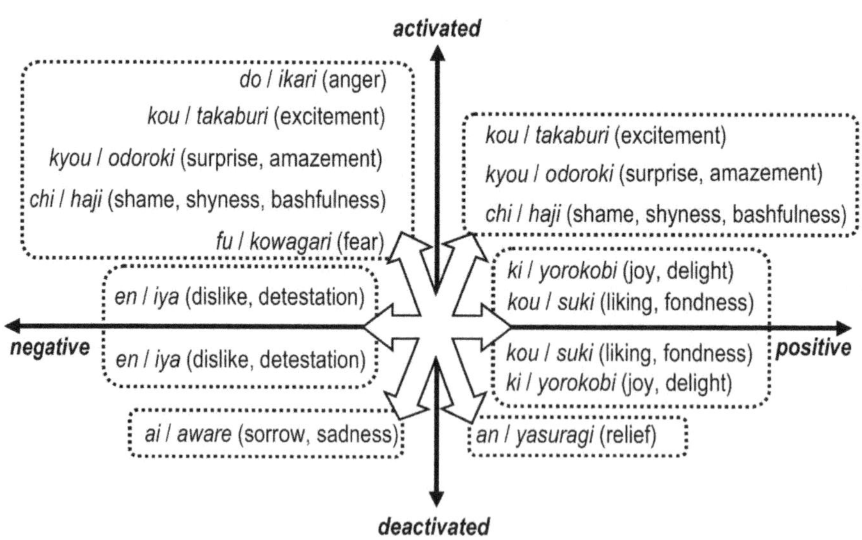

Secondly, in utterances classified as emotive (presence of at least one emoteme), the system uses the database of emotive expressions to search for all expressions describing emotional states. Here, emotions specified by CAO are added to the result of ML-Ask basic procedure. This determines the specific emotion type (or types) conveyed in the utterance. Examples of analysis performed by ML-Ask (system output) were represented in the following sections. In these examples, from top line there are: an example in Japanese, emotive information annotation (emotemes - underlined, emotive expressions-bold type font) and English translation.

Contextual Valence Shifters in ML-Ask

Additionally, to deal with the confusion in some cases of the valence of emotive expressions, resulting from the lack of processing of grammatical context, ML-Ask applies the idea of Contextual Valence Shifters (CVS). One example of such problematic case was presented below in example (3). In this sentence the emotive expression is the verb *akirameru* (to give up [verb]) but the phrase *-cha ikenai* (Don't- [particle+verb]) suggests that the speaker is in fact negating and forbidding the emotion expressed literally. Phrases negating evaluative expressions in grammatical context belong to the group of CVS.

The idea of CVS application in Sentiment Analysis for English was first proposed by Polanyi and Zaenen (2006), who distinguished such CVS as "not", "never", or "not quite" (negations), and "very", "very much", or "deeply" (intensifiers).

Examples of CVS negations in Japanese are grammatical structures such as: *-nai* (not-), *amari -nai* (not quite-), *-to wa ienai* (cannot say it is-), or *-te wa ikenai* (cannot+[verb]-). Intensifiers are: *totemo-* (very-), *sugoku-* (-a lot), or *kiwamete-* (extremely). A manually-crafted database of CVS in ML-Ask contains 71 negation structures.

Additionally, to specify the emotion types after changing polarity with CVS, we applied the idea of the 2-dimensional model of affect (Russell, 1980) which assumes that all emotions can be described in 2-dimensions: the emotion's valence polarity (positive/negative) and activation (activated/deactivated). An example of positive-activated emotion could be "excitement"; a positive-deactivated emotion is, e.g., "relief" (see Figure 2).

Emotion types distinguished in ML-Ask were mapped on this model and their affiliation to one of the spaces determined. The emotion types with ambiguous affiliation were mapped on two possible fields. When a CVS structure is discovered, ML-Ask changes the valence polarity of the detected emotion. The appropriate emotion after valence changing is determined as the one with valence polarity and activation parameters opposite to the contrasted emotion (note arrows in Figure 2).

CAO: Emoticon Analysis System

Since one of the most popular strategies of expressing emotions in online communication is using emoticons, we supported ML-Ask with emoticon analysis system, CAO. It is a system for estimation of emotions conveyed through emoticons, and was created by Ptaszynski et al. (2010). CAO, or *emotiCon Analysis and decOding of affective information*, extracts an emoticon from an input (a sentence) and determines specific emotion types expressed by it using a three-step procedure. Firstly, matching the input with a predetermined raw emoticon database containing over ten thousand emoticons. The emoticons, which could not be estimated with only the database are automatically divided into semantic areas, such as representations of "mouth" or "eyes," based on the idea of kinemes, or minimal meaningful body movements, applied from the theory of kinesics (Birdwhistell, 1952, 1970). The areas are automatically annotated according to their co-occurrence in database. The annotation is firstly based on eye-mouth-eye triplet. If no triplet is found, all semantic areas are estimated separately. This provides hints about potential groups of expressed emotions giving the system a coverage of over 3 million possibilities. CAO is used as a supporting procedure in ML-Ask to improve the performance of the affect analysis procedure in utterances, which do not include emotive expressions, like in the example (2) below (emotemes - underlined; emotive expressions - bold type font).

1. *Kyo wa nante **kimochi ii** hi nanda !*

   Today:TOP ML:nante **MX:joy** day:SUB ML:nanda ML:!
   Translation: Today is such a nice day!

2. *Iya~, sore wa sugoi desu ne– ! ^o^*

   ML:iya~ this:TOP ML:sugoi COP ML:ne– ML:! ML:^o^
   Translation: Whoa, that's great! ^o^ **MX:joy**

3. ***Akirame** cha ikenai yo !*

Table 3. Four examples of cyberbullying entries gathered during Internet Patrol from unofficial school BBS Websites. The upper three represent expressing strong sarcasm despite of the use of positive expressions in the sentence. Emotemes - underlined; Emotive expressions - bolt type font.

*>>104 Senzuri koi te shinu nante? sonna hageshii senzuri sugee naa. "Senzuri masutaa" toshite isshou **agamete** yaru yo.* Analysis results: Emotemes: nante, sugee, naa, -yo, senzuri; Emotive expression: **agameru** (worship, respect) → fondness ; Translation: >>104 Dying by 'flicking the bean'? Can't imagine how one could do it so fiercely. I'm gonna worship her as a 'master-bator', that's for sure.
*2-nen no tsutsuji no onna meccha busu **suki** na hito barashimashoka? 1-nen no anoko desu yo ne? kimogatteru n de yamete agete kudasai* Analysis results: Emotemes: meccha, -yo, -ne, -nde, kimogaru; Emotive expressions: ***suki*** (like) → **fondness** ; Translation: Wanna know who likes that awfully ugly 2nd-grade Azalea girl? It's that 1st-grader isn't it? He's disgusting, so let's leave him mercifully in peace.
*Aitsu wa busakute sega takai dake no onna, busakute se takai dake ya noni yatara otoko-**zuki** meccha tarashi de panko anna onna owatteru* Analysis results: Emotemes: yatara, meccha, busai, tarashi, panko; Emotive expressions:***-zuki*** (-lover; an amateur of-) → **fondness** ; Translation: She's just tall and a part from that she's so freakin' ugly, and despite of that she's such a cock-loving slut, she's finished already.
Shinde kureeee, daibu kiraware-mono de yuumei, subete ga itaitashii… Analysis results: Emotemes: -eee (syllable prolongation), … (elipsis);Emotive expressions: ***kiraware-mono*** (disliked by others) → **dislike**, ***itaitashii*** (pathetic,pitiful) → **gloom, sadness** ; Translation: Please, dieeee, you're so famous for being disliked by everyone, everything in you is so pathetic

MX:dislike ML:chal CVS:cha-ikenai{→joy} ML:yo ML:!
Translation: Don't give up!

4. ***Hitoribocchi*** nante ***iya*** da ~~

MX:sadness ML:nante–da **MX:dislike** COP ML:~~
Translation: Being alone sucks...

AFFECT ANALYSIS RESULTS

At first we calculated the number of all emotive entries among both sets of data. There was 956 emotive samples among 1,495 harmful (63.95%) and 1,029 among 1,504 non-harmful (68.42%) entries. The difference was not high and therefore the number of emotive entries cannot be considered as a highly distinctive feature for cyberbullying. However, we made a first weak assumption, that harmful data could be less emotively emphasized than non-harmful. This is a reasonable assumption, since cyberbullying is often based on irony or sarcasm, which is not highly emotive, however deliberately uses some amount of emotive information to slander the object of sarcasm. To confirm this hypothesis we performed other comparisons.

We calculated emotive values of all emotive entries. Although the number of emotive entries and emotive value, both relate to the idea of emotiveness of a corpus in general, they are not directly related. One can easily imagine the difference between one corpus that consists of many slightly emotive entries (high number of emotive entries, but low average emotive value) and another corpus with a small number of highly emotive entries (low number of emotive entries, but high average emotive value). The approximated emotive value for harmful and non-harmful data was 1.47 and 1.5, respectively. Here also the difference is not high, although, since both values are not directly related, this can moderately support the above hypothesis.

Next, we took a closer look at the extracted emotemes. There are four groups of emotemes distinguished in ML-Ask: i) interjections, ii) exclamations, iii) vulgarities and iv) mimetic expressions (*gitaigo* in Japanese) - arranged in order of their emotional weight. Distribution of the extracted emotemes within both sets is represented in Table 4. There were relatively more emotemes with high emotive weight in non-harmful data and more low weight emotemes in harmful data, which is another confirmation of the thesis presented at the beginning of this section.

The most visible difference between the number of extracted emotemes was found for vulgarities. Therefore we can say with certainty that vulgarities can be regarded as one distinctive feature of cyberbullying entries. This is one of the reasons we used it as the main feature in initial machine learning approach, described in later section.

A similar difference, although lower, appeared also in mimetic expressions, which could be included in further study on enlarging the lexicon for the machine learning system. As for interjections and exclamations, although they appeared in a large number in both datasets, more of them appeared in non-harmful entries. This could be caused by the fact that these two emoteme types are used to express emotive attitude in a straightforward way. Therefore, although there certainly are cyberbullying cases where the victims are slandered straightforwardly, non-emotional and cold sarcasm is also a frequent phenomenon.

Another comparison was made with the closer study of emotive utterances. ML-Ask is capable of detecting emotive utterances with a high reliability (previous research indicated *kappa* = 0.8), however, it specifies particular emotion types with low Recall (although with high Precision) (Ptaszynski et al., 2009). It is due to the use of a lexicon (Nakamura's "Dictionary of Emotive Expressions", cf. Nakamura, 1993) that is out of date. Therefore there is a certain number of samples always described as emotive but with no specified emotion types. Such a phenomenon is however reasonable from the linguistic point of view, since there are many sentences that are emotive, although the emotion they convey depends on their context.

We first compared how many specified vs unspecified emotive utterances there were in the data. The result was 13.18% vs 86.82% for cyberbullying and 11.95% vs 88.05% for the normal entries. The slightly higher ratio of specified emotion types in cyberbullying data might suggest that people more often use traditional emotive expressions to slander other people than they do to express emotions in normal situations.

Next, we compared the number of particular emotive expressions extracted by ML-Ask. The results were represented in Table 5. The analysis of the number of emotion types represented by the extracted emotive expressions revealed interesting tendencies, although here as well the strength of the proof was weak.

Anger scored much higher in the cyberbullying data than in the normal data, which is a reasonable result, since Internet entries meant to slander others are expected to express anger more often. Fear on the other hand scored very low in cyberbullying data. This is also reasonable, since it is difficult to bully others by expressing one's fears. Dislike scored slightly higher in the harmful data. As for the positive emotion types, e.g., joy scored higher in normal dataset, which was expectable. On the other hand, fondness scored unexpectedly higher in cyberbullying dataset. Detailed analysis revealed that people would often express strong sarcasm with the use of positive expressions. Some examples of such entries have been represented in Table 3.

Table 4. Distribution of the extracted emotemes within both entry sets

type of	**type of data**	
emoteme	**non-harmful**	**harmful**
interjections	**859**	784
exclamations	**284**	174
vulgarities	8	**149**
mimetic expressions	7	**23**

Table 5. The number of particular emotive expressions extracted by ML-Ask from both datasets

type of data			
non-harmful		harmful	
emotion type	no. extr.	emotion type	no. extr.
dislike	49	dislike	56
joy	32	fondness	49
fondness	21	joy	12
relief	18	relief	9
fear	11	anger	8
gloom/sadness	7	gloom/sadness	7
surprise	6	excitement	3
excitement	5	fear	3
anger	3	shame	3
shame	0	surprise	3

Finally, we compared tendencies in the annotated emotion types with regard to the two-dimensional affect space. The results were represented in Table 6. In the valence dimension, negative emotions were annotated most often on harmful data, and positive emotions, on non-harmful data, which is a reasonable and predictable result. The differences were not that obvious, however, after exclusion of fondness, which, as mentioned above, was often used mostly in sarcasm, the differences became clearer. The smallest difference was observed in emotion types which can be classified as both positive or negative, as their valence usually depends on the particular context.

As for the activation dimension, non-harmful data was annotated as more vivid in the groups of deeply activated and deeply deactivated emotions. On the other hand, harmful data was annotated more often with moderately activated emotions, which provides another proof for the hypothesis set on the beginning of this section, namely, that slandering is often expressed in non-emotional statements. Moreover, we were able to set the linguistic feature most distinguishable for cyberbullying activities, namely, vulgarities. This could be an important clue in future development of machine learning algorithm for cyberbullying detection.

Table 6. Comparison of tendencies in annotation of emotion types with regard to the two-dimensional affect space

valence (polarity) of emotions								
negative emotion			**negative/positive (both possible)**			**positive emotion**		
emotion type	non-harmful	harmful	emotion type	non-harmful	harmful	emotion type	non-harmful	harmful
gloom/sadness	7	7	excitement	**5**	3	joy	**32**	12
fear	**11**	3	shame	0	**3**	fondness	21	**49**
anger	3	**8**	surprize	**6**	3	relief	**18**	9
dislike	49	**56**				SUM	**71**	70
SUM	70	**74**	SUM	**11**	9	SUM (fondness excluded)	**50**	21

activation of emotions								
deactivated emotion			**moderately activated (deactivated/activated)**			**activated emotion**		
emotion type	non-harmful	harmful	emotion type	non-harmful	harmful	emotion type	non-harmful	harmful
gloom/sadness	7	7	joy	**32**	12	shame	0	**3**
relief	**18**	9	fondness	21	**49**	excitement	**5**	3
			dislike	49	**56**	fear	**11**	3
						anger	3	**8**
						surprize	**6**	3
SUM	**25**	16	SUM	102	**117**	SUM	**25**	20

BASELINE MACHINE LEARNING METHOD FOR CYBERBULLYING DETECTION

In this section we describe an initial machine learning method developed to handle cyberbullying activities. The method consists of several stages, including creation of a lexicon of vulgar, slanderous and abusive words, slanderous information detection module, ranking of the information according to the level of its harmfulness, and visualization of the harmful information. The system flow chart was represented in Figure 3. The creation of the system was separated into two general phases: training phase and processing (test) phase. Below we present the details of each phase.

1. Training phase:
    a. Crawling the school Web sites,
    b. Detecting manually cyberbullying entries,
    c. Extraction of vulgar words and adding them to lexicon,
    d. Estimating word similarity with Levenshtein distance,
    e. Part of speech analysis,
    f. Training with SVM.
2. Processing (test) phase:

a. Crawling the school Web sites,
b. Detecting the cyberbullying entries with SVM model,
c. Part of speech analysis of the detected harmful entry,
d. Estimating word similarity with Levenshtein distance,
e. Marking and visualization of the key sentence.

DEFINITION OF CYBERBULLYING ENTRY

Basing on the definition of cyberbullying provided by MEXT (2008) as well as the results of affect analysis from previous section, we created our own working definition of a cyberbullying entry. With this definition we aimed to embrace the features needed to deal with in research such as ours.

Firstly, the data needs to be appropriately divided and weighted. In our definition we divided entries into three types. Normal (N) entry is an entry not containing any harmful information and thus not needing any intervention. Doubtful (D) entry contains information that might be harmful, but it needs further analysis to make the decision whether to delete it or not. Finally, Harmful (H) entry is a type of entry towards which there is no doubt that it contains harmful information and the decision to delete it can be made without further analysis. We used the above tripartite annotation to classify different types of entry contents.

At first we recall the definition provided by MEXT, which generally assumes that cyberbullying happens when a person is personally offended on the Web. This includes disclosing the person's name, personal information and other areas of privacy. Therefore, as the first feature distinguishable for cyberbullying entry we define NAMES. This includes such information as:

- **Names and surnames of people**

  (e.g. "Michal Ptaszynski")
  H - When a person's name can be clearly distinguished

- **Initials and nicknames**

  (e.g. "M.P.", "Mich** Ptasz**ski", "Mr. P.")
  H - When a person's identity can be clearly distinguished
  D - When a person's identity cannot be clearly distinguished

- **Names of institutions and affiliations**

(e.g. "That Professor from Kitami Institute of Technology")
H - When a person's identity can be clearly distinguished
D - When a person's identity cannot be clearly distinguished

As the second type of a feature distinguishable for cyberbullying we define any other type of PERSONAL INFORMATION. This includes:

- **Address, phone numbers, etc.**

(e.g. "Koen-cho 165, Kitami, 090-8507, Japan", or "+81-0157-26-9327")
H - When the information refers to a private person,
D - When the information is public or refers to a public entity.

- **Questions about private persons**

(e.g. "Who is that tall foreigner walking around lately on the Department's corridor?")

H - Always considered as undesirable and harmful, including situations, in which the object is described in a positive way.

- **Entries revealing personal information**

(e.g. "I heard that guy is responsible for the new project.")
H - When a person's identity can be clearly distinguished,
D - When a person's identity cannot be clearly distinguished.

In the above section we were also able to find another distinctive feature of cyberbullying. Namely, the largest difference in extraction of linguistic features from both cyberbullying and normal data was noticed for vulgarities. Therefore we selected VULGARITIES as the keywords distinguishable for cyberbullying. Vulgarities are obscene or vulgar words which convey slurs against particular persons or society. Examples of such words in English are *shit, fuck, bitch*. Examples in Japanese include words like *uzai* (freaking annoying), or *kimoi* (freaking ugly). In our research we divided the entries containing vulgarities into two types, namely:

- **Entries containing any form of vulgar or offensive language**

D - Even when the object cannot be identified

- **Quarrels between two or more users**

D - Even when it happens between two anonymous users, a quarrel can lead to revealing personal information or other forms of cyberbullying

All entries not containing any of the above information are classified as normal (N).

Definition Testing

To test, whether the above definition is coherent, we performed an experiment. From the overall 2,998 entries (1,490 harmful and 1,508 non-harmful) we extracted randomly a sample of 500 entries. Then we asked six human annotators (5 males and 1 female) to annotate the sample according to the above definition. Finally, we calculated Cohen's *kappa* agreement coefficient for all participants. The agreement coefficient was 0.67, which is regarded as strong, and confirms that the definition is coherent. However, in some cases the participants did not agree completely, mostly in cases of vulgarity. Some words could be considered as vulgar or not depending on one's subculture and usual vocabulary (e.g., "gangster", or "pimp" can be perceived as normal in a hip-hop subculture). This indicates that the definition should be complemented in the future with more strict definitions of vulgarities.

Construction of Vulgarity Lexicon

Vulgar words are often not detected by part of speech (POS) taggers, or marked as "unknown words". We decided to create a list of vulgarities and add it to a basic lexicon of the POS tagger applied in this research (MeCab (Kudo, 2001)). This was performed according to the procedure described below.

At first, we performed a study on vulgar keywords constituting the harmful information. We read through our dataset of informal school Web pages and manually annotated vulgar words on this data. This way we obtained 255 unique vulgar keywords distinguishable for cyberbullying activity. The extracted keywords were finally added to the list of vulgarities. Finally, we added grammatical information to the extracted keywords and added them to the POS tagger. An example of addition of grammatical information is presented in Table 7.

Estimation of Word Similarity With Levenshtein Distance

A thorough analysis of the dataset revealed that the users would often change spelling of words and write them in a non-standard way. It is a part of jargonization of the language used online. Examples of this phenomenon in English, would be writing phrases like, "C.U." in the meaning of "See you [later]!" (usually at the end of e-mails or online messages), or "brah" in the meaning of "bro[ther], friend" (https://www.internetslang.com/), etc. Some examples of such colloquial transformations in the Japanese online language are shown in Table 8.

With this variation, words which have the same meaning would be classified as separate samples, which would cause hit-rate dispersion. Therefore to unify the same words written with slightly different spelling we calculated the similarity of the extracted words. The similarity was calculated using Levenshtein Distance (Levenshtein, 1965) in a way similar to Minoru and Hirohide (1997) and Ryozo, Koudai, and Tatsuya (2005). The Levenshtein Distance between two strings is calculated as the minimum number of operations required to transform one string into another, where the available operations are only deletion, insertion or substitution of a single character.

However, as Japanese is transcribed using three character types, Chinese characters (kanji) encapsulating from one to several syllables and two additional syllabary (katakana and hiragana), calculating the distance would become imprecise. To solve this problem, every word was automatically transformed into its alphabetical transcription. An example of distance calculation is presented on the back-transformation of the word *kimosu* to its original spelling *kimoi* in Table 9. The distance between both words is equal 2.

Table 7. Example of a newly registered word in POS tagger

kimoi (freaking ugly)
POS: Adjective;
Headword: *kimoi* (hit-rate: 294);
Reading: kimoi;
Pronunciation: kimoi;
Conjugated form: uninflected

Figure 3. Flow chart of the cyberbullying activity detecting system

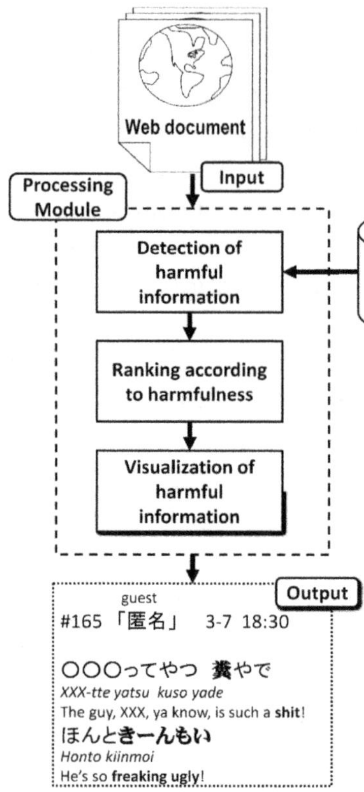

Table 8. Three examples of colloquial transformations of Japanese words in online jargon

original word	colloquial transformation
kimoi (freaking ugly, gross)	*kimosu, kishoi, kisho, ...*
uzai (freaking annoying)	*uzee, UZAI, uzakkoi, ...*
busaiku (ugly bitch)	*buchaiku, bussaiku, ...*

Table 9. An example of colloquial transformations of Japanese words in online jargon

transformed word performed operation	
kimosu	
→ *kimoiu*	substitution of 's' to 'i'; distance = 1;
→ *kimoi*	deletion of final 'u'; distance = 2;

SVM Based Classification of Cyberbullying

To classify the entries into either harmful (cyberbullying) or non-harmful, we used Support Vector Machines. Support Vector Machines (SVMs) are a method of supervised machine learning developed by Vapnik (1998) and used for classification of data. They are defined as follows. With a set of training samples, divided into two categories A and B, SVM training algorithm generates a model for prediction of whether test samples belong to either category A or B. In the traditional description of SVM model, samples are represented as points in space (vectors). SVM constructs a hyperplane, in a space of a higher dimension than the base one, with the largest distance to the nearest training data points (support vectors). The larger the margin the lower the generalization error of the classifier. Since SVM has been successfully used for text classification (Hirotoshi, Takafumi & Masahiko, 1998) we decided to use them in this research as well as a baseline. In our research category A contains cyberbullying cases and the category B contains all other cases, which do not consist of socially harmful information. As the software for building SVM models we used SVM light (http://svmlight.joachims.org).

Extraction of Key Sentences

In the process of automation of Internet Patrol, apart from the classification of cyberbullying entries, there is a need to appropriately determine how harmful a certain entry is. A ranking according to the harmfulness of entries is important to detect the most dangerous cases. In our approach an entry is considered as the more harmful, the more vulgar keywords appear in the entry.

The harmfulness of an entry is calculated using T-score. T-score is a measure that answers the question of how confident one can be that the association measured between two words is an actual collocation and not a matter of chance. The higher occurrence frequency a word has in a corpus, the higher is the value of T-score. A T-score of a word associating with words A and B is calculated according to the equation below:

$$T_{score} = \frac{a}{b} \tag{1}$$

where,

$$a = \left[word\ \ co'occurrence\ \ frequency\right] - \frac{\left(\left[occurrence\, of\ word\, A\right] * \left[occurrence\, of\ word\, B\right]\right)}{\left[all\ words\ in\ the\ corpus\right]}$$

and,

$$b = \sqrt{\left[word\ \ co'occurrence\ \ frequency\right]}$$

We calculate the harmfulness of the whole entry as a sum of T-scores calculated for all vulgar words. This way the more frequently occurring words there are in the entry, the higher rank the entry achieves in the ranking of harmfulness.

EVALUATION OF THE METHOD

To verify the performance of the method we evaluated three procedures:

1. Classification of cyberbullying entries with SVM,
2. Word similarity calculation with Levenshtein distance,
3. Extraction of key sentences.

Evaluation of SVM Model

To apply SVM to detect harmful information from unofficial school BBS sites, we needed to prepare the data for training the SVM model. At first we performed morphological analysis of the BBS entries to be used as the training data. For every part of speech from the analyzed and parsed data we used as features the POS labels with the original strings of characters. As the features in the part of speech identification we used parts of speech like nouns (person's name, or other than name), verbs and adjectives. In the identification of the whole entries we used feature sets consisting of the features of each part of speech and the strings of characters containing the whole entry. Based on the amount of identified features, SVM model calculates the probability of affiliation of a character string to a certain class.

As the features for training we used several combinations of main and additional features. Main features included: (1) words with POS, (2) words only, (3) POS only. Additional features included: (A) Occurrence frequency, calculated as in equation 2, (B) Relative frequency, calculated as in equation 3, (C) Inverse document frequency (IDF), calculated as in equation 4, and (D) Term frequency–inverse document frequency (TF-IDF), calculated as in equation 5.

$$(\mathbf{A})\ \textbf{\textit{Occurrence frequency}} = \textbf{\textit{Frequency of a POS within one document}} \tag{2}$$

$$(\mathbf{B})\ \textbf{\textit{Relative frequency}} = \frac{(A)}{\textbf{\textit{Frequency of a POS within all documents}}} \tag{3}$$

Figure 4. Results of the experiments with SVM for different features

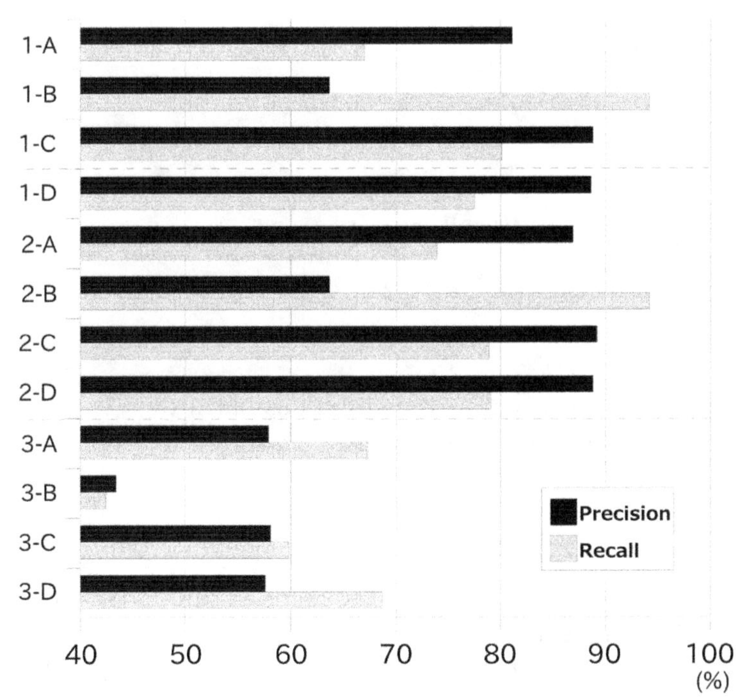

$$(C)\ IDF = log\left(\frac{number\ of\ all\ entries}{number\ of\ entries\ containing\ the\ POS} + 1\right) \tag{4}$$

$$(D)\ TF * IDF = (A) * (C) \tag{5}$$

As the training data we used all 2,998 entries gathered during an actual Internet Patrol, from which human annotators (Internet Patrol members) classified 1,490 entries as harmful and 1,508 as non-harmful. We did not, however, apply the string similarity calculation to the SVM model, to evaluate both techniques separately.

The above conditions were applied to test the model trained with SVM light. In the evaluation we calculated the system's result as balanced F-score, using 10-fold cross validation for Precision and Recall. In 10-fold cross validation data is first broken into 10 sets of size n/10. Then, 9 datasets are used for training on and 1 for testing. This procedure is repeated 10 times and the overall score is the mean accuracy from all 10 tests. The balanced F-score, Precision (P) and Recall (R) are calculated as follows,

$$F_{score} = 2 * \frac{P * R}{P + R} \tag{6}$$

where,

$$\textbf{Precision} = \frac{s}{n} \qquad \textbf{Recall} = \frac{n}{c}$$

and,

s = cases correctly classified by the system as harmful
n = all cases classified by the system as harmful
c = all harmful cases

The results were represented in Figure 4. The results for group 3 (only POS) were the lowest. Groups 1 (words+POS) and 2 (words only) were comparable. The highest Recall appeared in the experiments with Relative Frequency. However, the Precision in this case was not ideal (close to 65%).

Table 10. Two heuristic rules applied in optimization of similarity calculation algorithm

Rule	Example
1. deletion syllable prolongations	*kimoooi* → *kimoi*
2. unification of word first letter	In case of *uzai* we will consider only the words beginning with *u*

Experiments with IDF (C) and TF-IDF (D) gave the highest results with Recall close to 80%, Precision close to 90%. The highest score from all was for the combination words+POS with TF-IDF (Precision = 89%, Recall = 80%, F-score = 84.3%).

Evaluation of Similarity Calculation

When preparing the conditions for evaluation of word similarity calculation method with Levenshtein distance, we noticed that the larger was the threshold, the higher was the probability of matching a word with completely different meaning. Therefore we performed an optimization of the similarity

Figure 5. Precision of similarity calculation before and after applying the heuristic rules

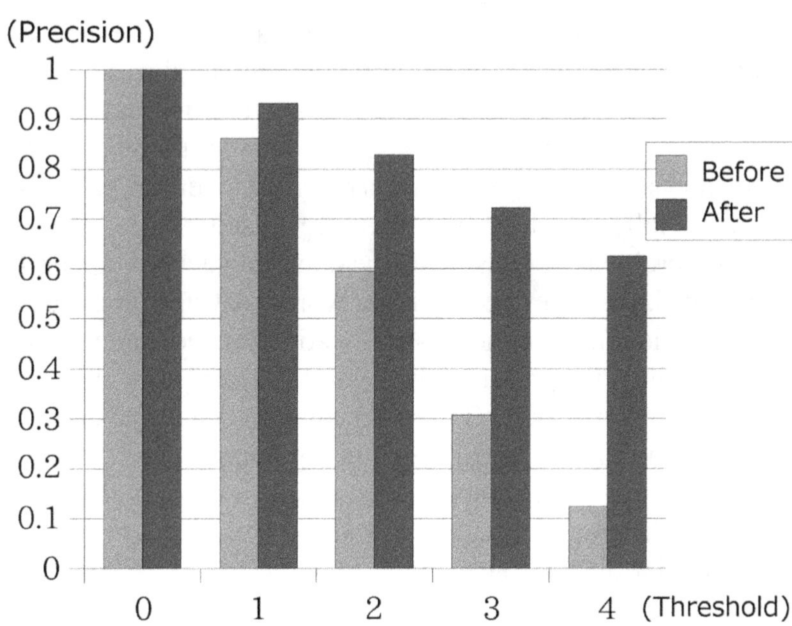

calculation algorithm. In the optimization we applied two heuristic rules shown in Table 10.

On BBS sites, where informal language is widely used, such as unofficial school Web sites, prolonging of syllables is used mostly to express changes in user attitude, or mood, usually highlighting the informal character of the entry. However, such operation has no influence on the semantics of a word. Therefore before the phase of similarity calculation we added a rule deleting all syllable prolongations.

The second rule was unification of the first letters of matched words. This was done because in Japanese language only the final letters change during conjugation. Therefore we could assume that it is irrelevant to calculate similarity for words differing with first letters.

The results for Precision of similarity calculation before and after applying the heuristic rules were presented on Figure 5. The Precision was greatly improved after applying the rules. With the threshold set on 2, the Precision before applying the rules was 58.9% and was improved to 85.0%.

Evaluation of Key Sentence Extraction

To set the ranking of cyberbullying entries according to how harmful they are, we calculated the T-score of vulgar vocabulary they contain. The results were represented in Table 11. As one can see in Table 11, the first three scores are much higher then the other ones. This is caused by numerous repetitions of the same vulgar words in one entry, which artificially increases the occurrence rate. Moreover, in the cases appearing in the table on places 4-6, one of the words was used repeatedly, which also caused artificial increase of occurrence and eventually the result of T-score, although smaller than for the first three cases. In such cases, although the occurrence of a certain pair is not high, T-score is artificially increased and therefore biased.

To solve this problem we considered the same vulgar words appearing in one entry as one word. However, some vulgar words may appear as collocations. In such cases the identical numerous collocations are considered as one. The change in the results is represented in Table 12. The results indicate the bias have disappeared. However, the T-score became too small causing many word pairs appear on the same place in the ranking making the ranks difficult to set. This is caused by the fact that the words with the same meaning appear on the Web sites in different transcription and therefore there is a large number of word sets with a small occurrence.

Table 11. The results of T-score calculation for sets of vulgar words. Words in Japanese can be usually transcribed in three different systems: hiragana, katakana and kanji. The differences in transcription are represented in the table as markers after the words, with [h] for hiragana, [k] katakana and [K] for kanji.

word A	word B	co-occurrence	T-score
baka [h] (stupid)	baka [h]	861	29.34
shine [K] (fuck you)	shine [K]	552	23.49
shine [h]	shine [h]	58	7.62
tarashi [k] (pimp)	shine [K]	17	4.12
busu [k] (ugly bitch)	shine [K]	16	4.00
kimosu [h]	shine [h]	16	4.00
shine [h]	busu [h]	6	2.45

Table 12. Change in the results of T-score calculation for sets of vulgar words, when two or more words were considered as one

word A	word B	co-occurrence	T-score
shine [K]	shine [K]	7	2.65
shine [h]	shine [h]	4	2.00
pashiri [k] (looser)	shine [K]	3	1.73
debu [k]	kiero [K]	3	1.73
kiero [K] (get lost)	kiero [K]	2	1.41
shine [K]	kiero [K]	2	1.41
uzai [h]	kimoi [k]	2	1.41

Table 13. Change in the results of T-score calculation for sets of vulgar words, with calculated word similarity

word A	word B	co-occurrence	T-score
shine [K]	shine [K]	11	3.32
kimoi [h]	shine [K]	11	3.32
kimoi [h]	busaiku [h]	8	2.83
uzai [h]	kimoi [h]	7	2.65
panko [k] (slut)	panko [k]	6	2.45
kimoi [h]	kimoi [h]	6	2.45
busaiku [h]	busaiku [h]	6	2.45

We solved this problem by calculating word similarity before calculating T-score. The results were represented in Table 13. Due to word similarity calculation a rise in T-score was observed and the number of diversified word pairs increased, which made rank setting much easier. There was 202 vulgar word pairs, from which 40 pairs occurred more than twice.

DISCUSSION

This time in morphological analysis of vulgar words we used only a small set of manually discovered words, which we added to the lexicon. It is difficult to include all existing vulgar words and more such vocabulary will appear in the future as well. Therefore as a further work we need to develop a method for automatic extraction of vulgar vocabulary from the Internet.

The results of SVM model used to distinguish between harmful and non-harmful information were 89% of Precision and 80% of Recall. However, on the unofficial school Web pages used as the data in this research there were numerous entries consisting of only one sentence, or even one word. Therefore the feature set for training was not sufficient and the overall result was not ideal (F-score = 84.3%).

As for word similarity calculation, many vulgar words are short and a change of even one letter might cause a change of meaning. Therefore, two different words would be matched as similar by Levenshtein distance, when the threshold is too wide. This problem might be solved by automatically setting the threshold according to the length of each word.

As for the extraction of key sentences, although we were able to calculate a non-biased T-score for vulgar expressions and set the ranking, over 80% of vulgar words appeared only once. This caused over half of the cases to be attached with similar ranks. This problem could be solved in future by increasing the number of training data or applying a different method of rank setting.

CONCLUSION AND FUTURE WORK

In this chapter we performed a study on datasets containing cyberbullying entries, described in a the literature. We found and described nine datasets, from which we chose one in particular, developed especially for the study on cyberbullying by one of the Human Rights Centers in Japan.

Looking for clues to select linguistic features to be used later in machine learning algorithm for cyberbullying detection, we performed a comparative affect analysis of the cyberbullying data and normal entries. As a result, we noticed that the harmful data was less emotively emphasized than non-harmful. This hypothesis is reasonable, since harmful entries are usually written with premeditation and aim not in expressing ones own emotions, but in evoking in other online community members negative emotions against the victim of cyberbullying. The results of comparing different dimensions of emotional emphasis suggested the hypothesis was true, although the reliability of the proof was not satisfactory and further analysis on more robust data is necessary.

Another discovery, although an expected one, was that positive emotions appeared more often in non-harmful data and negative emotions appeared more often in harmful data. However, detailed analysis revealed that, especially for fondness, the expressions of positive emotions were often used in strong sarcastic meaning. Therefore there is a need to analyze the data taking into consideration also other dimensions than the valence and the activation of an emotion. As one of such means in the future we plan to apply Ptaszynski et al's (2009, 2010, 2013) system for contextual affect analysis, which verifies whether an emotion expressed in an utterance is appropriate for its context. We assume this will help in developing a sufficient model of formalization of cyberbullying activities. For the first step of the research, we were able to select the most distinctive linguistic feature for cyberbullying, namely, vulgarities. We used this feature in the creation of the initial machine learning classifier for cyberbullying detection.

We created the machine learning-based system for cyberbullying detection and evaluated it. At first, we manually gathered a lexicon of vulgar words distinctive for cyberbullying entries. To recognize the vulgar words, but written in an informal or jargonized way, we calculated word similarity with Levenshtein distance. As the result, with the threshold equal 2 the system was able to correctly determine the similar words with a 85% of Precision. The Support Vector Machine model trained for discrimination between harmful and non-harmful data achieved the results of 89% of Precision and 80% of Recall (with balanced F-score = 84.3%). Finally the rank setting of the online entries according to their harmfulness was set using T-score. We were able to eliminate undesirable bias in the rank setting, unfortunately, the procedure is not yet ideal.

Since new vulgar words appear frequently, we need to find a way to automatically extract new vulgarities from the Internet to keep the lexicon up to date. There is also a need for more experiments with the system including its different variations and improvements (ex. Levenshtein distance threshold optimization).

In the following chapters we will focus firstly on improving the method for rank setting of online entries according to their harmfulness (Chapter 4), after which we propose an original method for cyberbullying inspired by a Brute Force Search algorithm (Chapter 5), and then with Convolutional Neural Networks (Chapter 6). We also describe our smartphone application for testing the developed methods (Chapter 7).

The problems concerning online security have been escalating ever since the birth of the Internet. Some of them are widely known to the society, such as spam e-mails or hacking, however more and more of such problems, including cyberbullying, appear by the day and awareness about them is not yet sufficient. There have been developed solutions for some of these problems (e.g., automatic spam e-mail filtering, firewall protection, etc.), while others, like cyberbullying, only keep escalating. Recognizing such problems and developing the remedy is an urgent matter and is desirable to come into focus of Artificial Intelligence.

REFERENCES

Abbasi, A., & Chen, H. (2007). Affect Intensity Analysis of DarkWeb Forums. IEEE Intelligence and Security Informatics, 282-288.

Bayzick, J., Kontostathis, A., & Edwards, L. (2011). Detecting the Presence of Cyberbullying Using Computer Software. Poster presentation at WebSci11, Koblenz Germany.

Birdwhistell, R. L. (1952). *Introduction to kinesics: an annotation system for analysis of body motion and gesture*. Univ. of Kentucky Press.

Birdwhistell, R. L. (1970). *Kinesics and Context*. Philadelphia: University of Pennsylvania Press.

Chen, H., Qin, J., Reid, E., Chung, W., Zhou, Y., Xi, W., ... Sageman, M. (2004). The dark web portal: Collecting and analyzing the presence of domestic and international terrorist groups on the web. *Proc. 7th IEEE Int. Conf. Intelligent Transportation Systems*, 106-111.

Chen, Y., Zhou, Y., Zhu, S., & Xu, H. (2012). Detecting offensive language in social media to protect adolescent online safety. *Privacy, Security, Risk and Trust (PASSAT), 2012 International Conference on and 2012 International Conference on Social Computing (SocialCom)*, 71-80. 10.1109/SocialCom-PASSAT.2012.55

Dinakar, K., Jones, B., Havasi, C., Lieberman, H., & Picard, R. (2012). Commonsense Reasoning for Detection, Prevention and Mitigation of Cyberbullying. ACM Transactions on Intelligent Interactive Systems, 2(3).

Dinakar, K., Reichart, R., & Lieberman, H. (2011). Modeling the detection of Textual Cyberbullying. *The Social Mobile Web, 11*(2).

Hinduja, S., & Patchin, J. W. (2009). *Bullying beyond the schoolyard: Preventing and responding to cyberbullying*. Corwin Press.

Hirotoshi, T., Takafumi, M., & Masahiko, H. (1998). Support Vector Machine ni yoru tekisuto bunrui [Text Categorization Using Support Vector Machines]. *IPSJ SIG Notes*, *98*(99), 173–180.

Hosseinmardi, H., Li, S., Yang, Z., Lv, Q., Ibn Rafiq, R., Han, R., & Mishra, S. (2014). A comparison of common users across Instagram and Ask.fm to better understand cyberbullying. *2014 IEEE Fourth International Conference on Big Data and Cloud Computing (BdCloud)*, 355-362.

Hosseinmardi, H., Mattson, S. A., Rafiq, R. I., Han, R., Lv, Q., & Mishra, S. (2015). Analyzing labeled cyberbullying incidents on the instagram social network. In *International Conference on Social Informatics* (pp. 49-66). Springer. 10.1007/978-3-319-27433-1_4

Ishisaka, T., & Yamamoto, K. (2010a). Detecting Nasty Comments from BBS Posts. PACLIC 2010, 645-652.

Ishisaka, T., & Yamamoto, K. (2010b). 2channeru wo taishō to shita waruguchi hyōgen no chūshutsu [Extraction of abusive expressions from 2channel] (in Japanese). *Proceedings of The Sixteenth Annual Meeting of The Association for Natural Language Processing (NLP2010)*, 178-181.

Kontostathis, A., Edwards, L., & Leatherman, A. (2010). *Text mining and cybercrime. Text Mining: Applications and Theory*. Chichester, UK: John Wiley & Sons, Ltd.

Kontostathis, A., Reynolds, K., Garron, A., & Edwards, L. (2013). Detecting Cyberbullying: Query Terms and Techniques. *Proceedings of the 5th ACM Web Science Conference (WEBSCI2013)*, 195-204. 10.1145/2464464.2464499

Kudo, T. (2001). *MeCab: Yet Another Part-of-Speech and Morphological Analyzer*. Retrieved from: http://taku910.github.io/mecab/

Levenshtein, V. I. (1965). Binary Code Capable of Correcting Deletions, Insertions and Reversals. *Doklady Akademii Nauk SSSR*, *163*(4), 845–848.

Matsuba, T., Satomi, N., Masui, F., Kawai, A., & Isu, N. (2009). Gakkō hikōshiki saito ni okeru yūgai jōhō kenshutsu [Detection of harmful information on school informal Websites] (in Japanese). Technical Report of The Institute of Electronics, Information and Communication Engineers, NLC2009-6, Vol.109, N.142, pp.93-98, 2009.07.

Matsuba, T., Satomi, N., Masui, F., Kawai, A., & Isu, N. (2010). Gakkō hikōshiki saito no yūgai na jōhō no kenshutsu [Harmful information detection on informal school websites] (in Japanese). *Proc. of The 16th Annual Meeting of The Association for Natural Language Processing (NLP2010)*, 383-386.

Matsuba, T., Satomi, N., Masui, F., Kawai, A., & Isu, N. (2011). Gakkō hikōshiki saito ni okeru yūgai jōhō kenshutsu wo mokuteki to shita kyokusei hantei moderu ni kansuru kenkyū [A study on the polarity classification model for the purpose of detecting harmful information on informal school sites] (in Japanese). *Proceedings of The Seventeenth Annual Meeting of The Association for Natural Language Processing (NLP2011)*, 388-391.

McGhee, I., Bayzick, J., Kontostathis, A., Edwards, L., McBride, A., & Jakubowski, E. (2011). Learning to identify Internet sexual predation. *International Journal of Electronic Commerce*, *15*(3), 103–122. doi:10.2753/JEC1086-4415150305

Ministry of Education, Culture, Sports, Science, and Technology (MEXT). (2008). *'Netto-jō no ijime' ni kansuru taiō manyuaru jirei shū (gakkō, kyōin muke)* ["Bullying on the Net" Manual for handling and collection of cases (for schools and teachers)] (in Japanese). MEXT.

Ministry of Education, Culture, Sports, Science, and Technology (MEXT). (2008). *'Netto jō no ijime' ni kansuru taiō manyuaru jirei shū (gakkō, kyōin muke)* ['Bullying on the Net' Manual for handling and collection of cases (for school teachers)] (in Japanese). MEXT.

Minoru, H., & Hirohide, E. (1997). Nihongo OCR bun ni okeru eiji, katakana no superu ayamari teiseihō [Spelling Correction Method for English and Katakana in Japanese OCR Text] (in Japanese). *Transactions of Information Processing Society of Japan, 38*(7), 1317–1327.

Nakamura, A. (1993). *Kanjō hyōgen jiten* [Dictionary of Emotive Expressions]. Tokyo: Tōkyōdō Publishing.

Nitta, T., Masui, F., Ptaszynski, M., Kimura, Y., Rzepka, R., & Araki, K. (2013). Detecting Cyberbullying Entries on Informal School Websites Based on Category Relevance Maximization. *Proceedings of the 6th International Joint Conference on Natural Language Processing (IJCNLP 2013)*, 579-586.

Patchin, J. W., & Hinduja, S. (2006). Bullies move beyond the schoolyard: A preliminary look at cyberbullying. *Youth Violence and Juvenile Justice, 4*(2), 148–169. doi:10.1177/1541204006286288

Ptaszynski, M., Dybala, P., Matsuba, T., Masui, F., Rzepka, R., Araki, K., & Momouchi, Y. (2010). In the Service of Online Order: Tackling cyberbullying with Machine Learning and Affect Analysis. *International Journal of Computational Linguistics Research, 1*(3), 135–154.

Ptaszynski, M., Dybala, P., Rzepka, R., & Araki, K. (2009). Affecting Corpora: Experiments with Automatic Affect Annotation System - A Case Study of the 2channel Forum. *Proc. of PACLING-09*, 223-228.

Ptaszynski, M., Dybala, P., Rzepka, R., Araki, K., & Masui, F. (2017). MLAsk: Open Source Affect Analysis Software for Textual Input in Japanese. *Journal of Open Research Software, 5*(1), 1–16.

Ptaszynski, M., Dybala, P., Shi, W., Rzepka, R., & Araki, K. (2009). Towards Context Aware Emotional Intelligence in Machines: Computing Contextual Appropriateness of Affective States. *Proceedings of Twenty-first International Joint Conference on Artificial Intelligence (IJCAI-09)*, 1469-1474.

Ptaszynski, M., Dybala, P., Shi, W., Rzepka, R., & Araki, K. (2010). Contextual Affect Analysis: A System for Verification of Emotion Appropriateness Supported with Contextual Valence Shifters. *International Journal of Biometrics, 2*(2), 134–154. doi:10.1504/IJBM.2010.031793

Ptaszynski, M., Maciejewski, J., Dybala, P., Rzepka, R., & Araki, K. (2010). CAO: A Fully Automatic Emoticon Analysis System Based on Theory of Kinesics. *IEEE Transactions on Affective Computing, 1*(1), 46–59. doi:10.1109/T-AFFC.2010.3

Ptaszynski, M., Masui, F., Kimura, Y., Rzepka, R., & Araki, K. (2015a). Brute force works best against bullying. *IJCAI 2015 Workshop on Intelligent Personalization (IP 2015)*, 28–29.

Ptaszynski, M., Masui, F., Kimura, Y., Rzepka, R., & Araki, K. (2015b). Extracting patterns of harmful expressions for cyberbullying detection. *Proceedings of 7th Language and Technology Conference (LTC'15)*, 370–375.

Ptaszynski, M., Masui, F., Nitta, T., Hatakeyama, S., Kimura, Y., Rzepka, R., & Araki, K. (2016). Sustainable cyberbullying detection with category-maximized relevance of harmful phrases and double-filtered automatic optimization. *International Journal of Child-Computer Interaction*, *8*, 15–30. doi:10.1016/j.ijcci.2016.07.002

Ptaszynski, M., Mazur, M., Dybala, P., Rzepka, R., Araki, K., & Momouchi, Y. (2013). Towards Computational Fronesis: Verifying Contextual Appropriateness of Emotions. *International Journal of Distance Education Technologies*, *11*(2), 16–47.

Reynolds, K., Kontostathis, A., & Edwards, L. (2011). Using machine learning to detect cyberbullying. *2011 10th International Conference on Machine Learning and Applications and Workshops (ICMLA), 2*.

Russell, J. A. (1980). A circumplex model of affect. *Journal of Personality and Social Psychology*, *39*(6), 1161–1178. doi:10.1037/h0077714

Ryozo, K., Koudai, H., & Tatsuya, S. (2005). Production Rule wo mochiita shisutemu hyōgen to koshō shindan e no ōyō [Modeling and Fault Diagnosis of Controlled Plant based on Production Rule] (in Japanese). *The Robotics and Mechatronics Conference 2005*, 16.

Vapnik, V. (1998). *Statistical Learning Theory*. Springer.

Xu, Z., & Zhu, S. (2010). Filtering offensive language in online communities using grammatical relations. *Proceedings of the Seventh Annual Collaboration, Electronic Messaging, Anti-Abuse and Spam Conference*.

Yin, D., Xue, Z., Hong, L., Davison, D. B., Kontostathis, A., & Edwards, L. (2009). Detection of Harassment on Web 2.0. *CAW 2.0 '09: Proceedings of the 1st Content Analysis in Web 2.0 Workshop*.

Zaenen, A., & Polanyi, L. (2006). Contextual Valence Shifters. In J. G. Shanahan, Y. Qu, & J. Wiebe (Eds.), *Computing Attitude and Affect in Text* (pp. 1–10). Dordrecht, The Netherlands: Springer Verlag.

Chapter 4
Web Mining-Based Method for Cyberbullying Detection

ABSTRACT

In this chapter, the authors present a method for automatic detection of cyberbullying entries based on a Web mining technique, in particular, on an extended SO-PMI-IR method calculating relevance of new input documents with training documents. The method uses seed words from three categories to calculate semantic orientation score and then maximizes the relevance of categories. The method outperformed previously proposed Web-mining-based methods in both laboratory and real-world conditions. The developed system is deployed and tested in practice. After a year of testing, the authors notice an over 30% point drop in its performance. They hypothesize on the reasons for the drop. To regain the lost performance and sustain it in the future, the authors propose additional improvements including automatic acquisition and filtering of seed words. Experimentally selected optimal improvements regained much of the lost performance.

INTRODUCTION

Web-mining-based methods have been widely acknowledged in document classification, particularly in sentiment and affect analysis (Turney, 2002; Pang & Lee, 2008; Ptaszynski et al., 2009), even in such novel fields as machine ethics (Komuda et al., 2010). Their advantage lies mostly in their high effectiveness and, most of all, efficiency. Web-mining methods usually

DOI: 10.4018/978-1-5225-5249-9.ch004

require minimal training data to perform a mass-level search on available Web data, such as the Internet (Ptaszynski et al., 2009), or large scale local corpora (Komuda, Rzepka & Araki, 2013) due to minimal human effort needed to achieve satisfactory results.

Here, we present our attempt of applying a Web mining method to the detection of cyberbullying. The reason for this attempt was backed by the main goal of our research, namely, to provide help to the members of Internet Patrol, which have been carried out mostly manually. It takes much time and effort to find harmful entries (entries that contain information and expressions aimed to harm other users) in a large amount of contents appearing on countless numbers of electronic Bulletin Board (BBS) pages. Moreover, the task comes with a great psychological burden on mental health to the net-patrol members.

To solve the above problem and decrease the burden of net-patrol members, we firstly proposed a preliminary method to detect harmful entries automatically (Matsuba et al., 2011). In this method we extended the method of relevance calculation SO-PMI-IR, developed by Turney (2002) to the relevance of a document with harmful contents. With the use of a small number of seed words we were able to detect large numbers of document candidates for harmful entries with satisfying effectiveness.

The initial method was demonstrated to determine harmful entries with an accuracy of 83% on test data for which about a half contained harmful entries. However, it was not verified how well the method would perform in real life conditions, where cyberbullying entries and normal contents do not appear in equal numbers.

In the research described in this chapter, initially introduced by Nitta et al. (2013) in 2013, we firstly proposed an optimization of the original method by maximizing the relevance scores. In the method we divided the seed words into multiple categories and calculated maximal relevance values for each seed word from each category. By calculating the maximized score, representing semantic orientation of harmfulness of an Internet entry, the method detected harmful entries more effectively than in the previous attempts. Moreover, we additionally evaluated our method on data sets with real-life ratios of harmful contents to verify the usability of the method in the most realistic way.

After confirming the performance, the method was deployed and tested "in the field" for over one year. Unfortunately, after re-evaluating the method after that time we found out that the performance significantly dropped by losing over 30-percentage-points when compared to its original performance measured in 2013. In the original evaluation process, applied also in this research and previously in Matsuba et al. (2011), Nitta et al. (2013) assigned the harmfulness score to all sentences from their dataset containing harmful and non-harmful entries, sorted all entries decreasingly and checked the performance looking at the top n entries, while increasing the number of n (further referred to as "threshold window") by 50 entries at a time. This way they were able to witness the fluctuation in performance when more data is applied in the evaluation. As the evaluation measures they used standard Precision and Recall. In particular, the originally confirmed high performance was on a level of 91% when it comes to Precision for low Recall values. Moreover, original performance from late 2013 was retained high (around 70%) even close to 50% of Recall, after which it decreased due to drop in Precision for higher thresholds. However, when the evaluation experiment was repeated in early 2015, the overall results greatly dropped. Precision did not exceed 60% for the whole threshold span. This made us introduce a number of further improvements to regain the lost performance and assure sustaining it on a sufficient level.

The outline of this chapter is as follows. Firstly, in Section "Web-mining Based Method for Cyberbullying Detection", we describe the proposed method. Next, in Section "Evaluation experiment", we construct evaluation data sets with different ratios of cyberbullying entries, perform evaluation experiments based on these data sets, and describe the results of those experiments. We also present a more detailed discussion of the results in Section "Discussion". Next, we present the re-evaluation of the method after over one year time. We discuss the potential reasons for the drop in performance (Section "Discussion on reasons for performance drop"), and then propose an optimization method to regain some of the performance. In particular we propose a method for automatic acquisition of seed words (Section "Automatic seed word acquisition and filtering") not only to improve the method performance this time, but to allow sustaining the performance for future use of the method. We conduct an additional series of experiments with the automatically obtained different seed word sets and experimentally choose the one with the best performance (Section "Optimization experiment and results"). Finally, in Section "Conclusions and future work" we conclude the chapter and propose some of the ideas for further improvement, and future applications of the method.

WEB-MINING-BASED METHOD FOR CYBERBULLYING DETECTION

In this section we present an overview of the Web-mining-based method we developed for detection of cyberbullying messages on the Internet. In the proposed method we extended the method developed by Turney (2002), which calculates the relevance of seed words with words contained in the input entries, in our case, entries from electronic Bulletin Board (BBS) pages. Turney's method is extended firstly in the sense that the relevance with seed word is calculated not for simple words, but for phrases automatically extracted by using dependency relations. Secondly, the score is maximized for each of the applied category of seed words. We apply multiple categories of harmful words and calculate the degree of association separately for each category. Finally, as the harmfulness score (or "harmful polarity") we choose the maximum value from those achieved by all categories. The method consists of three general steps:

1. Phrase extraction,
2. Categorization and harmful word detection together with harmfulness polarity determination,
3. Relevance maximization.

Each of the steps is explained in detail in the following paragraphs.

Phrase Extraction

For some explicit cases of cyberbullying entries the harmful character of an entry could be determined by looking at separate words, as it was demonstrated in previous research (Ptaszynski et al., 2010; Matsuba et al., 2011). For other cases however, even if a word in itself is not harmful, it gains harmful meaning when used in a specific context, or in combination with other words. For example, for a pair of words 性格が悪い (*seikaku ga warui*) "bad personality", neither "bad", nor "personality" on their own express harmful meaning. However, when these words are used together in a dependency relation to describe a specific individual, they become harmful (negative depiction of a person's personality). Therefore, methods for detecting harmful contents using separate words only, will fail when they encounter an entry which gained harmful meaning by such context dependent phrases containing words in dependency relations.

Table 1. Types of phrases applied in the proposed method with examples

Phrase	Example
noun-noun	サル顔 *(sarugao)* "monkey face" →Description ridiculing person's features
noun-verb	新田を殺す *(Nitta wo korosu)* "Kill Nitta" →Threatening expressions
noun-adjective	性格が悪い *(seikaku ga warui)* "bad personality" →Description criticizing person's features

To deal with this issue, we calculated the harmful polarity score not for single words, but for all combinations of morphemes[1] being in dependency relations. We define such combinations as "phrases" (one phrase consists of a morpheme pair in dependency relation). The dependency relation is calculated by using morphological information provided by a morphological analysis tool for Japanese (MeCab, developed by Kudo (2006) and parsed by a dependency parser for Japanese (Cabocha developed by Kudo (2010). The phrases defined this way were extracted from all target entries. The strength of this approach is that such basic language analysis tools (morphological analyzers and dependency parsers) exist for most of common languages, which makes the proposed method language independent. Examples of such extracted phrases are represented in Table 1.

Harmful Word Detection and Categorization

In this process we detect the words and phrases of potential bullying connotations, later referred to as "harmful words/phrases". Harmful words often include newly coined words (Fujii, Ando & Ito, 2010) or informal modifications of normal transcriptions (Ikeda & Yanagihara, 2010), thus are not recognized by standard preprocessing tools, such as morphological analyzers or dependency parsers. Therefore, it is possible such words would not be handled properly and would cause error in morphological analysis, unless specifically annotated. We investigated the entries of informal school Websites using the definition of harmful words proposed by the Japanese Ministry of Education, Culture, Sports, Science and Technology (later referred to as "Ministry of Education", or MEXT) (2008), and registered 255 harmful words (nouns, adjectives and verbs) in the dictionary of morphological analyzer.

In addition, we categorized harmful words into three categories: obscene, violent and abusive. In this regard we followed the definition provided by The Ministry of Education of Japan, which specifically mentions words frequently used in cyberbullying messages to include those three categories. In this study, we applied the above official definition as it follows the country's policy in handling of cyberbullying cases, thus we also classified harmful words into the three mentioned categories.

Next, from each category we automatically selected as seed words three words most often occurring in the context of cyberbullying and registered them in the system. The words we selected included: セックス (*sekkusu*) "[to have] sex", ヤリマン (*yariman*) "slut'", フェラ (*fera*) "fellatio/blowjob" for the obscene category, 死ね (*shine*) "die [imperative]'", 殺す (*korosu*) "[to] kill", 殴る (*naguru*) "[to] slap" for the violent category, and うざい (*uzai*) "annoying", きもい (*kimoi*) "gross", 不細工 (*busaiku*) "ugly" for the abusive category.

Maximization of Relevance Score

In this process we calculated the harmfulness polarity score of automatically extracted phrases with each seed word for all three categories. To measure the semantic orientation we applied the Pointwise Mutual Information (PMI) score, which in our implementation measures relevance between a phrase and harmfulness polarity words from each category. PMI here indicates a co-occurrence frequency of the queried phrase with the three words registered for each category. To calculate the co-occurrence frequency we used information retrieval (IR) score (co-occurrence hit rate). Since countless numbers of various Web pages exist on the Internet, and various words are written there, it is possible to obtain a high coverage for the method by using the IR score.

We calculated the relevance of a phrase with words from each category according to equation (1). In this equation p_i is a phrase extracted from the entry, w_j are the three words that were registered in one category of harmfulness polarity words, $hits(p_i)$ and $hits(w_j)$ are Web search hits for each category for p_i and w_j respectively, $hits(p_i\&w_j)$ is a number of hits when p_i and w_j appear on the same Web page. Finally, $PMI\text{-}IR(p_i,w_j)$ is the relevance of p_i and w_j .

$$\mathrm{PMI-IR}\left(p_i, w_j\right) = log_2 \left\{ \frac{hits\left(p_i \ \& \ w_j\right)}{hits\left(p_i\right) hits\left(w_j\right)} \right\} \quad (1)$$

From all three scores calculated for the phrase with seed words from the three categories, we select the category which achieved the highest score as the one of the highest relevance with the phrase. We calculate the relevance score this way for all phrases extracted from the entry. Finally we select the category with the maximal overall score as the one with the highest relevance with the entry. Thus the *score* is calculated according to the following equation (2).

$$score_{entry} = max_{all\_phrases}\left(max_{all\_categories}\left(PMI - IR\left(p_i, w_j\right)\right)\right) \quad (2)$$

In one of the previous research, which will be considered here as a baseline, Matsuba et al. (2011) calculated the relevance as a sum of all scores for all phrases with each harmful word separately. In this method instead of taking all words separately and calculating the score as the sum of all intermediate PMI scores, we grouped them in categories and calculated the relevance with three most common harmful words from each category. By incorporating this improvement during the Web search the retrieved pages are those for which the phrase appeared not only with at least one of the harmful words, but with all three words from one category. This reduces the processing time, and, what is more important, improves the calculation of the relevance score, since only the strongest (most harmful) phrases are selected. Moreover, since it is easier to find a Web page containing a phrase with only one harmful word, than a phrase with three words together, baseline method mistakenly allowed phrases with low actual relevance to bullying entries to achieve high scores. Maximization of the relevance *score* prevents low relevance phrases to erroneously achieve high scores.

Table 2. The numbers of entries on informal school BBS including the number and percentage of cyberbullying entries

BBS	Overall number of entries	Cyberbullying entries	Percentage (%)
BBS(1)	600	75	12.5
BBS(2)	736	90	12.2
BBS(3)	886	100	11.3

We explain the above process on the following example: 可愛いけど性格が悪い女 (*Kawaii kedo seikaku ga warui onna*) "Cute girl, but bad personality". Firstly, from the entry the extracted phrases are: 可愛い-女 (*kawaii-onna*) "cute-girl", 性格-悪い (*seikaku-warui*) "bad-personality", 悪い-女(*warui-onna*) "bad-girl". Next, we calculate the relevance between "cute-girl" and the three groups of words separately ("sex, slut, fellatio", "die, kill, slap", "annoying, gross, ugly"). The highest maximal score is selected as the relevance (harmfulness score) for this phrase. Similarly the score is calculated for "bad-personality" and "bad-girl". From all the scores for all phrases the highest overall score is considered as the maximized harmfulness *score* of the entry. All entries are then sorted beginning with the one with the highest harmfulness score. Finally, we set a harmfulness threshold *n* and consider *n* entries with the highest score as harmful, and discard other as irrelevant to check how many of the entries within the specified threshold are in fact harmful.

EVALUATION EXPERIMENT

We performed an experiment to evaluate the performance of the proposed method and compared the results with the baseline. In the experiment we used the full dataset described in Chapter 3. At first, we performed a preliminary study for carrying out the experiment (Section "Preliminary study"). Next, we explain the experiment settings (Section "Experiment settings") and report on the results of experiment (Section "Results").

Preliminary Study

After preparing the initial datasets for experiments, it was necessary to create test data with harmful and non-harmful entries mixed at an appropriate rate. In previous research the mixing was set at the same rate (half of the data contained cyberbullying entries). However, it cannot be assumed that harmful entries appear in real life with the same rate as normal ones. Therefore to evaluate our method in conditions closer to reality we performed a preliminary study to verify how much of the entries are harmful on actual Web pages. We counted the harmful entries mixing ratio on three informal school Websites, in particular we focused on informal school bulletin boards (BBS). The result of the study is represented in Table 2. We performed the study during four days between January 27 and 30, 2012. The number of obtained entries was 2,222.

As for the result of the study, the first BBS contained a total number of 600 entries from which 75 were harmful, which indicates that harmful entry appearance rate was 12.5%. Similarly, for the second BBS, 90 out of 736 total entries were harmful (12.2%). On the third BBS there were 886 total entries with 100 harmful ones (11.3%). From the above results, we concluded that about 12% of all entries appearing on informal school BBS can be accounted for cyberbullying. Therefore in the experiment we verified the performance of the method under the condition when harmful entries cover 12% of the whole data.

Experiment Setup

In the evaluation experiment we compared the performance of the proposed method to the baseline (Matsuba et al., 2011). We did this firstly for the case where the test data contained 50% of harmful entries, to first verify the performance under the same conditions as in the previous research. Next, we prepared a different test data, which contained 12% of harmful entries and compared the performance under this condition for both the baseline and the proposed method.

Firstly, on the prepared initial dataset we performed a 10-fold cross validation. We processed the dataset by both the baseline and the proposed method and calculated the harmful polarity score for entries where the phrases could be extracted. Then we ranked all entries decreasingly according to the harmful polarity score, and evaluated the performance looking at the top n entries and increased the threshold n by 50 entries each time.

Next, we prepared the datasets for the verification in real word condition (12% of harmful entries). We prepared five test sets by randomly extracting 60 harmful and 440 non-harmful, 500 entries in total from the original dataset. On these datasets we did not perform a 10-fold cross validation, since it would make the results not statistically significant (each set for cross validation would contain only six (one tenth) of harmful entries). Instead, we calculated the results for each of the five sets separately. This allowed us to include all entries from the original test set in the evaluation. We processed these datasets with both the baseline and the proposed method and calculated the harmfulness polarity score for entries for which the phrases could be extracted. Then, similarly to the original dataset, we ranked all entries based on the harmfulness polarity score and evaluated the performance by taking the top n and increasing the threshold n by 10 entries each time.

As evaluation criteria we used Precision (P) and Recall (R), calculated according to the equations (3) and (4). P and R are standard evaluation measures defined in 1955 (Perry, Kent & Berry, 1955), and from that time used as standard evaluation measures in many fields, including mathematics, statistics, and more recently information retrieval. Precision is traditionally defined as a ratio of all correctly retrieved documents to all retrieved documents. Recall on the other hand is the ratio of the all correctly retrieved documents to all correct documents available.

Within the context of present research, Precision is a ratio of the number of harmful entries that were correctly determined as harmful by the proposed method to the number of all entries determined by the system as harmful among the top *n* cases. For example, when the proposed system retrieves 50 documents (in other words classifies 50 documents as harmful), not all of them are classified correctly, some of them could be assigned a high harmfulness score mistakenly. If, for example 45 out of 50 entries are classified correctly, Precision is equal to 90% (45/50).

Recall in our research is understood as a ratio of the number of entries that were correctly determined by the proposed method as harmful to the overall number of harmful entries in the dataset (1,490). Therefore, if for the first threshold window (top 50 entries with the highest assigned harmfulness score) all are classified correctly, the Recall for this threshold window is about 3.4% (50/1490). However, if for the first threshold window, only 45 entries are harmful and the remaining five entries are mistakenly classified non-harmful entries, the Recall is equal to about 3% (45/1490).

The final performance is calculated as a harmonic mean of Recall and Precision for each test data in this experiment. As an additional evaluation mean we also looked at Area Under the Curve (AUC) for graph representing Precision and Recall on *y* and *x* axis respectively.

$$P = \frac{\textit{correct annotations}}{\textit{all system annotations}} \tag{3}$$

$$R = \frac{\textit{correct annotations}}{\textit{all harmful entries}} \tag{4}$$

Figure 1. Precision and Recall for both the baseline and the proposed method for both datasets (50% and 12% of cyberbullying entries). The horizontal axis and the vertical axis represent percentage of Recall and Precision for each threshold, respectively. All results were statistically significant. For the 50% data the results were extremely significant on 0.0001 level. For the 12% data the results were statistically significant on 0.05 level.

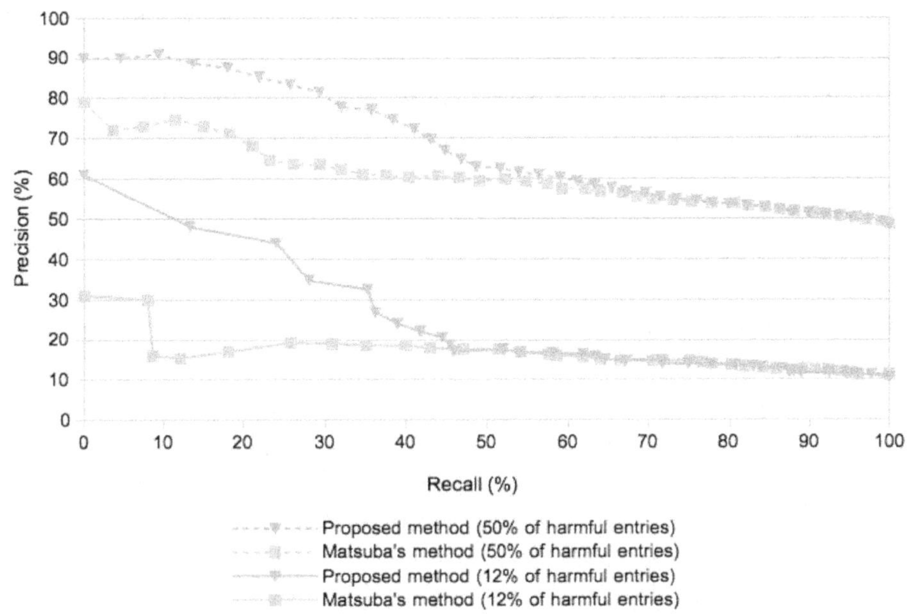

RESULTS

The results showing Precision and Recall for both the baseline and the proposed method for both datasets (50% and 12% of cyberbullying entries) are represented in Figure 1. The horizontal axis and the vertical axis represent percentage of Recall and Precision for each threshold, respectively.

For the test data containing 50% of harmful entries, Precision was between 49% - 79%, with Recall oscillating between 3% - 100% for the baseline, while for the proposed method Precision was between 49% - 88%, with Recall between 5% - 100%. For the test data containing 12% of harmful entries, Precision was between 11% - 31%, with Recall oscillating between 8% - 100% for the baseline, while for the proposed method Precision was between 10% - 61%, and Recall was between 13% - 100%. This suggests that the proposed method outperformed the baseline. AUC also indicated the same result. The results are further explained and discussed in detail in Section "Discussion".

DISCUSSION

The experiment results showed that the proposed method achieved higher overall performance comparing to the baseline. The shape of the correlation curve for Recall and Precision shows that the performance for the baseline was significantly lower in general comparing the test data containing 12% of harmful entries to the test data containing 50% of harmful entries. However, for the proposed method, although the performance is reduced as well, there was no sudden drop in the shape of the correlation curve when comparing both datasets.

This could suggest that the performance was more stable in the proposed method than in the baseline. There were several cases of threshold *n* where the Recall was slightly higher for the baseline than for the proposed method in the test data containing 12% of harmful entries. This happened because for some harmful entries the harmfulness score could not be calculated highly enough due to the fact that the score calculation is more strict (Precision-oriented) in the proposed method. Therefore, although Recall is slightly higher in the baseline for high thresholds, it is always still higher for the proposed method for small and medium thresholds, with the Precision being constantly higher for the proposed method. Therefore, it can be concluded that the proposed method achieved higher general performance than the baseline.

Next, we explain the results for the test data containing 12% of harmful entries. We investigated the threshold cases of entries where the Precision reaches 48%. Entries found there included, for example "アトピーのやつ死ねよ" (*atopii no yatsu shine yo*) "The bastard with atopy must die" and "ウザイキモイぶす" (*uzai kimoi busu*) "annoying, gross and ugly". From those entries high relevance score was calculated for phrases like "アトピー-死ね" (*atopii-shine*) "atopy-die" and " ウザイ-ぶす" (*uzai-busu*) "annoying-ugly". Since the phrases contained seed words as well, this most probably increased the polarity score of the harmful entry.

On the other hand, there were many non-harmful entries incorrectly classified as harmful with harmfulness polarity score equally high or higher than the actual harmful entries. An example of a non-harmful entry of this kind was "県外に住んでいる" (*Kengai ni sun de iru*) "Living outside of the prefecture". The phrase extracted from this entry was "外-住ん" (*soto-sun*) "outside-live". This is a neutral phrase, and appears often in non-harmful entries. However, it also appears in harmful entries in cases of exposing personal information about where a person lives. Therefore, the relevance of a harmful entry containing such phrase is increased, and as a result overall harmfulness polarity score of such non-harmful entry becomes higher.

As a countermeasure it could be considered to register some words, which appear only in non-harmful entries, like "beautiful" or "splendid", with non-harmful polarity and calculate the relevance of non-harmful entries as well. In particular, firstly, the non-harmful words could be registered in the dictionary. Then the relevance could be calculated for the phrases with both, non-harmful polarity words and harmful polarity words. In such cases the phrase could be considered as non-harmful when the relevance score of the phrase with non-harmful words was higher than the relevance with the harmful words. This could reduce the influence of neutral phrases on the overall performance.

We also investigated the cases where Recall reaches 100%. These cases include entries which contain personal information only such as school name or person's name, such as "Nitta of Kitami Institute of Technology, 4th grader" (name changed to only illustrate the example), etc. The relevance of such entries with harmful words registered at present in the dictionary is low, which influenced their overall harmfulness score as well. To solve this problem we plan to register in the dictionary words which have high relevance with personal information and use them in the relevance score calculation as well.

DEPLOYMENT AND RE-EVALUATION OF THE METHOD

After confirming the performance, the proposed method was deployed as a working system and tested "in the field" for over one year. It was used to analyze informal electronic forums and BBS of various universities including Kitami Institute of Technology (which the authors belong to), Asahikawa Medical University, Otaru University of Commerce, Obihiro University of Agriculture and Veterinary Medicine. Despite some successes at first, after some time we started to notice that less and less contents is picked up by the system each day. Therefore we decided to perform a re-evaluation of the system under the same conditions we evaluated it before in 2013. In the reevaluation we also applied the same metrics we used previously, namely Area Under the Curve (AUC) on the graph showing Precision and Recall.

After re-evaluating the method after over one and a half year we found out that the performance changed since the time of its development. The performance significantly dropped, losing over 30-percentage-points compared to its original performance. The result of the comparison is represented in Figure 2.

Discussion on Reasons for Performance Drop

In this section we discuss the possible reasons for the decrease in performance of the proposed method.

After thorough analysis of the experiment data we noticed that most of the information extracted in 2013 was not available in 2015. This could be due to the following reasons.

Firstly, fluctuation in page rankings could push the information lower making it not extractable anymore by the proposed method. Secondly, frequent deletion requests of harmful contents by Internet Patrol members could make their efforts pay off. However, the most probable is the third cause, which is the recent tightening of usage policies by most Web service providers, such as Google (n.d.), Twitter (2014) and *Yahoo!*, which is used in the proposed method in the Information Retrieval procedure. This also includes recently introduced DMARC (n.d.) policies related to e-mail spoofing and general improvements in policies aimed at decreasing Internet harassment. However, the fact that the performance decreased from over 90% to less than 60% during less than two years is an important warning also for other research based on Web mining. Probability of such problems have been indicated some time ago by Kilgarriff (2007), and could become a major problem in the future. This also advocates more focus on either corpus-based methods or methods providing optimization and constant update of applicable seed words (training features). In the following sections we focused on the latter, since it allows improving the method even when the performance drops again in the future.

AUTOMATIC SEED WORD ACQUISITION AND FILTERING

In this section we propose our re-implementation and performance improvement of the proposed method for cyberbullying detection. To improve the lost performance we firstly propose a method for automatic acquisition of seed words which we combine with optimization method based on single- and double-filtering of the seed words.

Figure 2. Performance comparison for the proposed method in late 2013 and re-evaluated in early 2015. The evaluation performed for fair condition with data balanced for harmful and non-harmful entries.

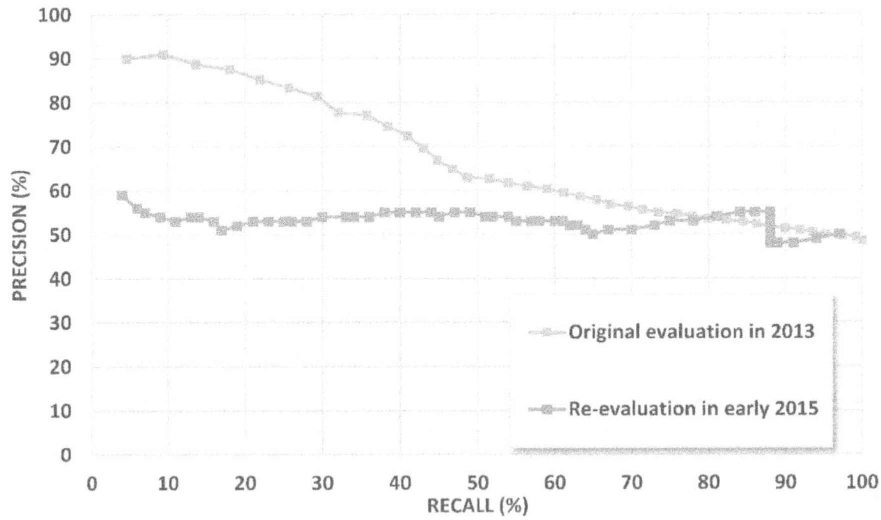

Table 3. Examples of extracted harmful statements. Japanese transcription (J), English translation (E, adjusted to express the original meaning as closely as possible)

1. J: *Busaiku dashi uta wa heta dashi dansu mo heta.* E: She's ugly, sings badly, and cannot even dance.
2. J: *Omake ni DQN darake.* E: Apart form that all moron.
3. J: *Kumamon ni kuwasero, baka dono!* E: Feed this to Kumamon [TV character], you ass*ole!
4. J: *Ramen mania tte shinsoko kimoi* E: That Ramen maniac is like completely gross
5. J: *Munou dakara darou.* E: That's 'cause his an impotent.

Automatic Acquisition of Harmful Words

To improve the performance of our method we first applied a method proposed by Ishisaka et al. (2011).

The method proposed by Ishisaka et al. extends the initial value based on n-gram statistics and uses it to automatically acquire harmful expressions from a large corpus (for example the Web). It calculates the SO-PMI-IR value (later referred to as "SO value") indicating the degree of harmfulness of a word in a document (for explanation of SO-PMI-IR see equation 1 in section "Maximization of relevance score"). The difference to our method is that Ishisaka et al. focuses on optimizing the relevance between words, not phrases. In particular, after obtaining an initial set of words (for example harmful and non-harmful), they calculate SO value between all words in the set to provide clusters of words being in close relevance. Originally, the method was successfully applied to harmful word acquisition from a large Japanese electronic bulletin board system (BBS), called "2 channel" (2 Channel, n.d.). Some of the examples of harmful statements extracted with this method are represented in Table 3. All example sentences contain harmful expressions.

The method of Ishisaka et al. allows modification and updating of the initial value in the proposed method, which consists of a set of harmful seed words used in the IR procedure (Web mining). Such words could be automatically acquired and updated regularly, which would greatly decrease the cost of collecting the seed word lists when the Web mining conditions change. We assumed this method could be used to optimize the seed word set used in the proposed method.

Double Filtering of Harmful Seed Words

We conducted an experiment using Ishisaka et al.'s method to verify its potential in the automatic selection of seed word candidates for the developed cyberbullying detection method.

Ishisaka et al. in their study at first conducted a questionnaire in which they asked three annotators to judge whether a word is harmful or not. In the questionnaire they used a set of 2,735 words automatically extracted from harmful BBS entries. From the initial set they retained only those words for which all three annotators agreed about. There were 76 of such words (we refer to them as harmful word candidates). These words were used as a base for automatic selection.

Next, Ishisaka et al. automatically selected a set of 14 most frequent harmful and 17 non-harmful basic words appearing in the original entries by using n-gram statistics (with n=7). They used those basic words to filter-out the most harmful out of the initial 76 harmful word candidates selected by human annotators. In our approach we added to the Ishisaka et al.'s 14 harmful basic words 9 harmful seed words used by Nitta et al. (2013). With overall 23 harmful and 17 non-harmful basic words we conducted first filtering of the basic words. We calculated SO values for each of the 76 harmful word candidates with every other basic word, and calculated the sum of SO values for each word candidate. From the words which obtained SO value higher than 0 we selected only those words which also appeared in the group of basic words. The basic word set used in filtering is represented in Table 4. The basic words that were filtered out are represented in Table 5. This first filtering provided a set of basic harmful words which were both harmful from the point of view of human annotators and were in the strongest relevance to harmful BBS entries.

In the second filtering we used as basic words the 17 harmful basic words obtained in the first filtering and the same 17 non-harmful basic words (later called "seed17"), and calculated the SO value again, this time for a dataset containing 76 harmful word candidates and 17 non-harmful basic words (93 words in total). We added the non-harmful words to verify whether the harmful basic words cause a bias in scoring. If it did, the non-harmful words would also achieve a high SO value. For a comparison, instead of the filtered out 17 basic words, we also used only the original set of 9 harmful seed words used in the originally developed method (later called "seed9"), and similarly calculated the SO value for the whole dataset (93 words). Having all SO values, we calculated arithmetic mean of SO values – μ and standard deviation – σ, and automatically set a threshold $\alpha 1$ as $\mu \pm \sigma$. Finally, we extracted harmful word candidates w and non-harmful word candidates h as $h \leq \alpha 1 \leq w$. A graph visualizing this operation is represented in Figure 3.

Figure 3. Graph visualizing the procedure for extraction of word candidates for set seed17

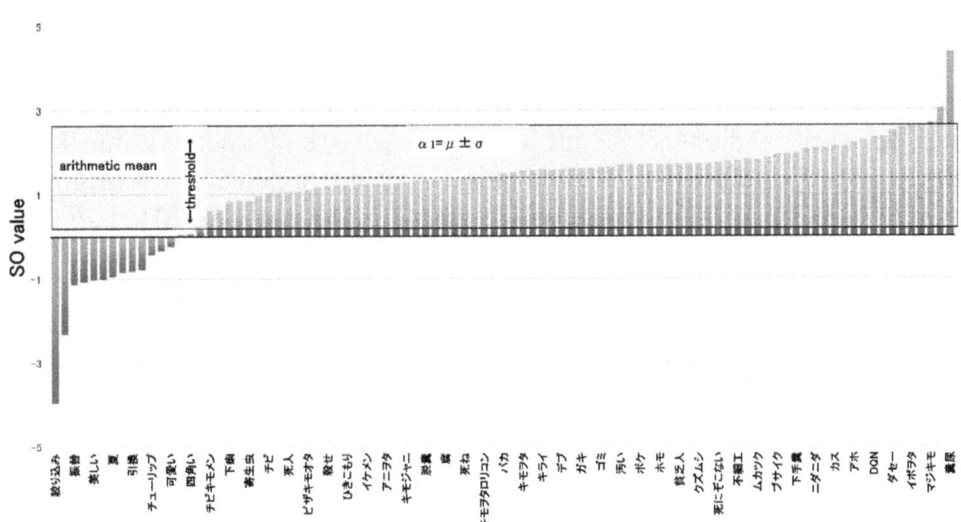

All words extracted this way for sets *seed17* and *seed9* are represented in Table 6. Worth mentioning is the fact that although one would expect the basic words to come on top, since they would be expected to obtain higher SO value due to perfect relevance score with themselves, in result the candidate words extracted according to this procedure did not contain even one word from the basic harmful word set. Instead, the words which were in the highest general relevance at the time (present Web condition) with the words used for optimization appeared on top. This indicates that the filtering optimized the search and can be considered as useful procedure.

Optimization Experiment and Results

After obtaining seed word sets described in section "Automatic seed word acquisition and filtering", we conducted an experiment to verify whether and to what extent does the change in the selection of seed words affect the originally developed method. Moreover, we calculated the statistical significance of the results using the McNemar Test (McNemar, 1947).

Experiment Setup

The experiment was designed as follows. Using the filtered out seed words we prepared six different harmful word candidate sets (later referred to as "cases"), applied them as seed words in originally developed method and verified its performance. *Case1* contained 7 double-filtered harmful words (all harmful words from *seed17* in Table 6). *Case2* contained 12 harmful words obtained by single-filtering out the words with the highest harmful relevance using only the original seed word set (all harmful words from seed9 in Table 6). *Case3* contained original 9 seed words and 7 double-filtered harmful word candidates (overall 16 words). *Case4* contained original 9 seed words and 12 single-filtered candidates. *Case5* contained 5 words originally used by Ishisaka et al. in their paper (Ishisaka & Yamamoto, 2011). Finally, *Case6* contained only the original 9 seed words without any modification or optimization. All sets were additionally described in Table 7.

We used each case as a seed word set in the proposed cyberbullying detection method and conducted the analysis using the original dataset of 2998 entries. We decided to use the whole set, not the set containing 12% of harmful entries to verify how each change in the seed word set influences the results in a fair balanced condition. Moreover, as the original experiment

Table 4. Harmful and non-harmful basic words used in the experiment. English translations added by the authors to represent a meaning as close to original as possible. Capital letters indicate different characters used to write a word.

	Harmful basic word candidates	Non-harmful basic word candidates
Ishisaka et. al [20]	*kiero* (get lost), *ujimushi* (worm), *kasu* (scum), *shineyo* (just die!), *doutei* (virgin), *UZAi* (ANNOYing), *KIMOi* (UGLy), *kichigai* (fucking crazy), *chon* (f*ckin' Chinese), *kuzu* (trash), *munou* (impotent), *BUSAIKU* (ugly), *busu* (ugly hag), *kirai* (hate)	*hikikae* (exchange), *kaiage* (purchase), *shiborikomi* (narrowing), *kawaii* (cute), *furikae* (transfer), *koujun* (descending), *suteki* (nice), *ikemen* (handsome), *akai* (red), *subarashii* (wonderful), *utsukushii* (beautiful), *tsukue* (desk), *suppai* (sour), *chuurippu* (tulip), *taiyou* (sun), *natsu* (summer), *shikakui* (square)
Proposed	*sekkusu* (sex), *yariman* (slut), *fera* (bl*wjob), *shine* (die), *korosu* (kill), *naguru* (beat the crap out of somebody), *uzai* (annoying), *kimoi* (gross), *busaiku* (ugly)	

Table 5. Harmful 17 basic words with SO value ≥ 0

*kiero (get lost), shineyo (just die!), munou (incompetent), busaiku (ugly), busu (ugly hag), doutei (virgin), chon (f*ckin' Chinese), BUSAIKU (ugly), shine (die), uzai (annoying), UZAi (ANNOY- ing), KIMOi (UGLy), kichigai (fucking crazy), kimoi (ugly), kasu (scum), korosu (kill), kuzu (trash)*

Table 6. Harmful and non-harmful seed words obtained according to the double filtering procedure (seed17) and single filtering procedure (with original seed words used in the final filtering (seed9))

	Harmful seed words	Non-harmful seed words
Seed-17	*dasee* (hopeless), *bakasayo* (stupid communist), *fun-nyou* (dung), *majikimo* (seriously gross), *ibo-ota* (warty nerd), *kuzumasugomi* (shitty mass-mudia), *goki-ota* (cockroachy nerd)	*shiborikomi* (narrowing), *kaiage* (purchase), *furikae* (transfer), *koujun* (descending), *natsu* (summer), *suteki* (nice), *utsukushii* (beautiful), *kawaii* (cute), *hikikae* (exchange), *akai* (red), *taiyou* (sun), *chuurippu* (tulip), *tsukue* (desk)
Seed-9	*bicchi* (bitch), *ibo-ota* (warty nerd), *mekuso* (eye gum), *dappun* (feces), *kusomushi* (dung beetle), *bakasayo* (stupid communist), *dasee* (hopeless), *fun-nyo* (dung), *goki-ota* (cockroachy nerd), *maji-kimo* (seriously gross), *kuzumasugomi* (shitty mass-mudia), *gumin* (ignorant)	*shiborikomi* (narrowing), *chuurippu* (tulip), *kaiage* (pur-chase), *suteki* (nice), *taiyou* (sun), *tsukue* (desk), *natsu* (summer), *akai* (red), *shikakui*(square), *koujun* (descending), *kawaii* (cute), *hikikae* (exchange), *furikae* (transfer), *kiseichuu* (parasite), *utsukushii* (beautiful)

from section "Evaluation experiment" showed, the results scale similarly for both kinds of evaluation datasets. Thus the differences between the change in performance depending on different cases will remain similar. Also, when more than two cases are compared, smaller and less balanced dataset could cause difficulties in finding valid differences between the cases for higher thresholds, and, most importantly, in testing the statistical significance of the results.

In the evaluation we looked at several metrics to choose the best seed word set. We calculated Precision (P), Recall (R) and balanced F-score (F) for each case. Then we first (1) checked which case obtained the highest F-score for the longest threshold span. Next, (2) we looked at which case obtained the highest break-even point (BEP) on a plot with P and R. Thirdly, (3) we looked at which of the cases obtained the highest Precision in general. Finally, (4) as the last mean of evaluation we used the same metrics as previously, namely, area under the curve (AUC) on a plot with P and R on y and x axis respectively. We also asked a question (5) whether it was always better to simply add more words, or whether the automatic filtering of harmful word candidates improved the method and to what extent.

Results

Below we address the five questions from Section "Experiment setup," one by one:

1. The highest F-score in general was obtained by *case2* (68%). Also *case5* and *case6* obtained similarly high F-score once, however, for most of the threshold, F for *case2* was always the highest, while for *case5* and *case6* mostly the lowest.
2. All cases obtained similar BEP, with cases 1, 2 and 6 = 54% and cases 3, 4, 5 = 53%. Therefore BEP did not appear sufficiently informative, although *case2* being in the higher group could indicate a minor support for the result from (1), where *case2* appeared the best.

Table 7. Description of six seed word sets (case1–case6) applied in the experiment with the proposed cyberbullying detection method

case1	7 words from *seed17* (Table 5)
case2	12 words from *seed9* (Table 5)
case3	16 words (7 words from *seed17* + original 9 words)
case4	21 words (12 words from *seed9* + original 9 words)
case5	5 words originally used by Ishisaka et al. [20]
case6	9 words originally used in the developed method

3. The highest Precision was obtained by *case4* (80%). However, despite obtaining the highest score once, Precision in *case4* quickly decreases, ending with one of the worst results in general. The second best P was obtained by *case2* (76%). Moreover, *case2* retains high P for most of the threshold span. This supports the previous result indicating *case2* as the best choice.
4. When it comes to AUC, *case2* outperformed all other cases for most of the threshold span. We consider this as a final support for *case2* obtaining the best performance. The results were represented in Figure 4

Figure 4. Results of all compared cases

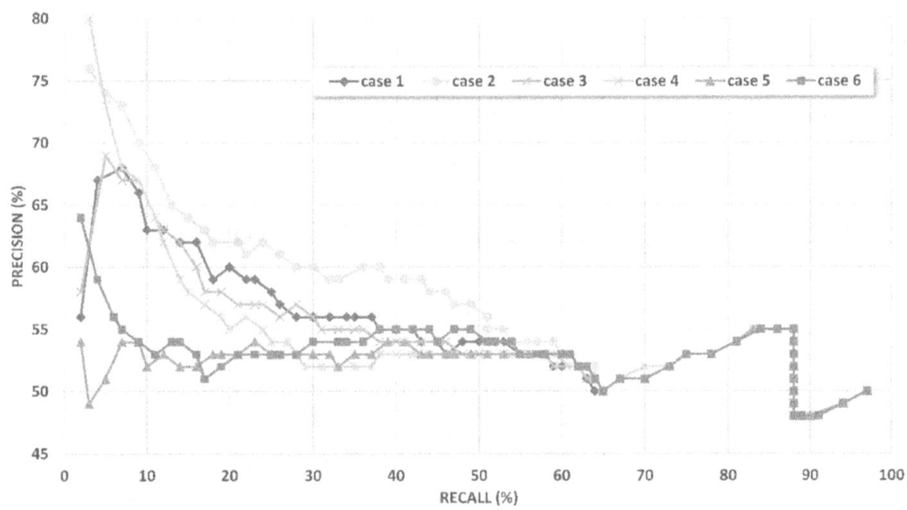

*Table 8. McNemar Test results (for cases 5 and 6 as baselines), *p≤0.5, **p≤0.1, ***p≤0.01*

	case1	*case2*	*case3*	*case4*	*case5*	*case6*
case5	189.00 ***	26.88 ***	0.83	0.30	-	16.98 ***
case6	145.00 ***	5.80 *	9.47 **	10.29 **	18.56 ***	-

DISCUSSION OF THE EXPERIMENT RESULTS

Finally, we verified whether simply adding words to the original method improved its performance. After analyzing all evaluation metrics, the cases' performances were in order: case2 (12 words), case1 (7 words), case3 (16 words), case4 (21 words), case6 (9 words), case5 (5 words). This suggests the following conclusions. Simply adding words does not improve the performance. Moreover, the two best scores were obtained by the cases applying the proposed automatic acquisition and optimization method. Here, case1 applies the full filtering procedure (seed17). Case2 applies single filtering with final set of harmful seed words extracted with the help of original seed word set instead of double-filtered word set. This suggests that the filtering improves the performance of the cyberbullying detection method in general. Moreover, shortening the filtering from double- to single-filtering positively influences not only the performance, but also efficiency of the method. Applying only single-filtering instead of double-filtering saves much of the processing time needed to extract the final set of words.

Statistical Significance Verification With McNemar Test

We verified the statistical significance of the results using McNemar Test (1947), which is a standard test used for calculating statistical significance for paired nominal data. We considered *case5* and *case6* as baselines and calculated the significance for all other cases.

All cases except 3 and 4 compared to case5-baseline were statistically significant on at least 5% level. The results were always extremely significant for *case1*, which we consider as the one with second-best performance. The results of the best performing *case2* were significant when compared to baseline-*case6* and extremely significant when compared to baseline-*case5*.

CONCLUSION AND FUTURE WORK

In this chapter, we presented a method of maximization of category relevance to automatically detect cyberbullying entries. The method contributes especially to reducing the burden of Internet Patrol personnel who make efforts to manually detect harmful entries appearing on the Internet. In order to verify the actual usefulness of the proposed method we evaluated the performance for the test data containing similar percentage of harmful entries as in reality.

Firstly, in a preliminary study we verified the usual ratio of harmful entries on the Internet. Next, we prepared test datasets containing the same amount of cyberbullying entries as in reality and evaluated the method on these test sets. In addition, we reproduced the baseline method and compared the performance to the proposed method.

The experiment results showed that the proposed method obtained higher results than the baseline. Under the fair condition (test dataset with 50% of harmful entries) the proposed method achieved over 90% of Precision at 10% Recall and retained high Precision (80-70%) at Recall close to 50%. Under the real world condition (test dataset with 12% of harmful entries) the method achieved nearly 50% of Precision at about 10% of Recall. The relevance curve have decreased slowly with growing Recall for the proposed method, while for the baseline the relevance curve has dropped suddenly from 30% to around 15% at the same Recall rate. As for drawbacks in the proposed method, harmful entries consisting of personal information were scored as less harmful due to the appearance of neutral phrases which appear often in both harmful and non-harmful entries.

After deploying and testing the system for over a year we re-evaluated it and noticed a sudden drop in performance (over 30% points). The loss could be caused by several factors, including tightening of usage policies by many Internet services. To deal with this problem we proposed a method for automatic acquisition and optimization of seed words based on the method by Ishisaka et al. (2011), and performed an experiment on multiple automatically constructed seed word sets. The results clearly showed that simply adding more words to the original method is not effective. On the other hand, the proposed filtering method was significantly effective, although shortening the filtering from double to single improved not only efficiency of the method, but also its performance, regaining much of the originally achieved performance. Moreover, the optimization not only improved the proposed method for the present time, but it can be used to improve it in the future, if the results drop again due to fluctuations in Web information.

As for future plans regarding this method in particular, we plan to deal with the remaining drawbacks. These include registering non-harmful polarity words which have a high relevance with non-harmful entries. This would lower the overall harmfulness polarity score of non-harmful entries containing neutral phrases. We will also investigate a method for assessing the harmfulness score to entries including personal information. Furthermore, by continuous testing of the method in practice we plan to semi-automatically collect additional datasets and determine the optimal threshold automatically by using machine learning methods. We also plan to repeat the experiments by Ishisaka et al. to eliminate any potential ambiguities in human judgments about the harmfulness of words. Finally, we plan to apply the proposed optimization method to other Web mining-based tasks and verify its potential and limitations in improving such methods in general.

REFERENCES

2channel. (n.d.). Retrieved from: https://www.2ch.net/

Adam Kilgarriff, K. (2007). Googleology is bad science. *Computational Linguistics, 33*(1), 147–151. doi:10.1162/coli.2007.33.1.147

DMARC. (n.d.). *dmarc.org – Domain Message Authentication Reporting & Conformance*. Retrieved from: http://www.dmarc.org/

Fujii, Y., Ando, S., & Ito, T. (2010). Yūgai jōhō firutaringu no tame no 2-tangokan no kyori oyobi kyōki jōhō ni yoru bunshō bunrui shuhō no teian [Developing a method based on 2-word co-occurence information for filter harmful information] (in Japanese). *Proceedings of The 24th Annual Conference of The Japanese Society for Artificial Intelligence (JSAI2010)*, 1-4.

Google. (n.d.). *Google Event Community Guidelines and Anti-Harassment Policy*. Retrieved from: https://www.google.com/events/policy/anti-harassmentpolicy.html

Ikeda, K., & Yanagihara, T. (2010). Kakuyōso no chūshōka ni motozuku ihō-, yūgaibunsho kenshutsu shuhō no teian to hyōka [Proposal and evaluation of method for illegal and harmful document detection based on the abstraction of case elements] (in Japanese). *Proceedings of 72nd National Convention of Information Processing Society of Japan (IPSJ72)*, 71-72.

Komuda, R., Ptaszynski, M., Momouchi, Y., Rzepka, R., & Araki, K. (2010). Machine Moral Development: Moral Reasoning Agent Based on Wisdom of Web- Crowd and Emotions. *International Journal of Computational Linguistics Research, 1*(3), 155–163.

Komuda, R., Rzepka, R., & Araki, K. (2013, March). Aristotelian Approach and Shallow Search Settings for Fast Ethical Judgment. *International Journal of Computational Linguistics Research, 4*(1), 14–22.

Kudo, T. (2006). MeCab: Yet Another Part-of-Speech and Morphological Analyzer. Retrieved from: http://taku910.github.io/mecab/

Kudo, T. (2010). *CaboCha: Yet Another Japanese Dependency Structure Analyzer*. Retrieved from: http://taku910.github.io/cabocha/

Matsuba, T., Masui, F., Kawai, A., & Isu, N. (2011). Gakkō hi-kōshiki saito ni okeru yūgai jōhō kenshutsu wo mokuteki to shita kyokusei hantei moderu ni kansuru kenkyū [Study on the polarity classification model for the purpose of detecting harmful information on informal school sites] (in Japanese). *Proceedings of The Seventeenth Annual Meeting of The Association for Natural Language Processing (NLP2011)*, 388-391.

McNemar, Q. (1947). Note on the sampling error of the difference between correlated proportions or percentages. *Psychometrika*, *12*(2), 153–157. doi:10.1007/BF02295996 PMID:20254758

Ministry of Education, Culture, Sports, Science, and Technology (MEXT). (2008). *'Netto-jō no ijime' ni kansuru taiō manyuaru jirei shū (gakkō, kyōin muke)* ["Bullying on the Net" Manual for handling and collection of cases (for schools and teachers)] (in Japanese). MEXT.

Nitta, T., Masui, F., Ptaszynski, M., Kimura, Y., Rzepka, R., & Araki, K. (2013). Detecting Cyberbullying Entries on Informal School Websites Based on Category Relevance Maximization. *Proceedings of the 6th International Joint Conference on Natural Language Processing (IJCNLP 2013)*, 579-586.

Pang, B., & Lee, L. (2008). Opinion mining and sentiment analysis. *Foundations and Trends in Information Retrieval*, *2*(1–2), 1–135. doi:10.1561/1500000011

Perry, J. W., Kent, A., & Berry, M. M. (1955). Machine literature searching X. Machine language; factors underlying its design and development. *American Documentation*, *6*(4), 242–254. doi:10.1002/asi.5090060411

Ptaszynski, M., Dybala, P., Matsuba, T., Masui, F., Rzepka, R., Araki, K., & Momouchi, Y. (2010). In the Service of Online Order: Tackling Cyber-Bullying with Machine Learning and Affect Analysis. *International Journal of Computational Linguistics Research*, *1*(3), 135–154.

Ptaszynski, M., Dybala, P., Shi, W., Rzepka, R., & Araki, K. (2009). A System for Affect Analysis of Utterances in Japanese Supported with Web Mining. *Journal of Japan Society for Fuzzy Theory and Intelligent Informatics, 21*(2), 30-49.

Tatsuya Ishisaka, T., & Yamamoto, K. (2011). Automatic detection of sentences representing slandering on the Web. *The 17th Annual Meeting of the Association for Natural Language Processing*, 131-134. (In Japanese)

Turney, P. D. (2002). Thumbs Up or Thumbs Down? Semantic Orientation Applied to Unsupervised Classification of Reviews. *Proceedings of the 40th Annual Meeting of the Association for Computational Linguistics*, 417-424.

Twitter. (2014). *Building a safer Twitter*. Retrieved from: https://blog.twitter.com/2014/building-a-safer-twitter

ENDNOTE

[1] In this chapter, we use the words "word" and "morpheme" in the same meaning, as they are processed similarly by morphological analysis tools for Japanese language.

Chapter 5
Brute Force Search Method for Cyberbullying Detection

ABSTRACT

In this chapter, the authors present a method for automatic detection of malicious internet contents, based on a combinatorial approach resembling brute force search algorithms, with application to language classification. The method automatically extracts sophisticated patterns from sentences and applies them in classification. The experiments performed on actual cyberbullying data showed advantage of this method to previous methods, including the one described in Chapter 4. Pros and cons of this method when compared to previous ones are also discussed in this chapter.

INTRODUCTION

Brute-force search algorithms, also known as exhaustive search algorithms, are a general group of algorithms applying combinatorial approach to problem solving. In particular, such algorithms firstly generate all possible answers to a problem, and then test the answer for its success. Combinatorial algorithms are especially useful in tasks where it is difficult to estimate a probable answer to narrow the scope of search. Therefore they have been traditionally used in password breaking and data decryption (Narayanan & Shmatikov, 2005; Paar, Pelzl & Preneel, 2010).

DOI: 10.4018/978-1-5225-5249-9.ch005

However, due to their minimal requirements when it comes to initial knowledge base, combinatorial algorithms have been also useful in Natural Language Processing, for example, in dependency parsing (Covington, 2001), stemming (Mishra & Prakash, 2012), or specific and novel tasks, such as extraction and analysis of emoticons (Ptaszynski et al., 2010).

However, brute-force approach often faces the problem of exponential and rapid growth of function values during combinatorial manipulations. This phenomenon is known as combinatorial explosion (Krippendorff, 1986). Since this phenomenon often results in very long processing time, combinatorial approaches have been often disregarded. We assumed however, that combinatorial explosion can be handled on modern hardware to the extent needed in our research. Moreover, optimizing the combinatorial approach algorithm specifically to problem requirements should shorten the processing time making it advantageous in the task of processing harmful language.

The method proposed in this chapter is original in following regards. As was pointed out by previous research (Ptaszynski et al., 2010), language used in cyberbullying messages is often deceptive and messy, and it is difficult to grasp a simple set of features to detect it. Therefore, to create a flexible model of cyberbullying, we applied a novel automatic feature extraction procedure. In research on machine learning, or applying any kind of machine learning to solve real world problems, one can use one of two approaches to feature extraction, namely, either automatic feature extraction (later called bottom-up approach) or select some custom predefined features (later called top-down approach, e.g., hand-crafting a lexicon of characteristic terms, etc.). The latter, although sometimes providing satisfying results, requires deep knowledge of the problem beforehand, meaning that the researchers need to figure out valid features themselves, which is inefficient.

In grand majority of NLP research, also in cyberbullying detection, applying the bottom-up approach, the features extracted automatically are typically based on separate words (as in e.g., bag-of-words) (Ptaszynski et al., 2010). Although instead of simple words one can use in text classification parts-of-speech or concepts (Sahlgren & Cöster, 2004), the sophistication of extracted pattern still does not exceed one token. A smaller number of research applies ngrams (usually unigrams to tetragrams of words or letters) (Damashek, 1995; Ponte & Croft, 1998; Siu & Ostendorf, 2000).

Recently, researchers have started to apply slightly more generalized version of ngrams, namely, skip-grams (Guthrie et al., 2006), which allow one controlled “skip”, or a gap of a controlled distance. This however is still far from the definition of a pattern proposed here, namely, allowing any number

Figure 1. A graphical summary of the whole method

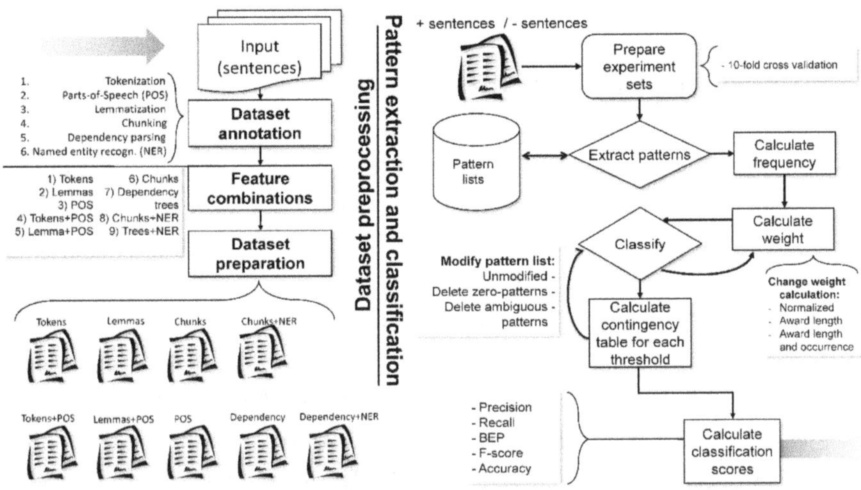

of "skips" with a flexible dynamic distance, which in mathematical terms refers to "ordered combinations without repetitions." This kind of pattern extraction has not been widely applied till now due to the computational cost it requires to train. The method proposed here takes advantage of the recent computing technologies allowing multiple cores and large amounts of memory to overcome this problem and compute such patterns in a sufficient time. We assumed this method of feature extraction will provide features of the sophistication level previously unused in cyberbullying detection research.

Outline of the chapter is as follows. Firstly, we describe the proposed method and the ways we decided to preprocess the applied dataset in this research. We explain the evaluation settings, and thoroughly analyze the results. Finally, we discuss the pros and cons of the method proposed in this chapter.

SENTENCE PATTERN EXTORTION METHOD DESCRIPTION

In this section we explain all parts of the proposed method, step by step. At first we describe general types of features we apply in this research and explain our feature extraction method. Next, we describe all ways of weight calculation for the applied features. Then, we present the applied classifier. Finally we describe the threshold optimization as a method to optimize the classifier performance. A graphical summary of the whole method was represented in Figure 1.

Sophistication of Language Model

Features applied in building a language model for classification can be in general viewed from two different points of view.

Firstly, a general sophistication of all features must be addressed. This applies to whether the applied features represent single words/tokens, or n-grams (sequences of tokens), or some other more sophisticated kinds of patterns.

Secondly, a specific kind of information encoded in the features needs to be recognized. For example, features can consist of words, but also of lemmas (undeclensed dictionary form of words), parts-of-speech (POS), etc. Combinations of those kinds of information are also allowed. For example it is possible to use combined features of words with POS, or lemmas with POS.

The latter, as being more related to the dataset rather than to the method itself, will be explained further in section describing "Dataset Preprocessing." Below we explain the former, being the core of the method.

Computationally simplest language model is called Bag-of-Words (BoW) (Zellig, 1954). It considers a piece of text or document as an unordered collection of words. BoW thus disregards grammar and word order. Although recently there has been proposed a generalization of BoW model using semantic concepts instead of words (Bag-of-Concepts) (Cambria & Hussain, 2012), the general rule remains the same, disregarding the order of elements within input, and longer strings of elements (e.g., phrases).

An approach in which word order is retained is broadly called the n-gram approach. In terms of probabilistic theory its basis was firstly formulated by Markov (1971). The n-gram approach perceives a given input (e.g., sentence) as a set of n-long ordered sub-sequences of words. This allows matching the words while retaining the sentence word order. However, the n-gram approach when applied to language, still allows only for simple sequence matching, while disregarding more sophisticated sentence structure.

An example of such sophisticated pattern, can be explained as follows. A following sentence (in Japanese) *Kyō wa nante kimochi ii hi nanda !* (What a pleasant day it is today!) contains a common and widely studied language pattern *nante * nanda !* (asterisk "*" used as a marker of disjointed elements). Similar cases can be easily found in other languages, for instance, in English.

An exclamative sentence "Oh, she is so pretty, isn't she?", contains a pattern "Oh * is so * isn't *?" which is a typical example of a *wh*-exclamative sentence pattern (Beijer, 2002; Sasai, 2006; Potts & Schwarz, 2008). The existence of such patterns in language is common and well recognized in linguistics. However, it is not possible to discover them using n-gram approach.

An example of a language model aimed to go beyond BoW and n-grams is the skip-gram model (sometimes also called skipped n-gram or distanced n-gram). It assumes that some words within an n-gram could be not adjacent, but skipped over. In theory this should allow extraction of most of frequent language patterns from a corpus. However, there are some major drawbacks in research studying skip-gram modeling. These include for example, assuming that a skip can appear only in one place (Huang et al., 1992). The above-mentioned English sentence example clearly indicates that frequent and easily recognizable language patterns can consist of elements appearing sometimes on the beginning of a sentence, another time in the middle, or at the end. Multiple gaps between them are also common, which cannot be covered by the skip-gram language model. Moreover, the number of skipped elements is recorded for each gap. For example, a 2-skip-3-gram can only allow 2 skips (omitting two words) between the elements, which means that the model considers as different patterns two cases in which the first gap has 2 skips, and second has 5 skips. Since the model assumes full control of the skip-length, the 2-skip-3-gram and 5-skip-3-gram consisting of the same elements (words) are represented as different entities and can never refer to the same pattern in a corpus. This assumption is unrealistic, since one can easily imagine that the same pattern, appearing in two sentences of different length, will be separated by gaps of different sizes. To illustrate this problem in Table 1 we compared which of the above-mentioned language models is capable of discovering particular patterns present in the two sentences below. The last column on the right represents capability of the language model based on the idea of language combinatorics (LC), applied in this research.

1. John went to school today.
2. John went to this awful place many people tend to generously call school today.

The language modeling method discussed in this chapter is capable of dealing with any of the sophisticated patterns. This is due to the fact that we define sentence pattern as *any ordered non-repeated frequently occurring combination of sentence elements.* This definition allows extraction of all

Table 1. Comparison of capabilities of different language models to capture certain patterns from a hypothetical corpus consisting of two sentences, (1) and (2) (○ = capable, × = incapable)

pattern	model			
	BoW	n-gram	skip-gram	LC
John	○	○	○	○
John went	×	○	○	○
John * to	×	×	○	○
John * school	×	×	×	○
John * to * today	×	×	×	○

possible frequent meaningful linguistic patterns from unrestricted text. Moreover, by a "frequent pattern" we consider a combination which occurs in a corpus at least twice. This differs from the traditional approach to building BoW language models, where one usually uses all extracted words, even if their occurrence is equal to 1. This is due to the fact that single words usually do not reach high occurrence rates, and most of them are rare. Therefore not using all of them, or using only those with occurrence = 2 or higher, could significantly decrease the Recall rate in classification process (not many features would be found). With sophisticated patterns the situation is different. They are extracted in enormous numbers and using all of them would make the classification process inefficient. By using the above cut-off rate, we conform to the general definition of "a pattern" (as something that appears repeatedly, or "at least twice"), get rid of the least useful patterns, and retain those which in fact appear most often.

Feature Extraction With Language Combinatorics

To extract the patterns of cyberbullying messages we first applied the idea of Language Combinatorics (Ptaszynski et al., 2011). This idea assumes that linguistic entities, such as sentences can be perceived as bundles of ordered non-repeated combinations of elements (words, punctuation marks, etc.). Furthermore, the most frequent combinations appearing in many different sentences can be defined as sentence patterns. The idea was applied in SPEC or **S**entence **P**attern **E**xtraction ar**C**hitecture – a custom feature extraction and classification system, which we also applied in the experiment.

We assumed that for the task of cyberbullying detection, where actual harmful meaning is often hidden and indirect, applying such sophisticated patterns with disjointed elements should provide better results than the usual bag-of-words or n-gram approach. As long as patterns are defined as ordered combinations of sentence elements, they could be automatically extracted by generating all ordered combinations of sentence elements, verifying their occurrences within a corpus, and filtering out those the combinations which appear only once.

From the fact that the method first extracts all possible patterns from a sentence with brute force inspired algorithm, we decided to call the method ***pattern extortion***, to distinguish it from typical *pattern extraction* methods based on n-grams or single tokens.

Formally, in this method, firstly, ordered non-repeated combinations are generated from all elements of all input sentences in a training set. In every n-element sentence there is k-number of combination clusters, such as that $1 \leqq k \leqq n$, where k represents all k-element combinations being a subset of n. The number of combinations generated for one k-element cluster of combinations is equal to binomial coefficient, represented in equation 1. In this procedure the system creates all combinations for all values of k from the range of $\{1, \ldots, n\}$. Therefore the number of all combinations is equal to the sum of combinations from all k-element clusters of combinations, like in equation 2.

$$\binom{n}{k} = \frac{\boldsymbol{n}!}{\boldsymbol{k}!(\boldsymbol{n}-\boldsymbol{k})!} \tag{1}$$

$$\sum_{k=1}^{n} \binom{n}{k} = \frac{n!}{1!(n-1)!} + \frac{n!}{2!(n-2)!} + \ldots + \frac{n!}{n!(n-n)!} = 2^n - 1 \tag{2}$$

Next, all non-subsequent elements are separated with an asterisk ("*"). All patterns generated this way are used to extract frequent patterns appearing in a given corpus.

For comparison, we also applied more traditional n-gram model.

Weight Calculation

After combinatorial patterns are extracted, their occurrences O are calculated, separately for the positive (here, meaning "harmful") side O_{pos} and the negative side (here meaning "non-harmful") side O_{neg}. The occurrences of each pattern j are further used to calculate normalized pattern weight w_j according to equation 3.

$$w_j = \left(\frac{O_{pos}}{O_{pos} + O_{neg}} - 0.5 \right) * 2 \tag{3}$$

The weight can be later modified in several ways. Two features are important in weight calculation. A pattern is the more representative for a corpus when, firstly, the longer the pattern is (length k), and the more often it appears in the corpus (occurrence O). Thus the weight can be modified by

- Awarding length (later: LA), by multiplying normalized weight w_j by pattern length k_j, which provides a weight with awarded length W_{LA}, like in equation 4, or
- Awarding length and occurrence (later: LOA), by multiplying normalized weight w_j by pattern length k_j and overall pattern occurrence (O_{pos} +O_{neg}), which provides a weight with awarded length and occurrence w_{LOA}, like in equation 5.

$$w_{LA} = w_j * k_j \tag{4}$$

$$w_{LOA} = w_j * k_j * \left(O_{pos} + O_{neg} \right) \tag{5}$$

The list of frequent patterns generated in the process of pattern generation and extraction can be also further modified. When two collections of sentences of opposite features (such as "positive vs. negative" or "harmful vs. non-harmful") are compared, a generated list of patterns will contain patterns that appear uniquely in only one of the sides (e.g. uniquely positive patterns and uniquely negative patterns) or in both (ambiguous patterns). Therefore the pattern list can be further modified by

- Erasing all ambiguous patterns[1] (later: AMB),
- Erasing only ambiguous patterns which appear in the same number on both sides (later zero patterns, or 0P).

Moreover, a list of patterns will contain both the sophisticated patterns (with disjointed elements) as well as more common n-grams. Therefore the experiments on the proposed method were performed with both

- Patterns (PAT), and
- N-grams (NGR) only.

Classification

The proposed classifier is a function defined as a sum of weights of patterns found in the input sentence, like in equation 6.

$$\text{score} = \sum w_j, \left(1 \geq w_j \geq -1\right) \tag{6}$$

It produces a harmfulness score for each analyzed sentence. The score alone does not yet specify whether a sentence should be considered harmful or not, however, a good guess is that the higher above zero is the score the more harmful patterns it contains, or, to put it in more straightforward terms, the more it resembles a style of writing usually found in cyberbullying. On the other hand, the lower below zero the score, the more it resembles non-harmful way of writing. However, an intuitive rule of thumb, with zero as a universal threshold does not apply to pattern-based method, since even a one word difference in a sentence can produce much larger number of patterns on one of the sides (harmful or non-harmful), and thus cause an imbalance in the data. Therefore we also performed a threshold optimization to specify which threshold should be used for the applied data.

Threshold Optimization and Heuristic Rules

If the initial collection of sentences was biased toward one of the sides (e.g., more sentences of one kind, or the sentences were longer, etc.), there will be significantly more patterns of a certain kind. Thus to avoid bias in the results, instead of applying a static rule of thumb, threshold was optimized automatically.

All above settings were automatically verified in the process of evaluation, based on 10-fold cross validation, to choose the best model. The metrics used in evaluation were standard Precision (P), Recall (R), balanced F-score (F) and Accuracy (A). These scores were calculated for every threshold and compared to choose the optimal model.

Finally, to deal with the combinatorial explosion mentioned on the beginning of this chapter we applied two heuristic rules. In the preliminary experiments (Ptaszynski et al., 2011), we found out that the most valuable (frequently appearing) patterns in language are up to six element long, thus we limited the scope of pattern extraction to $k \leq 6$. Therefore, the procedure of pattern generation will (1) generate up to six elements patterns, or (2) terminate at the point where no frequent patterns were found.

EVALUATION EXPERIMENT

Dataset Preprocessing and Feature Selection

The proposed method takes as an input sentences separated into elements (words, tokens, etc.). In original transcription of Japanese language (the language of applied dataset) spaces, like in English are not used. Therefore we needed to preprocess the dataset and make the sentences separable into elements. We did this in several ways to check how the preprocessing would influence the results. We used MeCab[2], a morphological analyzer for Japanese and CaboCha[3], a Japanese dependency structure analyzer, to preprocess the sentences from the dataset in the following ways.

- **Tokenization:** All words, punctuation marks, etc. are separated by spaces (later: TOK).
- **Lemmatization:** Like the above but the words are represented in their generic (dictionary) forms, or "lemmas" (later: LEM).
- **Parts of Speech:** Words are replaced with their representative parts of speech (later: POS).
- **Tokens With POS:** Both words and POS information is included in one element (later: TOK+POS).
- **Lemmas With POS:** Like the above but with lemmas instead of words (later: LEM+POS).

- **Chunks:** Larger sub-parts of sentences divided in grammatical clusters, such as noun phrase, verb phrase, predicates, etc., but without dependency relations (later: CHUNK).
- **Dependency Structure:** Same as above, but with information regarding in what relation a chunk is with previous one, the following one, and other chunks (later: DEP).
- **Chunks With Named Entities:** Chunks with added information on what named entities (private name of a person, organization, numericals, etc.) appear in the sentence. The information is provided by the dependency structure analyzer (later: CHUNK+NER).
- **Dependency Structure With Named Entities:** Both dependency relations and named entities are provided (later: DEP+NER).

Feature extraction from sentences is done automatically, according to procedure explained in section "Feature Extraction with Language Combinatorics." Next, language model is generated automatically using the extracted features. In this context, the dataset preprocessing methods represented above can be understood as feature selection preset for the experiment.

Five examples of preprocessing are represented in Table 2. Theoretically, the more generalized a sentence is, the less unique and frequent patterns it will produce, but the produced patterns will be more frequent. This can be explained by comparing tokenized sentence with its POS representation. For example, in the sentence from Table 2 we can see that a simple phrase *kimochi_ii hi* ("pleasant day") is be represented by a POS pattern as ADJ N. We can easily assume that there will be more ADJ N patterns than *kimochi_ii hi*, because many word combinations can be represented by this POS pattern. On the other hand, there are more words in the dictionary than POS labels. Therefore POS patterns will come in less variety but with higher occurrence frequency. By comparing the result of the classification using different preprocessing methods we can find out whether it is better to represent sentences as more generalized or as more specific.

Experiment Setup

The preprocessed original dataset provides nine separate training and test sets for the experiment (tokenized, POS-tagged, tokens with POS, lemmatized, lemmas with POS, chunks, dependency relations, chunks with named entities, dependency with named entities). The experiment was performed nine times, one time for each kind of preprocessing to choose the best option. For each version of the dataset a 10-fold cross validation was performed and the results were calculated using standard Precision, Recall, balanced F-score and Accuracy for each threshold within the whole threshold span. In one experiment 14 different versions of the proposed classifier are compared with 10-fold cross validation condition. Versions of the classifier represent combinations of weight calculation and pattern list modification explained in section "Weight Calculation," and are in order: PAT, PAT-0P, PAT-AMB, PAT-LA, PAT-LA-0P, PAT-LA-AMB, PAT-LOA, NGR, NGR-0P, NGR-AMB, NGR-LA, NGR-LA-0P, NGR-LA-AMB, NGR-LOA. Since the experiment was performed for nine different versions of preprocessing, we obtained overall number of 1260 experiment runs (9 datasets * 14 classifier versions in 10-fold cross-validation). There were several evaluation criteria. Firstly, we looked at which version of the algorithm achieved highest balanced F-score, and highest Accuracy within the threshold span. This is referred to as threshold optimization. However, theoretically, an algorithm could achieve its best score for one certain threshold, while for others it could perform poorly. Therefore we also looked at break-even points (BEP) of Precision and Recall. This shows which version of the algorithm is more balanced. Finally, we checked the statistical significance of the results. We used paired t-test because the classification results could represent only one of two classes (harmful or non-harmful). To choose the best version of the algorithm we compared separately the results achieved by each group of modifications, eg., "different pattern weight calculations", "pattern list modifications" and "patterns vs n-grams". We also compared the performance to previous methods, which we consider a baseline. This refers primarily to SO-PMI-IR based methods (Matsuba et al., 2011; Nitta et al., 2013; Ptaszynski et al., 2016), including the method described in previous chapter, which were based on the same data.

RESULTS AND DISCUSSION

We analyzed the results in a number of ways to obtain as objective perspective as possible.

Firstly, we analyzed the results for each feature set separately, to find out which weight calculation method and which pattern list modification achieved highest results for each set. We looked at the highest F-score and Accuracy. We also checked break-even point of Precision and Recall (BEP) for each

*Table 2. Three examples of preprocessing of a sentence in Japanese; N = noun, PP = postpositional particle, ADV = adverb, ADJ = adjective, AUX = auxiliary verb, SYM = symbol, 1D, 2D, ... = depth of dependency relation, *0, *1, *2, ... = phrase number.*

Sentence: 今日はなんて気持ちいい日なんだ!
Transcription in alphabet: *Kyōwanantekimochiiihinanda!*
Glosses: Today TOP what pleasant day COP EXCL
Translation: What a pleasant day it is today!

Preprocessing examples

–**Tokenization:** *Kyō wa nante kimochiii hi nanda !*
–**POS:** N PP ADV ADJ N AUX SYM
–**Tokens+POS:** *Kyō* [N] *wa*[PP] *nante*[ADV] *kimochi_ii*[ADJ] *hi*[N] *nanda*[AUX] *!*[SYM]
–**Chunks:** *Kyō wa nante kimochi_ii hi_nanda!*
–**Dependency relations:** *0 3D *Kyō wa* *1 2D *nante* *2 3D *kimochi_ii* *3 -1D *hi nanda!*

version of the classifier. We also calculated statistical significance between all results within each feature set.

Secondly, we compared the results among all feature sets to find out whether there exists a stable pattern in results, e.g., if patterns were always better than n-grams, or if it is more effective to use all patterns, or only the unique ones, etc.

Following, we analyzed, whether the method works better on more generalized of more specific feature sets.

Finally, we calculated statistical significance between the best results of each feature set.

Lastly, we compared the best and the worst results of the proposed method to previous methods.

Results Separately for Each Feature Set

Tokenized Set

At first, we looked at the dataset preprocessed with the simplest method, namely, tokenization.

Highest achieved Precision was 0.861 and was obtained by both patterns and n-grams when zero-patterns were deleted from pattern lists. Second best Precision was achieved by pattern list containing all patterns/n-grams (0.858). However, when all ambiguous patterns were deleted, the highest achieved Precision suddenly dropped to 0.820. Awarding length usually caused drop in Precision. The results for best Precision were represented in Table 3.

The highest achieved F-score was 0.778 and was obtained by patterns when zero-patterns were deleted from pattern lists. Second best F-score was achieved by pattern list containing all patterns/n-grams (0.724). Deleting all ambiguous patterns caused drop in F-score to 0.690. Awarding length also caused drop in F-score. The results for best F-score were represented in Table 4.

The highest achieved Accuracy was 0.776 and was obtained by patterns when all ambiguous patterns were deleted from pattern lists. This stands in contradiction to the above results for best Fscore, however, second best Accuracy was achieved by pattern list containing all patterns/n-grams (0.766). Awarding length, similarly to above results, caused drop in Accuracy. The results for best Accuracy were represented in Table 5.

When it comes to statistical significance, differences between most results were statistically significant, meaning, they could not be considered as a matter of chance. Pairs which tended to be not statistically significant included those which differed only in one kind of characteristics, e.g., PAT-0P and NGR-0P, which were also two best scores for highest Precision and highest F-score (former). Results of T-test for F-scores and Accuracies among all system results for tokenized dataset were represented in Table 6.

Table 3. Comparison of best Precision within the threshold span for each version of the classifier for tokenized dataset. Best classifier version within each preprocessing kind - highlighted in bold type font

Highest Precision within threshold				
	Pr	**Re**	**F1**	**Acc**
PAT-ALL	0.858	0.242	0.377	0.610
PAT-0P	**0.861**	**0.249**	**0.387**	**0.614**
PAT-AMB	0.820	0.491	0.614	0.699
PAT-LA-0P	0.838	0.150	0.255	0.571
PAT-LA	0.839	0.143	0.244	0.568
PAT-LA-AMB	0.755	0.562	0.644	0.697
NGR-ALL	0.859	0.243	0.378	0.611
NGR-0P	**0.861**	**0.249**	**0.387**	**0.614**
NGR-AMB	0.820	0.491	0.614	0.699
NGR-LA	0.840	0.144	0.245	0.568
NGR-LA-0P	0.838	0.150	0.254	0.570
NGR-LA-AMB	0.754	0.563	0.645	0.697

Table 4. Comparison of best F-score within the threshold span for each version of the classifier for tokenized dataset. Best classifier version within each preprocessing kind - highlighted in bold type font. In case of identical results for F-score, the best score was optimized for Accuracy.

Highest F-score within threshold				
	Pr	**Re**	**F1**	**Acc**
PAT-ALL	0.724	0.842	0.778	0.766
PAT-0P	**0.724**	**0.842**	**0.778**	**0.766**
PAT-AMB	0.690	0.889	0.777	0.751
PAT-LA-0P	0.697	0.796	0.743	0.73
PAT-LA	0.656	0.856	0.742	0.709
PAT-LA-AMB	0.666	0.826	0.738	0.712
NGR-ALL	0.723	0.842	0.778	0.766
NGR-0P	0.724	0.841	0.778	0.765
NGR-AMB	0.690	0.889	0.777	0.751
NGR-LA	0.654	0.855	0.741	0.708
NGR-LA-0P	0.696	0.796	0.743	0.730
NGR-LA-AMB	0.666	0.826	0.737	0.711

Table 5. Comparison of best Accuracy within the threshold span for each version of the classifier for tokenized dataset. Best classifier version within each preprocessing kind - highlighted in bold type font. In case of identical results for Accuracy, the best score was optimized for F-score.

Highest Accuracy within threshold				
	Pr	**Re**	**F1**	**Acc**
PAT-ALL	0.724	0.842	0.778	0.766
PAT-0P	**0.785**	**0.718**	**0.750**	**0.766**
PAT-AMB	0.778	0.760	0.769	0.776
PAT-LA-0P	0.736	0.713	0.724	0.734
PAT-LA	0.740	0.708	0.723	0.735
PAT-LA-AMB	0.715	0.703	0.709	0.718
NGR-ALL	0.723	0.842	0.778	0.766
NGR-0P	0.784	0.718	0.749	0.766
NGR-AMB	0.777	0.759	0.768	0.776
NGR-LA	0.740	0.708	0.723	0.735
NGR-LA-0P	0.737	0.713	0.725	0.735
NGR-LA-AMB	0.714	0.702	0.708	0.717

Table 6. Results of t-test (p-values) for F-scores and Accuracies among all system results for tokenized dataset.

F-score	PAT-ALL	PAT-AMB	PAT-LA	PAT-LA-AMB	PAT-LA-0P	NGR-ALL	NGR-AMB	NGR-LA	NGR-LA-AMB	NGR-LA-0P	NGR-0P	PAT-0P
PAT-ALL		.000***	.002**	.002**	.002**	.920	.000***	.002**	.002**	.002**	.005**	.004**
PAT-AMB			.000***	.128	.000***	.000***	.068	.000***	.130	.000***	.000***	.000***
PAT-LA				.004**	.001***	.002**	.000***	.429	.004**	.001***	.003**	.003**
PAT-LA-AMB					.004**	.002**	.128	.004**	.023*	.004**	.002**	.002**
PAT-LA-0P						.002**	.000***	.001***	.004**	.147	.002**	.002**
NGR-ALL							.000***	.002**	.002**	.002**	.005**	.005**
NGR-AMB								.000***	.130	.000***	.000***	.000***
NGR-LA									.004**	.001***	.003**	.003**
NGR-LA-AMB										.004**	.002**	.002**
NGR-LA-0P											.002**	.002**
NGR-0P												.853
PAT-0P												
Accuracy												
PAT-ALL		.000***	.006**	.000***	.005**	.998	.000***	.006**	.000***	.005**	.001***	.001***
PAT-AMB			.000***	.272	.000***	.000***	.110	.000***	.265	.000***	.000***	.000***
PAT-LA				.000***	.000***	.006**	.000***	.697	.000***	.000***	.008**	.008**
PAT-LA-AMB					.000***	.000***	.268	.000***	.004**	.000***	.000***	.000***
PAT-LA-0P						.005**	.000***	.000***	.000***	.225	.006**	.006**
NGR-ALL							.000***	.006**	.000***	.004**	.001***	.001***
NGR-AMB								.000***	.261	.000***	.000***	.000***
NGR-LA									.000***	.000***	.009**	.009**
NGR-LA-AMB										.000***	.000***	.000***
NGR-LA-0P											.006**	.006**
NGR-0P												.802
PAT-0P												

$*p \leq 0.05$, $**p \leq 0.01$, $***p \leq 0.001$

Lemmatized Set

The second simplest way of data preprocessing, after tokenization, was lemmatization. In this process all declensed and conjugated words are simplified to their dictionary forms. Therefore, lemmatization provides less specific, thus less numerous, but more frequently appearing features. This makes lemmatization more generalized than tokenization.

The highest achieved Precision for lemmatized dataset was higher than for tokens, and reached 0.902 when patterns were used with length awarded weighting and zero-patterns deleted. Differently to tokenized dataset, where different weighting and pattern list modifications caused negative influence, for lemmas the influence was in most cases positive, especially when it comes to awarding length in weight calculation.

The highest achieved F-score for lemmatized dataset was also higher then for tokenized set, and reached 0.79 for n-grams. Highest scores of pattern-based classifier ranged lower in general. Similarly to tokenized dataset, awarding length caused drop in highest achieved F-score. Also, deleting either zero-patterns or all ambiguous patterns/n-grams caused occasional drop in scores, indicating that such patterns usually contribute positively to classification with lemmas. The results for best F-score were represented in Table 8.

Results for the highest Accuracy within threshold confirm the above results for F-score. The highest result was achieved by n-grams, and reached 0.79. Here also pattern list and weighting modifications decreased the results in general. The results for best Accuracy were represented in Table 9.

The differences among all versions of the classifier were in most cases statistically significant, usually on 0.1% level. Similarly to tokenized dataset, the results, when not significant usually had only one difference, e.g., PAT-0P and NGR-0P, or NGR-AMB and NGR-LA-AMB. Unfortunately, version of the classifier which achieved the highest top scores, namely, NGR-ALL (using all ngrams in classification), did not reach statistical significance with pattern-based classifiers, which decreases the reliability of n-gram-based scores. The results of T-test (p-values) for F-scores and Accuracies among all system results for lemmatized dataset were represented in Table 10.

Table 7. Comparison of best Precision within the threshold span for each version of the classifier for lemmatized dataset. Best classifier version within each preprocessing kind - highlighted in bold type font.

Highest Precision within threshold				
	Pr	**Re**	**F1**	**Acc**
PAT-ALL	0.871	0.276	0.419	0.627
PAT-0P	0.871	0.276	0.419	0.627
PAT-AMB	0.872	0.207	0.334	0.598
PAT-LA-0P	**0.902**	**0.208**	**0.338**	**0.602**
PAT-LA	0.872	0.293	0.438	0.633
PAT-LA-AMB	0.886	0.236	0.372	0.612
NGR-ALL	0.887	0.307	0.457	0.642
NGR-0P	0.886	0.329	0.48	0.651
NGR-AMB	0.810	0.597	0.687	0.735
NGR-LA	0.894	0.25	0.391	0.619
NGR-LA-0P	0.896	0.187	0.31	0.592
NGR-LA-AMB	0.807	0.609	0.694	0.738

Table 8. Comparison of best F-score within the threshold span for each version of the classifier for lemmatized dataset. Best classifier version within each preprocessing kind - highlighted in bold type font.

Highest F-score within threshold				
	Pr	Re	F1	Acc
PAT-ALL	0.715	0.82	0.764	0.753
PAT-0P	0.715	0.82	0.764	0.753
PAT-AMB	0.717	0.818	0.764	0.753
PAT-LA-0P	0.701	0.797	0.746	0.734
PAT-LA	0.714	0.811	0.76	0.749
PAT-LA-AMB	0.707	0.789	0.746	0.737
NGR-ALL	**0.713**	**0.885**	**0.79**	**0.77**
NGR-0P	0.713	0.885	0.79	0.769
NGR-AMB	0.713	0.864	0.781	0.763
NGR-LA	0.722	0.851	0.781	0.767
NGR-LA-0P	0.722	0.851	0.781	0.766
NGR-LA-AMB	0.724	0.818	0.768	0.758

Table 9. Comparison of best Accuracy within the threshold span for each version of the classifier for lemmatized dataset. Best classifier version within each preprocessing kind - highlighted in bold type font.

Highest Accuracy within threshold				
	Pr	Re	F1	Acc
PAT-ALL	0.765	0.724	0.744	0.756
PAT-0P	0.765	0.724	0.744	0.756
PAT-AMB	0.765	0.724	0.744	0.756
PAT-LA-0P	0.748	0.718	0.732	0.744
PAT-LA	0.763	0.717	0.740	0.753
PAT-LA-AMB	0.749	0.717	0.733	0.745
NGR-ALL	**0.787**	**0.781**	**0.784**	**0.790**
NGR-0P	0.785	0.783	0.784	0.789
NGR-AMB	0.759	0.786	0.772	0.773
NGR-LA	0.770	0.762	0.766	0.773
NGR-LA-0P	0.769	0.766	0.768	0.773
NGR-LA-AMB	0.755	0.771	0.763	0.766

Table 10. Results of t-test (p-values) for F-scores and Accuracies among all system results for lemmatized dataset.

F-score	PAT-ALL	PAT-AMB	PAT-LA	PAT-LA-AMB	PAT-LA-0P	NGR-ALL	NGR-AMB	NGR-LA	NGR-LA-AMB	NGR-LA-0P	NGR-0P	PAT-0P
PAT-ALL		.002**	.000***	.000***	.000***	.422	.001**	.001***	.001***	.001***	.222	.000***
PAT-AMB			.005**	.000***	.000***	.741	.001**	.001***	.001***	.001***	.421	.002**
PAT-LA				.000***	.000***	.803	.001**	.001**	.001***	.001**	.842	.000***
PAT-LA-AMB					.001***	.002**	.014*	.014*	.003**	.024*	.002**	.000***
PAT-LA-0P						.002**	.009**	.034*	.002**	.065	.003**	.000***
NGR-ALL							.002**	.001**	.001**	.001**	.005**	.422
NGR-AMB								.004**	.002**	.005**	.002**	.001**
NGR-LA									.002**	.001***	.001**	.001***
NGR-LA-AMB										.003**	.001**	.001***
NGR-LA-0P											.001**	.001***
NGR-0P												.222
PAT-0P												
Accuracy												
PAT-ALL		.000***	.000***	.000***	.000***	.310	.002**	.004**	.000***	.002**	.443	.000***
PAT-AMB			.003**	.000***	.000***	.202	.003**	.009**	.000***	.004**	.296	.000***
PAT-LA				.000***	.000***	.087	.007**	.045*	.000***	.020*	.135	.000***
PAT-LA-AMB					.000***	.000***	.165	.001***	.421	.001***	.000***	.000***
PAT-LA-0P						.000***	.283	.001**	.224	.002**	.000***	.000***
NGR-ALL							.000***	.000***	.000***	.000***	.000***	.310
NGR-AMB								.008**	.000***	.013*	.000***	.002**
NGR-LA									.000***	.000***	.000***	.004**
NGR-LA-AMB										.000***	.000***	.000***
NGR-LA-0P											.000***	.002**
NGR-0P												.443
PAT-0P												

$*p \leq 0.05, **p \leq 0.01, ***p \leq 0.001$

POS-Tagged Set

Comparing to previous datasets, POS-tagging provides the most generalized way of preprocessing. A small number of features is extracted, however their occurrences are very high.

When it comes to comparison of the highest achieved scores, the highest Precision reached 0.934 (although for Recall = 0.031), however, all other compared measures were in general much lower than for tokenized, and lemmatized datasets, and reached at best 0.677 and 0.612, for F-score and Accuracy, respectively. This dataset also had the highest number of cases where differences between classifier versions were not statistically significant. There was also no consistency to which version of the classifier performs best for this dataset.

This could suggest that the classifier performs poorly for highly generalized datasets, or in practice, for low number of features, even if their occurrences are numerous.

Results for highest Precision, F-score and Accuracy were represented in Tables 11, 12 and 13. Results for T-test were represented in Table 14.

Tokenized Set With POS

Dataset containing both tokens and POS information provides a feature set more specific than the original tokenized dataset.

Precision score was better for this dataset and reached 0.89 when either all patterns or all n-grams were used. Further modifications only decreased the results, although for second best Precision, corresponding F-score and Accuracy were much higher. The results for best Precision were represented in Table 15.

For F-score as well as for Accuracy, the highest results were obtained when zero-patterns were deleted from pattern list, and reached 0.796 and 0.784, respectively. Using all patterns, as well as deleting all ambiguous patterns caused decrease in results. Other modifications also did not cause any improvement.

Unfortunately, many of T-test results indicated lack of statistical significance. For the two best classifier versions (PAT-0P, NGR-0P) the differences were

Table 11. Comparison of best Precision within the threshold span for each version of the classifier for POS-tagged dataset. Best classifier version within each preprocessing kind - highlighted in bold type font.

Highest Precision within threshold				
	Pr	**Re**	**F1**	**Acc**
PAT-ALL	0.776	0.048	0.091	0.518
PAT-0P	0.776	0.048	0.091	0.518
PAT-AMB	0.796	0.019	0.037	0.507
PAT-LA-0P	0.761	0.114	0.198	0.539
PAT-LA	0.776	0.048	0.091	0.518
PAT-LA-AMB	0.758	0.119	0.205	0.540
NGR-ALL	0.917	0.022	0.042	0.510
NGR-0P	0.917	0.021	0.041	0.510
NGR-AMB	0.652	0.196	0.302	0.546
NGR-LA	**0.934**	**0.031**	**0.060**	**0.514**
NGR-LA-0P	0.910	0.032	0.062	0.514
NGR-LA-AMB	0.656	0.308	0.419	0.574

Table 12. Comparison of best F-score within the threshold span for each version of the classifier for POS-tagged dataset. Best classifier version within each preprocessing kind - highlighted in bold type font.

Highest F-score within threshold				
	Pr	Re	F1	Acc
PAT-ALL	0.526	0.950	0.677	0.547
PAT-0P	0.526	0.950	0.677	0.547
PAT-AMB	**0.528**	**0.946**	**0.677**	**0.550**
PAT-LA-0P	0.524	0.952	0.676	0.543
PAT-LA	0.526	0.950	0.677	0.547
PAT-LA-AMB	0.526	0.949	0.677	0.547
NGR-ALL	0.518	0.959	0.672	0.533
NGR-0P	0.520	0.954	0.673	0.537
NGR-AMB	0.500	1.000	0.666	0.500
NGR-LA	0.528	0.935	0.675	0.551
NGR-LA-0P	0.530	0.930	0.675	0.552
NGR-LA-AMB	0.565	0.764	0.650	0.588

Table 13. Comparison of best Accuracy within the threshold span for each version of the classifier for POS-tagged dataset. Best classifier version within each preprocessing kind - highlighted in bold type font.

Highest Accuracy within threshold				
	Pr	Re	F1	Acc
PAT-ALL	0.577	0.779	0.663	0.604
PAT-0P	0.577	0.779	0.663	0.604
PAT-AMB	0.578	0.776	0.663	0.605
PAT-LA-0P	0.639	0.461	0.536	0.600
PAT-LA	0.577	0.779	0.663	0.604
PAT-LA-AMB	0.640	0.463	0.537	0.600
NGR-ALL	**0.635**	**0.528**	**0.576**	**0.612**
NGR-0P	0.635	0.527	0.576	0.612
NGR-AMB	0.545	0.774	0.640	0.564
NGR-LA	0.624	0.539	0.578	0.607
NGR-LA-0P	0.626	0.540	0.580	0.609
NGR-LA-AMB	0.587	0.650	0.617	0.596

Table 14. Results of t-test (p-values) for F-scores and Accuracies among all system results for POS-tagged dataset.

F-score	PAT-ALL	PAT-AMB	PAT-LA	PAT-LA-AMB	PAT-LA-0P	NGR-ALL	NGR-AMB	NGR-LA	NGR-LA-AMB	NGR-LA-0P	NGR-0P	PAT-0P
PAT-ALL		.146	.000***	.009**	.009**	.086	.001***	.002**	.001**	.002**	.090	.000***
PAT-AMB			.146	.009**	.009**	.088	.001***	.002**	.001**	.002**	.093	.146
PAT-LA				.009**	.009**	.086	.001***	.002**	.001**	.002**	.090	.000***
PAT-LA-AMB					.076	.014*	.004**	.000***	.002**	.000***	.014*	.009**
PAT-LA-0P						.014*	.004**	.000***	.002**	.000***	.014*	.009**
NGR-ALL							.001**	.003**	.002**	.003**	.576	.086
NGR-AMB								.082	.005**	.092	.001**	.001***
NGR-LA									.014*	.007**	.003**	.002**
NGR-LA-AMB										.015*	.002**	.001**
NGR-LA-0P											.003**	.002**
NGR-0P												.090
PAT-0P												
Accuracy												
PAT-ALL		.065	.000***	.000***	.000***	.501	.000***	.000***	.000***	.000***	.474	.000***
PAT-AMB			.065	.000***	.000***	.656	.000***	.000***	.000***	.000***	.629	.065
PAT-LA				.000***	.000***	.501	.000***	.000***	.000***	.000***	.474	.000***
PAT-LA-AMB					.152	.000***	.043*	.628	.000***	.845	.000***	.000***
PAT-LA-0P						.000***	.052	.729	.000***	.965	.000***	.000***
NGR-ALL							.000***	.000***	.000***	.000***	.854	.501
NGR-AMB								.055	.000***	.040*	.000***	.000***
NGR-LA									.001***	.002**	.000***	.000***
NGR-LA-AMB										.001***	.000***	.000***
NGR-LA-0P											.000***	.000***
NGR-0P												.474
PAT-0P												

$*p \leq 0.05$, $**p \leq 0.01$, $***p \leq 0.001$

usually significant only for cases with no weight modifications. The results of T-test (p-values) for F-scores and Accuracies among all system results for tokenized dataset with POS information were represented in Table 18.

Lemmatized Set With POS

The dataset preprocessed to contain both lemmas and POS information (LEM+POS) is theoretically more generalized then TOK+POS, but more specific then tokenized only (TOK) or lemmatized only (LEM). The results for previous ways of preprocessing (TOK, LEM, POS) indicated, that lemmas alone, although being more generalized than tokens, were more effective. On the other hand, parts-of-speech, although providing even higher level of generalization, scored much lower. By combining lemmas with POS and comparing the results to TOK+POS we can evaluate, whether POS, although causing negative influence alone, could contribute positively to overall results,

Table 15. Comparison of best Precision within the threshold span for each version of the classifier for dataset containing tokens with POS information. Best classifier version within each preprocessing kind - highlighted in bold type font.

Highest Precision within threshold				
	Pr	Re	F1	Acc
PAT-ALL	**0.890**	**0.336**	**0.487**	**0.647**
PAT-0P	0.885	0.342	0.494	0.649
PAT-AMB	0.873	0.417	0.565	0.678
PAT-LA-0P	0.868	0.121	0.212	0.551
PAT-LA	0.868	0.092	0.167	0.539
PAT-LA-AMB	0.837	0.434	0.572	0.675
NGR-ALL	**0.890**	**0.336**	**0.487**	**0.647**
NGR-0P	0.886	0.344	0.496	0.650
NGR-AMB	0.873	0.417	0.565	0.678
NGR-LA	0.868	0.092	0.167	0.539
NGR-LA-0P	0.868	0.121	0.212	0.551
NGR-LA-AMB	0.837	0.434	0.572	0.675

Table 16. Comparison of best F-score within the threshold span for each version of the classifier for dataset containing tokens with POS information. Best classifier version within each preprocessing kind - highlighted in bold type font.

Highest F-score within threshold				
	Pr	Re	F1	Acc
PAT-ALL	0.754	0.840	0.795	0.783
PAT-0P	**0.756**	**0.839**	**0.796**	**0.784**
PAT-AMB	0.717	0.844	0.775	0.755
PAT-LA-0P	0.706	0.767	0.735	0.724
PAT-LA	0.700	0.775	0.736	0.722
PAT-LA-AMB	0.709	0.728	0.719	0.715
NGR-ALL	0.754	0.840	0.795	0.783
NGR-0P	**0.756**	**0.839**	**0.796**	**0.784**
NGR-AMB	0.717	0.844	0.775	0.755
NGR-LA	0.700	0.775	0.736	0.721
NGR-LA-0P	0.706	0.768	0.736	0.724
NGR-LA-AMB	0.709	0.728	0.719	0.715

Table 17. Comparison of best Accuracy within the threshold span for each version of the classifier for dataset containing tokens with POS information. Best classifier version within each preprocessing kind - highlighted in bold type font.

Highest Accuracy within threshold				
	Pr	**Re**	**F1**	**Acc**
PAT-ALL	0.809	0.743	0.775	0.784
PAT-0P	**0.756**	**0.839**	**0.796**	**0.784**
PAT-AMB	0.741	0.809	0.774	0.763
PAT-LA-0P	0.736	0.708	0.722	0.727
PAT-LA	0.731	0.715	0.723	0.726
PAT-LA-AMB	0.718	0.710	0.714	0.715
NGR-ALL	0.809	0.744	0.775	0.784
NGR-0P	**0.756**	**0.839**	**0.796**	**0.784**
NGR-AMB	0.741	0.809	0.774	0.763
NGR-LA	0.731	0.715	0.723	0.726
NGR-LA-0P	0.735	0.707	0.721	0.726
NGR-LA-AMB	0.717	0.710	0.714	0.715

Table 18. Results of t-test (p-values) for F-scores and Accuracies among all system results for tokenized dataset with POS information.

F-score	PAT--ALL	PAT--AMB	PAT--LA	PAT-LA-AMB	PAT--LA-0P	NGR--ALL	NGR--AMB	NGR--LA	NGR-LA-AMB	NGR--LA-0P	NGR--0P	PAT--0P
PAT-ALL		.000***	.906	.128	.815	.583	.000***	.905	.128	.825	.001***	.001***
PAT-AMB			.000***	.005**	.000***	.000***	.530	.000***	.005**	.000***	.000***	.000***
PAT-LA				.031*	.005**	.905	.000***	.783	.031*	.018*	.956	.964
PAT-LA-AMB					.034*	.128	.005**	.031*	.315	.033*	.146	.145
PAT-LA-0P						.814	.000***	.005**	.034*	.218	.949	.941
NGR-ALL							.000***	.904	.128	.824	.001***	.001***
NGR-AMB								.000***	.005**	.000***	.000***	.000***
NGR-LA									.031*	.016*	.957	.965
NGR-LA-AMB										.033*	.146	.145
NGR-LA-0P											.958	.950
NGR-0P												.101
PAT-0P												
Accuracy												
PAT-ALL		.000***	.074	.010*	.064	.577	.000***	.074	.010*	.066	.001**	.001**
PAT-AMB			.000***	.486	.000***	.000***	1.000	.000***	.487	.000***	.000***	.000***
PAT-LA				.005**	.001***	.074	.000***	.834	.005**	.002**	.093	.091
PAT-LA-AMB					.006**	.010*	.486	.005**	.575	.006**	.013*	.013*
PAT-LA-0P						.064	.000***	.001***	.006**	.048*	.081	.080
NGR-ALL							.000***	.074	.010*	.065	.002**	.002**
NGR-AMB								.000***	.487	.000***	.000***	.000***
NGR-LA									.005**	.002**	.093	.092
NGR-LA-AMB										.006**	.013*	.013*
NGR-LA-0P											.082	.081
NGR-0P												.208
PAT-0P												

$*p \leq 0.05$, $**p \leq 0.01$, $***p \leq 0.001$

when they are combined with other features. From the results on TOK+POS we could hypothesize that there might be some improvement.

Best achieved Precision reached 0.956 and was the highest of all previous results for any dataset. This score was achieved by pattern-based dataset with all ambiguous patterns removed. However, both unmodified pattern- or n-gram-based classifier also achieved very high scores, 0.954 and 0.948, respectively. The results for best Precision were represented in Table 19.

Results for both best achieved F-score and Accuracy indicated similar tendencies, with n-gram-based unmodified classifier achieving F1=0.803 and A=0.808. These results confirm positive influence of lemmas comparing to simple tokens and further support contribution of POS information, but only when it is used with other features as well. The results for best F-score and Accuracy were represented in Tables 20 and 21, respectively.

T-test results for both F-score and Accuracy were in most cases either extremely statistically significant ($p \leqq 0.001$) or very statistically significant ($p \leqq 0.01$). The results of T-test for F-scores and Accuracies among all system results for lemmatized dataset with POS information were represented in Table 22.

Table 19. Comparison of best Precision within the threshold span for each version of the classifier for dataset containing lemmas with POS information. Best classifier version within each preprocessing kind - highlighted in bold type font.

Highest Precision within threshold				
	Pr	Re	F1	Acc
PAT-ALL	0.954	0.114	0.204	0.565
PAT-0P	0.954	0.114	0.204	0.565
PAT-AMB	**0.956**	**0.119**	**0.212**	**0.567**
PAT-LA-0P	0.929	0.200	0.330	0.602
PAT-LA	0.954	0.114	0.204	0.565
PAT-LA-AMB	0.929	0.209	0.341	0.606
NGR-ALL	0.948	0.233	0.374	0.619
NGR-0P	0.948	0.119	0.212	0.567
NGR-AMB	0.932	0.205	0.336	0.604
NGR-LA	0.922	0.197	0.325	0.600
NGR-LA-0P	0.923	0.167	0.283	0.587
NGR-LA-AMB	0.892	0.266	0.409	0.626

Table 20. Comparison of best F-score within the threshold span for each version of the classifier for dataset containing lemmas with POS information. Best classifier version within each preprocessing kind - highlighted in bold type font.

Highest F-score within threshold				
	Pr	Re	F1	Acc
PAT-ALL	0.752	0.817	0.783	0.779
PAT-0P	0.752	0.817	0.783	0.779
PAT-AMB	0.759	0.813	0.785	0.782
PAT-LA-0P	0.725	0.809	0.765	0.756
PAT-LA	0.752	0.817	0.783	0.779
PAT-LA-AMB	0.732	0.805	0.766	0.760
NGR-ALL	**0.807**	**0.798**	**0.803**	**0.808**
NGR-0P	0.808	0.795	0.802	0.808
NGR-AMB	0.754	0.809	0.781	0.778
NGR-LA	0.733	0.794	0.763	0.756
NGR-LA-0P	0.720	0.825	0.769	0.757
NGR-LA-AMB	0.729	0.800	0.763	0.757

Table 21. Comparison of best Accuracy within the threshold span for each version of the classifier for dataset containing lemmas with POS information. Best classifier version within each preprocessing kind - highlighted in bold type font.

Highest Accuracy within threshold				
	Pr	Re	F1	Acc
PAT-ALL	0.817	0.737	0.775	0.791
PAT-0P	0.817	0.737	0.775	0.791
PAT-AMB	0.818	0.733	0.773	0.790
PAT-LA-0P	0.757	0.765	0.761	0.765
PAT-LA	0.817	0.737	0.775	0.791
PAT-LA-AMB	0.762	0.759	0.761	0.766
NGR-ALL	**0.807**	**0.798**	**0.803**	**0.808**
NGR-0P	0.808	0.795	0.802	0.808
NGR-AMB	0.788	0.764	0.776	0.784
NGR-LA	0.783	0.738	0.760	0.770
NGR-LA-0P	0.776	0.760	0.768	0.775
NGR-LA-AMB	0.729	0.800	0.763	0.757

Table 22. Results of t-test for F-scores and Accuracies among all system results for lemmatized dataset with POS information.

F-score	PAT--ALL	PAT--AMB	PAT--LA	PAT-LA-AMB	PAT--LA-0P	NGR--ALL	NGR--AMB	NGR--LA	NGR-LA-AMB	NGR--LA-0P	NGR--0P	PAT--0P
PAT-ALL		.000***	.000***	.001***	.001***	.034*	.000***	.001***	.000***	.001***	.048*	.000***
PAT-AMB			.000***	.001***	.001***	.024*	.000***	.001**	.001***	.002**	.032*	.000***
PAT-LA				.001***	.001***	.034*	.000***	.001***	.000***	.001***	.048*	.000***
PAT-LA-AMB					.002**	.001***	.282	.001***	.000***	.001***	.001**	.001***
PAT-LA-0P						.001***	.340	.001***	.000***	.001***	.001**	.001***
NGR-ALL							.001***	.001**	.001***	.002**	.001**	.034*
NGR-AMB								.058	.038*	.002**	.001***	.000***
NGR-LA									.000***	.001***	.002**	.001***
NGR-LA-AMB										.000***	.001***	.000***
NGR-LA-0P											.003**	.001***
NGR-0P												.048*
PAT-0P												
Accuracy												
PAT-ALL		.002**	.000***	.000***	.000***	.018*	.000***	.000***	.000***	.001**	.027*	.000***
PAT-AMB			.002**	.000***	.000***	.012*	.000***	.001***	.000***	.002**	.016*	.002**
PAT-LA				.000***	.000***	.018*	.000***	.000***	.000***	.001**	.027*	.000***
PAT-LA-AMB					.000***	.000***	.098	.000***	.000***	.000***	.000***	.000***
PAT-LA-0P						.000***	.128	.000***	.000***	.000***	.000***	.000***
NGR-ALL							.000***	.000***	.000***	.001***	.003**	.018*
NGR-AMB								.010*	.019*	.000***	.000***	.000***
NGR-LA									.000***	.000***	.000***	.000***
NGR-LA-AMB										.000***	.000***	.000***
NGR-LA-0P											.001**	.001**
NGR-0P												.027*
PAT-0P												

$*p \leq 0.05$, $**p \leq 0.01$, $***p \leq 0.001$

Chunk-Separated Set

While tokenization and lemmatization divide sentence by words or morphemes, sentence parsing splits a sentence by unified meaningful chunks, thus usually consisting of more than one word. The simplest way of parsing is shallow parsing, or chunking, in which chunks are simply separated by spaces with no additional information provided on relations between the chunks.

Chunking provides more generalized preprocessing than tokenization or lemmatization, but is less generalized then POS.

Highest achieved Precision was 0.875, which is higher than for tokens alone, but lower than for lemmas or POS. The results for best Precision were represented in Table 23.

Results for F-score and Accuracy were much lower than for all other sets, with F1=0.658 and A=0.640 (Tables 24 and 25, respectively). Similarly, the differences between the classifier versions were rarely statistically significant (Table 26).

Table 23. Comparison of best Precision within the threshold span for each version of the classifier for chunk-separated dataset. Best classifier version within each preprocessing kind - highlighted in bold type font.

Highest Precision within threshold				
	Pr	Re	F1	Acc
PAT-ALL	0.852	0.109	0.194	0.548
PAT-0P	0.845	0.112	0.198	0.548
PAT-AMB	0.849	0.087	0.158	0.534
PAT-LA-0P	0.845	0.115	0.202	0.549
PAT-LA	0.851	0.110	0.195	0.548
PAT-LA-AMB	0.850	0.088	0.160	0.535
NGR-ALL	0.848	0.110	0.195	0.547
NGR-0P	0.873	0.071	0.131	0.532
NGR-AMB	0.808	0.107	0.188	0.541
NGR-LA	0.856	0.111	0.197	0.549
NGR-LA-0P	**0.875**	**0.072**	**0.133**	**0.533**
NGR-LA-AMB	0.819	0.106	0.188	0.541

Table 24. Comparison of best F-score within the threshold span for each version of the classifier for chunk-separated dataset. Best classifier version within each preprocessing kind - highlighted in bold type font.

Highest F-score within threshold				
	Pr	Re	F1	Acc
PAT-ALL	0.490	1.000	0.658	0.490
PAT-0P	0.490	1.000	0.658	0.490
PAT-AMB	0.490	1.000	0.658	0.490
PAT-LA-0P	**0.490**	**1.000**	**0.658**	**0.490**
PAT-LA	0.490	1.000	0.658	0.490
PAT-LA-AMB	0.490	0.999	0.658	0.490
NGR-ALL	0.490	1.000	0.658	0.490
NGR-0P	0.490	1.000	0.658	0.490
NGR-AMB	0.490	1.000	0.658	0.490
NGR-LA	**0.490**	**1.000**	**0.658**	**0.490**
NGR-LA-0P	**0.490**	**1.000**	**0.658**	**0.490**
NGR-LA-AMB	0.490	0.999	0.658	0.490

Table 25. Comparison of best Accuracy within the threshold span for each version of the classifier for chunk-separated dataset. Best classifier version within each preprocessing kind - highlighted in bold type font.

Highest Accuracy within threshold				
	Pr	**Re**	**F1**	**Acc**
PAT-ALL	0.656	0.587	0.620	0.638
PAT-0P	0.656	0.587	0.620	0.638
PAT-AMB	0.644	0.604	0.624	0.631
PAT-LA-0P	**0.658**	**0.589**	**0.622**	**0.640**
PAT-LA	0.655	0.587	0.619	0.638
PAT-LA-AMB	0.645	0.605	0.625	0.631
NGR-ALL	0.655	0.586	0.619	0.638
NGR-0P	0.657	0.586	0.620	0.639
NGR-AMB	0.606	0.635	0.620	0.613
NGR-LA	0.656	0.589	0.621	0.639
NGR-LA-0P	0.657	0.587	0.620	0.639
NGR-LA-AMB	0.606	0.637	0.621	0.613

Table 26. Results of t-test for F-scores and Accuracies among all system results for chunk-separated dataset.

F-score	PAT-ALL	PAT-AMB	PAT-LA	PAT-LA-AMB	PAT-LA-0P	NGR-ALL	NGR-AMB	NGR-LA	NGR-LA-AMB	NGR-LA-0P	NGR-0P	PAT-0P
PAT-ALL		.006**	.084	.005**	.002**	.187	.030*	.035*	.015*	.005**	.109	.002**
PAT-AMB			.007**	.045*	.015*	.005**	.215	.008**	.048*	.014*	.007**	.009**
PAT-LA				.005**	.002**	.003**	.034*	.083	.017*	.008**	.227	.012*
PAT-LA-AMB					.010**	.004**	.413	.006**	.079	.009**	.006**	.007**
PAT-LA-0P						.001***	.056	.002**	.026*	.255	.048*	.007**
NGR-ALL							.026*	.000***	.013*	.003**	.051	.002**
NGR-AMB								.036*	.044*	.055	.031*	.042*
NGR-LA									.018*	.011*	.372	.071
NGR-LA-AMB										.025*	.017*	.021*
NGR-LA-0P											.009**	.025*
NGR-0P												.940
PAT-0P												
Accuracy												
PAT-ALL		.098	.342	.057	.000***	.000***	.126	.004**	.102	.000***	.002**	.000***
PAT-AMB			.113	.044*	.857	.026*	.151	.229	.111	.349	.986	.459
PAT-LA				.066	.000***	.000***	.132	.025*	.107	.000***	.003**	.000***
PAT-LA-AMB					.582	.015*	.199	.134	.147	.645	.696	.290
PAT-LA-0P						.000***	.277	.001***	.232	.012*	.641	.011*
NGR-ALL							.084	.000***	.067	.000***	.000***	.000***
NGR-AMB								.165	.117	.392	.276	.210
NGR-LA									.135	.001***	.017*	.063
NGR-LA-AMB										.331	.231	.173
NGR-LA-0P											.005**	.001***
NGR-0P												.058
PAT-0P												

$*p \leq 0.05, **p \leq 0.01, ***p \leq 0.001$

Dependency Parsed Set

Dependency parsing of a sentence, or deep parsing, refers to splitting a sentence into chunks with their syntactic interrelations. It is more specific than chunking, however, unless really large dataset is in use, it often provides lower results than simple tokenization, due to small number of extracted frequent features to build a reliable language model.

Results of our experiment confirmed this. While the highest Precision reached 0.868, best Fscore and Accuracy were the worst of all datasets, and reached F=0.658 and A=0.58, meaning that cyberbullying classification with the use of dependency parsing is close to random coin flipping. T-test results were also almost never statistically significant.

Results for highest Precision, F-score and Accuracy were represented in Tables 27, 28 and 29, respectively. Results for T-test were represented in Table 30.

Table 27. Comparison of best Precision within the threshold span for each version of the classifier with dependency parsed dataset. Best classifier version within each preprocessing kind - highlighted in bold type font.

Highest Precision within threshold				
	Pr	**Re**	**F1**	**Acc**
PAT-ALL	0.865	0.070	0.130	0.537
PAT-0P	0.865	0.070	0.130	0.537
PAT-AMB	0.860	0.069	0.129	0.537
PAT-LA-0P	0.866	0.071	0.131	0.537
PAT-LA	**0.868**	**0.071**	**0.131**	**0.537**
PAT-LA-AMB	0.860	0.069	0.129	0.537
NGR-ALL	0.865	0.071	0.130	0.537
NGR-0P	0.850	0.070	0.129	0.537
NGR-AMB	0.860	0.069	0.129	0.537
NGR-LA	0.865	0.070	0.130	0.537
NGR-LA-0P	0.862	0.069	0.129	0.537
NGR-LA-AMB	0.856	0.069	0.128	0.537

Table 28. Comparison of best F-score within the threshold span for each version of the classifier with dependency parsed dataset. Best classifier version within each preprocessing kind - highlighted in bold type font.

Highest F-score within threshold				
	Pr	Re	F1	Acc
PAT-ALL	0.490	1.000	0.658	0.490
PAT-0P	0.490	1.000	0.658	0.490
PAT-AMB	0.490	1.000	0.658	0.490
PAT-LA-0P	**0.491**	**1.000**	**0.658**	**0.491**
PAT-LA	**0.491**	**1.000**	**0.658**	**0.491**
PAT-LA-AMB	**0.491**	**1.000**	**0.658**	**0.491**
NGR-ALL	0.490	1.000	0.658	0.490
NGR-0P	0.490	1.000	0.658	0.490
NGR-AMB	0.490	1.000	0.658	0.490
NGR-LA	**0.491**	**1.000**	**0.658**	**0.491**
NGR-LA-0P	**0.491**	**1.000**	**0.658**	**0.491**
NGR-LA-AMB	**0.491**	**1.000**	**0.658**	**0.491**

Table 29. Comparison of best Accuracy within the threshold span for each version of the classifier with dependency parsed dataset. Best classifier version within each preprocessing kind - highlighted in bold type font.

Highest Accuracy within threshold				
	Pr	Re	F1	Acc
PAT-ALL	0.671	0.336	0.448	0.580
PAT-0P	0.671	0.336	0.448	0.580
PAT-AMB	0.659	0.340	0.448	0.574
PAT-LA-0P	**0.671**	**0.336**	**0.448**	**0.580**
PAT-LA	0.670	0.335	0.447	0.579
PAT-LA-AMB	0.659	0.340	0.449	0.574
NGR-ALL	0.671	0.336	0.448	0.580
NGR-0P	0.672	0.335	0.447	0.580
NGR-AMB	0.659	0.340	0.449	0.574
NGR-LA	0.671	0.336	0.448	0.580
NGR-LA-0P	0.672	0.335	0.448	0.580
NGR-LA-AMB	0.659	0.340	0.449	0.574

Table 30. Results of t-test for F-scores and Accuracies among all system results for dependency parsed dataset.

F-score	PAT-ALL	PAT-AMB	PAT-LA	PAT-LA-AMB	PAT-LA-0P	NGR-ALL	NGR-AMB	NGR-LA	NGR-LA-AMB	NGR-LA-0P	NGR-0P	PAT-0P
PAT-ALL		.176	.576	.238	.969	.000***	.184	.211	.180	.010**	.000***	.023*
PAT-AMB			.136	.057	.160	.108	.177	.154	.492	.240	.242	.219
PAT-LA				.186	.291	.186	.143	.862	.139	.016*	.025*	.062
PAT-LA-AMB					.218	.152	.221	.209	.000***	.318	.321	.294
PAT-LA-0P						.014*	.168	.462	.163	.011*	.019*	.045*
NGR-ALL							.113	.020*	.113	.000***	.000***	.000***
NGR-AMB								.161	.253	.253	.255	.231
NGR-LA									.157	.000***	.000***	.010*
NGR-LA-AMB										.240	.244	.222
NGR-LA-0P											.814	.533
NGR-0P												.354
PAT-0P												
Accuracy												
PAT-ALL		.600	.998	.516	.007**	.000***	.529	.149	.568	.036*	.136	.029*
PAT-AMB			.598	.000***	.818	.653	.003**	.631	.187	.790	.714	.673
PAT-LA				.514	.023*	.190	.528	.351	.566	.081	.260	.230
PAT-LA-AMB					.713	.566	.704	.543	.000***	.685	.615	.581
PAT-LA-0P						.048*	.728	.010*	.780	.403	.018*	.005**
NGR-ALL							.580	.591	.620	.142	.405	.475
NGR-AMB								.557	.165	.700	.629	.594
NGR-LA									.598	.058	.270	.235
NGR-LA-AMB										.751	.677	.638
NGR-LA-0P											.015*	.053
NGR-0P												.360
PAT-0P												

$*p \leq 0.05$, $**p \leq 0.01$, $***p \leq 0.001$

Chunk-Separated Set With Named Entities

Named entities, such as private names of people, companies, dates, numericals, etc., provide additional level of generalization for analyzed sentence. We applied named entity recognition (NER) to shallow and deep parsing to find out how such additional generalization would influence the results.

The results were in general lower than for chunks alone, but higher than for dependency parsing.

Results for highest Precision, F-score and Accuracy were represented in Tables 31, 32 and 33, respectively. Results for T-test were represented in Table 34.

Table 31. Comparison of best Precision within the threshold span for each version of the classifier for chunks with NER. Best classifier version within each preprocessing kind - highlighted in bold type font.

Highest Precision within threshold				
	Pr	**Re**	**F1**	**Acc**
PAT-ALL	0.637	0.165	0.262	0.546
PAT-0P	0.637	0.167	0.265	0.546
PAT-AMB	0.644	0.199	0.304	0.551
PAT-LA-0P	0.540	0.783	0.639	0.545
PAT-LA	0.592	0.698	0.641	0.543
PAT-LA-AMB	0.546	0.761	0.635	0.542
NGR-ALL	**0.768**	**0.242**	**0.368**	**0.586**
NGR-0P	0.749	0.251	0.376	0.585
NGR-AMB	0.724	0.186	0.297	0.558
NGR-LA	0.736	0.252	0.375	0.582
NGR-LA-0P	0.730	0.270	0.395	0.585
NGR-LA-AMB	0.644	0.209	0.315	0.552

Table 32. Comparison of best F-score within the threshold span for each version of the classifier for chunks with NER. Best classifier version within each preprocessing kind - highlighted in bold type font.

Highest F-score within threshold				
	Pr	**Re**	**F1**	**Acc**
PAT-ALL	0.551	0.902	0.684	0.575
PAT-0P	0.552	0.903	0.685	0.577
PAT-AMB	0.541	0.913	0.680	0.565
PAT-LA-0P	0.508	0.964	0.666	0.511
PAT-LA	0.507	0.984	0.669	0.515
PAT-LA-AMB	0.508	0.967	0.666	0.513
NGR-ALL	**0.563**	**0.879**	**0.686**	**0.603**
NGR-0P	0.560	0.864	0.680	0.599
NGR-AMB	0.554	0.851	0.671	0.587
NGR-LA	0.579	0.820	0.678	0.616
NGR-LA-0P	0.546	0.904	0.681	0.583
NGR-LA-AMB	0.523	0.906	0.664	0.548

Table 33. Comparison of best Accuracy within the threshold span for each version of the classifier for chunks with NER. Best classifier version within each preprocessing kind - highlighted in bold type font.

Highest Accuracy within threshold				
	Pr	**Re**	**F1**	**Acc**
PAT-ALL	0.596	0.668	0.630	0.602
PAT-0P	0.598	0.670	0.632	0.603
PAT-AMB	0.593	0.708	0.645	0.602
PAT-LA-0P	0.540	0.783	0.639	0.545
PAT-LA	0.592	0.698	0.641	0.543
PAT-LA-AMB	0.546	0.761	0.635	0.542
NGR-ALL	**0.659**	**0.647**	**0.653**	**0.655**
NGR-0P	0.655	0.646	0.650	0.651
NGR-AMB	0.622	0.568	0.594	0.613
NGR-LA	0.625	0.596	0.610	0.623
NGR-LA-0P	0.626	0.605	0.616	0.625
NGR-LA-AMB	0.588	0.663	0.624	0.603

Table 34. Results of t-test for F-scores and Accuracies among all system results for dataset separated by chunks with NER.

F-score	PAT-ALL	PAT-AMB	PAT-LA	PAT-LA-AMB	PAT-LA-0P	NGR-ALL	NGR-AMB	NGR-LA	NGR-LA-AMB	NGR-LA-0P	NGR-0P	PAT-0P
PAT-ALL		.006**	.021*	.021*	.021*	.017*	.051	.153	.127	.599	.017*	.016*
PAT-AMB			.026*	.026*	.025*	.010*	.018*	.020*	.339	.073	.010**	.008**
PAT-LA				.047*	.088	.004**	.003**	.009**	.009**	.012*	.004**	.021*
PAT-LA-AMB					.088	.004**	.003**	.010**	.010**	.013*	.004**	.022*
PAT-LA-0P						.004**	.003**	.010**	.009**	.012*	.004**	.021*
NGR-ALL							.027*	.008**	.005**	.005**	.046*	.015*
NGR-AMB								.026*	.002**	.008**	.027*	.041*
NGR-LA									.013*	.000***	.007**	.099
NGR-LA-AMB										.030*	.004**	.142
NGR-LA-0P											.004**	.438
NGR-0P												.015*
PAT-0P												
Accuracy												
PAT-ALL		.911	.029*	.026*	.031*	.031*	.010**	.002**	.000***	.000***	.028*	.046*
PAT-AMB			.023*	.021*	.025*	.033*	.011*	.003**	.000***	.000***	.031*	.559
PAT-LA				.028*	.063	.003**	.000***	.002**	.000***	.001***	.003**	.028*
PAT-LA-AMB					.214	.003**	.001***	.003**	.000***	.001***	.003**	.025*
PAT-LA-0P						.004**	.001***	.003**	.000***	.001***	.003**	.030*
NGR-ALL							.462	.334	.392	.863	.374	.034*
NGR-AMB								.520	.456	.659	.497	.012*
NGR-LA									.866	.000***	.345	.002**
NGR-LA-AMB										.089	.403	.000***
NGR-LA-0P											.921	.000***
NGR-0P												.031*
PAT-0P												

$*p \leq 0.05$, $**p \leq 0.01$, $***p \leq 0.001$

Dependency Parsed Set With Named Entities

When it comes to dependency parsing supported with named entity recognition, the results were in general lower than for chunks with NER, but higher than for dependency parsing. The differences between the results were also more often statistically significant.

This suggests, that named entities, even for not very big datasets, contribute positively to dependency parsing-based classification, although the contribution is not strong enough to make the classification much better than random guessing.

Results for highest Precision, F-score and Accuracy were represented in Tables 35, 36 and 37, respectively. Results for T-test were represented in Table 38.

Break-Even Point Analysis

Except detailed analysis for each dataset, we also looked at the results from a wider perspective.

Table 35. Comparison of best Precision within the threshold span for each version of the classifier for dependency parsed set with NER. Best classifier version within each preprocessing kind - highlighted in bold type font.

Highest Precision within threshold				
	Pr	**Re**	**F1**	**Acc**
PAT-ALL	0.529	0.160	0.246	0.513
PAT-0P	0.547	0.167	0.256	0.516
PAT-AMB	0.611	0.185	0.284	0.531
PAT-LA-0P	0.513	0.805	0.627	0.529
PAT-LA	0.513	0.805	0.627	0.528
PAT-LA-AMB	0.518	0.507	0.513	0.527
NGR-ALL	0.699	0.100	0.174	0.521
NGR-0P	0.688	0.101	0.176	0.520
NGR-AMB	0.619	0.216	0.320	0.536
NGR-LA	**0.718**	**0.010**	**0.020**	**0.513**
NGR-LA-0P	0.708	0.010	0.019	0.513
NGR-LA-AMB	0.647	0.196	0.301	0.536

Table 36. Comparison of best F-score within the threshold span for each version of the classifier for dependency parsed set with NER. Best classifier version within each preprocessing kind - highlighted in bold type font.

Highest F-score within threshold				
	Pr	**Re**	**F1**	**Acc**
PAT-ALL	0.500	0.983	0.662	0.509
PAT-0P	0.499	0.980	0.661	0.508
PAT-AMB	0.490	1.000	0.658	0.490
PAT-LA-0P	0.499	0.982	0.662	0.509
PAT-LA	0.499	0.982	0.662	0.509
PAT-LA-AMB	0.490	0.999	0.657	0.490
NGR-ALL	0.500	0.981	0.662	0.509
NGR-0P	**0.500**	**0.982**	**0.663**	**0.510**
NGR-AMB	0.490	1.000	0.658	0.490
NGR-LA	0.500	0.981	0.662	0.509
NGR-LA-0P	0.500	0.981	0.662	0.509
NGR-LA-AMB	0.490	0.999	0.657	0.490

Table 37. Comparison of best Accuracy within the threshold span for each version of the classifier for dependency parsed set with NER. Best classifier version within each preprocessing kind - highlighted in bold type font.

Highest Accuracy within threshold				
	Pr	**Re**	**F1**	**Acc**
PAT-ALL	0.519	0.766	0.618	0.534
PAT-0P	0.519	0.769	0.620	0.535
PAT-AMB	0.611	0.185	0.284	0.531
PAT-LA-0P	0.513	0.805	0.627	0.529
PAT-LA	0.513	0.805	0.627	0.528
PAT-LA-AMB	0.518	0.507	0.513	0.527
NGR-ALL	0.547	0.615	0.579	0.556
NGR-0P	**0.551**	**0.617**	**0.582**	**0.559**
NGR-AMB	0.533	0.512	0.522	0.540
NGR-LA	0.548	0.614	0.579	0.557
NGR-LA-0P	0.549	0.616	0.581	0.558
NGR-LA-AMB	0.536	0.516	0.526	0.543

Table 38. Results of t-test for F-scores and Accuracies among all system results for dependency parsed dataset with NER.

F-score	PAT--ALL	PAT--AMB	PAT--LA	PAT-LA-AMB	PAT--LA-0P	NGR--ALL	NGR--AMB	NGR--LA	NGR-LA-AMB	NGR--LA-0P	NGR--0P	PAT--0P
PAT-ALL		.444	.063	.515	.063	.015*	.056	.021*	.079	.023*	.019*	.019*
PAT-AMB			.000***	.017*	.000***	.672	.005**	.735	.007**	.786	.718	.378
PAT-LA				.008**	.246	.019*	.000***	.018*	.000***	.020*	.021*	.072
PAT-LA-AMB					.007**	.216	.004**	.224	.004**	.239	.230	.557
PAT-LA-0P						.019*	.000***	.018*	.000***	.020*	.021*	.072
NGR-ALL							.353	.093	.458	.014*	.000***	.015*
NGR-AMB								.277	.002**	.251	.323	.048*
NGR-LA									.373	.005**	.506	.019*
NGR-LA-AMB										.340	.422	.067
NGR-LA-0P											.098	.022*
NGR-0P												.018*
PAT-0P												
Accuracy												
PAT-ALL		.045*	.010*	.381	.009**	.001**	.000***	.001***	.000***	.001***	.001***	.065
PAT-AMB			.003**	.042*	.002**	.883	.000***	.955	.000***	.979	.979	.079
PAT-LA				.036*	.356	.001***	.000***	.001***	.000***	.001***	.001***	.008**
PAT-LA-AMB					.034*	.584	.000***	.533	.000***	.495	.496	.484
PAT-LA-0P						.001***	.000***	.001***	.000***	.001***	.001***	.007**
NGR-ALL							.017*	.079	.006**	.004**	.005**	.001***
NGR-AMB								.023*	.002**	.035*	.037*	.000***
NGR-LA									.008**	.019*	.307	.001***
NGR-LA-AMB										.014*	.015*	.000***
NGR-LA-0P											.999	.001***
NGR-0P												.001***
PAT-0P												

$*p \leq 0.05, **p \leq 0.01, ***p \leq 0.001$

Table 39. Break-even points for all feature sets and all classifier versions

	TOK	LEM	POS	TOK +POS	LEM +POS	CHUNK	DEP	CHUNK +NER	DEP +NER
PAT	0.761	0.751	0.613	0.785	0.781	**0.633**	0.566	0.603	0.510
PAT-0P	0.763	0.751	0.613	**0.786**	0.781	0.632	0.551	0.605	0.512
PAT-AMB	**0.770**	0.751	0.613	0.764	0.782	0.629	**0.591**	0.603	0.514
PAT-LA	0.729	0.748	0.613	0.726	0.781	0.632	0.568	--	0.505
PAT-LA-0P	0.729	0.737	0.596	0.726	0.760	**0.633**	0.549	--	0.505
PAT-LA-AMB	0.711	0.737	0.594	0.715	0.761	0.629	**0.591**	--	0.516
NGR	0.761	**0.784**	**0.614**	0.785	**0.802**	0.632	0.566	**0.655**	0.547
NGR-0P	0.762	**0.784**	0.613	**0.786**	**0.802**	0.632	0.551	0.652	**0.548**
NGR-AMB	**0.770**	0.767	0.570	0.764	0.777	0.612	**0.591**	0.610	0.526
NGR-LA	0.729	0.767	0.605	0.726	0.762	**0.633**	0.551	0.619	0.546
NGR-LA-0P	0.729	0.768	0.607	0.726	0.769	0.631	0.559	0.622	**0.548**
NGR-LA-AMB	0.711	0.762	0.596	0.715	0.750	0.613	0.589	0.589	0.529

One of the popular methods of evaluation in text classification studies has been estimation of a break-even point, or BEP. It is a cross point of Precision and Recall, where both those scores (and F-score in result) are in equality, meaning that the classifier is the most balanced. The higher the BEP, the more balanced the classifier can be considered.

We calculated BEP for all versions of the proposed classifier. The results were represented in Table 39. Since versions with weight modified by awarding both pattern length and occurrence rarely obtained BEP within threshold range, we excluded them from further analysis.

In the analysis we looked at four things, namely, 1) which classifier version got the highest BEP, 2) which classifier version usually got the highest BEP for different dataset preprocessing, 3) which preprocessing usually provided highest BEP, and 4) what was the highest achieved BEP, and by which dataset/classifier combination.

When it comes to classifier version most often achieving top scores, although often pattern-based and n-gram-based classifiers achieved similar, or even the same BEP scores, n-grams more often achieved the highest score. Moreover, the highest score of all was also achieved by n-gram-based classifier, and reached P=R=F1=0.802.

When it comes to dataset preprocessing method that usually scored highest, it was the lemmatized dataset combined with part-of-speech information. The highest score of all, mentioned above was also achieved by this feature set.

Also, clustering the dataset preprocessing methods into more generalized (POS, CHUNK, DEP, CHUNK+NER, DEP+NER, with BEP scores below 70%) and more specific (TOK, LEM, TOK+POS, LEM+POS, with BEP scores above 70%), provides a meaningful insight. The classifier usually performs better on more specific feature sets. In other words, the method provides better results when it can extract large number of features, even if their occurrence is not very high.

Although tokens with POS were the most numerous, the fact that lemmas with POS achieved the highest result needs to be addressed. Lemmatizing a sentence means that declensed and conjugated forms of words are unified. This makes it not only easier to extract frequent patterns, but is also advantageous in classification, since a pattern consisting of dictionary word forms applied to also lemmatized test data has much broader coverage. This provides the optimal setting for a classifier to use multiple specific features on the one hand, but on the other hand also be generalized to the extent allowing it to capture a broad range of cases.

Figure 2. Best F-scores for each dataset preprocessing, ordered from left to right, with corresponding Precision, Recall and Accuracy. Classifier version that achieved the score - in brackets.

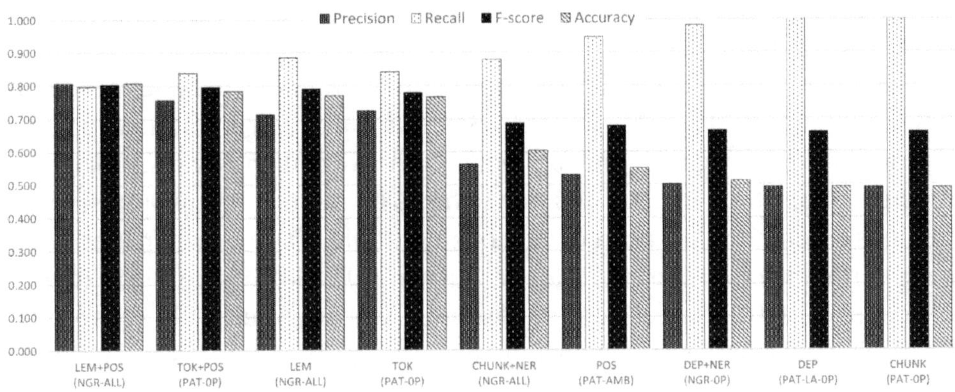

Comparison Between Feature Sets

Apart from analyzing BEPs, we also compared the highest achieved F-scores for each dataset. These two evaluation measures rarely go together, since it would be difficult to have the highest F-score in the place of BEP. However, we can see which of the best achieved F-scores is closest to BEP. We can also follow the tendencies in results and check if they correlate between the two evaluation measures. The results were represented in Figure 2. We ordered the datasets by their highest F-score from left to right.

The best score was achieved by lemmatization with POS information. The results was F1=0.803 with P=0.807, R=0.798, and A=0.808. This confirms the winning setting for BEP, with nearly identical F-score (0.802).

Interestingly, while the winning settings showed high consistency between Precision and Recall, close to BEP, for other dataset preprocessing settings, the lower was the F-score, the wider was also the gap between Precision and Recall. This is meaningful not only for the fact that the F-score, and therefore the general performance, of such a dataset is lower, but also provides further insight into the influence of generalization on results. Here, similarly to BEPs, the results can be clustered into two groups: with a small gap between P and R, and with a wide gap. This grouping is the same as for BEP analysis.

When it comes to the question whether it is more useful to use pattern- of n-gram-based classifier, although the very best score was achieved by n-grams, both settings appeared as the highest interchangeably. For example, second best was pattern-based classifier using pattern list with zero-patterns deleted, which achieved F1=0.796, P=0.756, R=0.839, and A=0.784. Third best was n-gram based classifier, fourth - again - patterns, etc. This suggests that we need to perform more experiments, most desirably on a wider threshold span to answer this question.

The most optimal classifier settings were the unmodified one, or the one with zero-patterns deleted. This suggests, that, although ambiguous patterns appear both in cyberbullying as well as in normal messages, it is more effective to use then in classification. This is an interesting insight, since, in previous research it has been often considered that only words/patterns that are specifically characteristic to cyberbullying should be used. For example, Fujii et al. (2010) refereed to them as "gray words/patterns" in comparison to "black words/patterns" appearing only in harmful messages and opted for disregarding gray words as noise.

Table 40. Analysis of influence of dataset generalization on results

Feature sophistication	Dataset Preprocessing	No. of unique unigrams	No. of all unigrams	Feature Density	Highest achieved F-score	Highest unmodified F-score	BEP
	DEP	12802	13957	0.917	0.658	0.658	0.591
	DEP+NER	12160	13956	0.871	0.663	0.662	0.548
high→	CHUNK	11389	13960	0.816	0.658	0.658	0.633
	CHUNK+NER	10657	13872	0.768	0.686	0.684	0.655
	TOK+POS	6565	34874	0.188	0.796	0.795	0.786
	TOK	6464	36234	0.178	0.778	0.778	0.770
←low	LEM+POS	6227	36426	0.171	0.803	0.783	0.802
	LEM	6103	36412	0.168	0.790	0.764	0.784
	POS	13	26650	0.000	0.677	0.677	0.614

	unique 1ngr with			FD with		
	F1	F1-unmod.	BEP	F1	F1-unmod.	BEP
Pearson Correlation Coefficient (ρ-value)	-0.450 (p=0.224)	-0.453 (p=0.221)	-0.431 (p=0.247)	-0.735 (p=0.0242)	-0.736 (p=0.024)	-0.706 (p=0.0336)
with statistical significance (p-value)			F1 & BEP 0.9681 (p=0.00002)		F1-unmod. & BEP 0.9595 (p=0.00004)	

Influence of Generalization on Results

To get a better grasp on the results we also analyzed the influence of how a dataset was preprocessed on the results.

To achieve this we needed a quantifiable dataset generalization measure. A dataset is the more generalized, the fewer number of frequently appearing unique features is used in its preprocessing. Therefore to estimate dataset generalization level we decided to calculate feature sophistication level. As the exact measure of feature sophistication level we applied the Lexical Density (LD) score (Ure, 1971). It is a score representing an estimated measure of content per lexical units for a given corpus, and is calculated as the number of all unique words from the corpus divided by the number of all words in the corpus. However, since in our research we use a variety of different features, not only words (tokens), and the LD can vary depending on which features or feature combinations were used, we will further call this measure Feature-based Lexical Density, or shortly, Feature Density (FD).

After calculating FD for all used datasets we calculated Pearson's correlation coefficient (ρ- value) to see if there is any correlation between dataset generalization (FD) and the results. Pearson's coefficient can achieve scores from 1.0 (meaning there is a perfect positive correlation), through 0.0 (no correlation) to -1.0 (perfect negative correlation).

As the results we used the highest achieved F-scores. However, since the highest overall F-scores were sometimes achieved by different versions of the classifier (all patterns, or zero-patterns deleted; with length awarded, or not, etc.), we also used an unmodified version of the classifier (PAT-ALL). As an equivalent set of results we also used BEPs. Finally, we verified whether the correlations were statistically significant.

The first intuition about the correlation of dataset generalization with the results was that the less unique features are used in its preprocessing the lower the results would be. However, there was no correlation between unique unigrams of datasets and the overall results.

On the other hand, Feature Density score revealed an interesting correlation. There was a somewhat strong negative correlation (around -0.7) between the results and FD. This means that the results are better when the feature density is low. The correlation was not ideal due to the fact that the preprocessing method resulting in the lowest FD (POS-tagged dataset) achieved some of the lowest results. Interestingly, preprocessing methods resulting in very high

FD (dependency parsing, etc.) also achieved similarly low results. This could suggest that there could be an even better way of preprocessing.

For the given datasets the scores are growing along with decreasing FD, until the lowest FD is reached, which also obtained low results. Therefore in the future we plan to use the FD measure to find a preprocessing method with optimal Feature Density, resulting in even better results.

The analysis of influence of dataset generalization on results is represented in Table 40.

Statistical Significance of Results

As a final step in analysis of results of the proposed method, we analyzed statistical significance of the highest achieved F-scores for each dataset preprocessing. As a measure of significance we used Student's paired T-test, since the results represented either one of two sides (cyberbullying/ harmful or non-harmful), and we compared all pairs of optimized methods (that achieved the highest F-scores for the certain dataset). Results of T-test for best F-scores for each dataset was represented in Table 41. We were most interested in how the best method (LEM+POS/NGR-ALL) compared to other methods, especially the worst ones. The worst methods (based on chunking, dependency parsing and only POS), always differed significantly with better methods (based on tokens, lemmas and those combined with POS). Usually the difference was very significant ($p \leqq 0.01$), or even extremely significant ($p \leqq 0.001$). There were some cases, where the difference did not reach significance (eg., CHUNK/PAT-0P vs. LEM+POS/NGR-ALL), which indicates we need to perform further experiments on wider threshold span to obtain more result samples for comparison.

Comparison With Previous Methods

After specifying optimal settings for the proposed method, we compared it to previous methods. In the comparison we used the methods proposed in Matsuba et al., (2011) and Nitta et al. (2013) and their most recent improvement in Ptaszynski et al. (2016), all of which were explained and presented together in previous Chapter. Moreover, since these methods extract cyberbullying relevance values from the Web (in particular Yahoo! API), apart from comparison to the reported results we also repeated their experiment to find out how the performance of the Web-based method changed during

Table 41. Results of T-test for best F-scores for each dataset

	TOK+POS (PAT-0P)	LEM (NGR-ALL)	TOK (PAT-0P)	CHUNK+NER (NGR-ALL)	POS (PAT-AMB)	DEP+NER (NGR-0P)	DEP (PAT-LA-0P)	CHUNK (PAT-0P)
LEM+POS (NGR-ALL)	0.0005 ***	0.0284 *	0.0353 *	0.3062	0.0028 **	0.0878	0.0001 ***	0.1416
TOK+POS (PAT-0P)		0.7225	0.091	0.0035 **	0.0004 ***	0.4689	0.0001 ***	0.0001 ***
LEM (NGR-ALL)			0.0214 *	0.0102 *	0.0031 *	0.5168	0.0001 ***	0.0018 **
TOK (PAT-0P)				0.0576	0.0027 **	0.2423	0.0001 ***	0.0018 **
CHUNK+NER (NGR-ALL)					0.003 **	0.0329 *	0.0001 ***	0.0004 ***
POS (PAT-AMB)						0.002 **	0.0213 *	0.0091 **
DEP+NER (NGR-0P)							0.0001 ***	0.0013 **
DEP (PAT-LA-0P)								0.0001 ***

$*p \leq 0.05$, $**p \leq 0.01$, $***p \leq 0.001$

the years. The details on the re-evaluation experiment were explained in previous Chapter. Finally, to make the comparison more fair, we compared both best and worst results of the method proposed here. As the evaluation metrics we used the same one used in the previous research, namely, area under the curve (AUC) on the graph showing Precision and Recall together. The results were represented in Figure 3.

Figure 3. Comparison between the proposed method (best and worst performance) and previous methods.

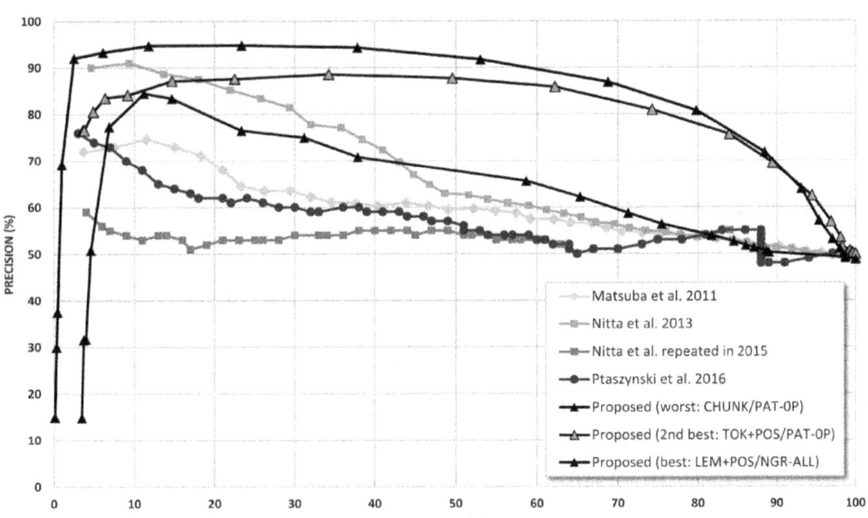

The highest overall results when it comes to AUC were obtained by the best settings of the proposed method (based on all n-grams and normalized feature weight). Although the method starts low, it quickly reaches over 95% of Precision and keeps this score even around 60% of Recall. Moreover, even when the method loses Precision, the loss is not sudden or steep, but decreases slowly, keeping a high Precision around 70% even when Recall reaches 90%. This method also outperformed all of the previous methods.

The second-best method (tokens with POS, all patterns, no weight modification) starts from a high 77% and also retains the Precision between 80% and 90% for most of the threshold. Although the highest originally reported Precision score (Nitta et al., 2013) was better than this second-best, the performance of that previous method quickly decreased due to quick drop in Precision for higher thresholds. What is important, even the worst method proposed here (based on separation by chunks with zero-patterns deleted) was still better then all other previous research except the original ones reported in 2013.

Finally, while the numerical results were in favor of the proposed approach, we also wanted to know to what extent the patterns automatically recognized by the proposed method cover the manually selected seed words in the previous research (Matsuba et al., 2010, 2011; Nitta et al., 2013). The comparison of the extracted patterns with seed word list applied in previous research revealed that all seed words applied in previous methods appeared in the list of patterns automatically extracted by the proposed method. This can be interpreted as follows. Firstly, the official governmental definition of cyberbullying (Ministry of Education, Culture, Sports, Science and Technology, 2008) and the intuition of researchers, on which previous approaches were mostly based, were generally correct. Secondly, using the automatically extracted patterns it could be possible to improve previous approaches in the future.

CONCLUSION AND FUTURE WORK

In this chapter we proposed a novel method for automatic detection of Internet forum entries that contain cyberbullying (CB). The proposed method applies a combinatorial algorithm, resembling brute force search algorithms, in automatic extraction of sophisticated sentence patterns, and used those patterns in text classification of CB entries. We tested the method on actual CB data obtained from Human Rights Center. We performed experiments on nine different feature sets. The settings that came out as optimal consisted of word lemmas with part-of-speech information. The results showed the proposed method outperformed all previous methods. Moreover, even the worst version of the proposed method achieved higher scores than previous methods. Apart from achieving much better performance, the proposed method was also more efficient as it requires minimal human effort.

For the near future we consider the following paths of further development of this particular method. To improve the detection method itself, we plan to apply different ways of dataset preprocessing to find out whether the performance can be further improved and to what extent. We have found out that too few highly generalized features (such as parts-of-speech alone), resulting in low Feature Density (FD), as well as too much of over-specific features (sentence chunks with dependency relations), resulting in very high Feature Density, cause similarly low performance. On the other hand, feature set that is to some extent generalized but also plentiful (lemmas with POS) resulting in not-too-high and not-too-low FD, achieves the highest scores. We will pursue this path to find out optimal FD for the applied dataset, and for the proposed method in general.

REFERENCES

Cambria, E., & Hussain, A. (2012). *Sentic Computing: Techniques, Tools, and Applications*. Dordrecht, The Netherlands: Springer. doi:10.1007/978-94-007-5070-8

Covington, M. A. (2001). A fundamental algorithm for dependency parsing. *Proceedings of the 39th annual ACM southeast conference*, 95-102.

Damashek, M. (1995). Gauging similarity with n-grams: Language-independent categorization of text. *Science*, *267*(5199), 843–848. doi:10.1126cience.267.5199.843 PMID:17813910

Fabian Beijer, F. (2002). *The syntax and pragmatics of exclamations and other expressive/ emotional utterances*. Working Papers in Linguistics 2, The Dept. of English in Lund.

Fujii, Y., Ando, S., & Ito, T. (2010). Yūgai jōhō firutaringu no tame no 2-tangokan no kyori oyobi kyōki jōhō ni yoru bunshō bunrui shuhō no teian [Developing a method based on 2-word co-occurence information for filtering harmful information] (in Japanese). *Proceedings of The 24th Annual Conference of The Japanese Society for Artificial Intelligence (JSAI2010)*, 1-4.

Guthrie, D., Allison, B., Liu, W., Guthrie, L., & Wilks, Y. (2006). A closer look at skipgram modelling. *Proceedings of the 5th international Conference on Language Resources and Evaluation (LREC-2006)*, 1-4.

Huang, X., Alleva, F., Hon, H.-W., Hwang, M.-Y., & Rosenfeld, R. (1992). The SPHINX-II Speech Recognition System: An Overview, Computer. *Speech and Language*, *7*(2), 137–148. doi:10.1006/csla.1993.1007

Klaus Krippendorff, K. (1986). Combinatorial Explosion. In *Web Dictionary of Cybernetics and Systems*. Principia Cybernetica Web.

Markov, A. A. (1971). Extension of the limit theorems of probability theory to a sum of variables connected in a chain. John Wiley and Sons.

Matsuba, T., Masui, F., Kawai, A., & Isu, N. (2010). Gakkō hikōshiki saito ni okeru yūgai jōhō kenshutsu [Detection of harmful information on informal school websites] (in Japanese). *Proc. of The 16th Annual Meeting of The Association for Natural Language Processing (NLP2010)*.

Matsuba, T., Masui, F., Kawai, A., & Isu, N. (2011). Gakkō hi-kōshiki saito ni okeru yūgai jōhō kenshutsu wo mokuteki to shita kyokusei hantei moderu ni kansuru kenkyū [A study on the polarity classification model for the purpose of detecting harmful information on informal school sites] (in Japanese). *Proceedings of The Seventeenth Annual Meeting of The Association for Natural Language Processing (NLP2011)*, 388-391.

Ministry of Education, Culture, Sports, Science, and Technology (MEXT). (2008). *'Netto-jō no ijime' ni kansuru taiō manyuaru jirei shū (gakkō, kyōin muke)* ["Bullying on the Net" Manual for handling and collection of cases (for schools and teachers)] (in Japanese). MEXT.

Mishra, U., & Prakash, C. (2012). MAULIK: An effective stemmer for Hindi language. *International Journal on Computer Science and Engineering*, *4*(5), 711.

Narayanan, A., & Shmatikov, V. (2005, November). Fast dictionary attacks on passwords using time-space tradeoff. In *Proceedings of the 12th ACM conference on Computer and communications security* (pp. 364-372). ACM. 10.1145/1102120.1102168

Nitta, T., Masui, F., Ptaszynski, M., Kimura, Y., Rzepka, R., & Araki, K. (2013). Detecting Cyberbullying Entries on Informal School Websites Based on Category Relevance Maximization. *Proceedings of the 6th International Joint Conference on Natural Language Processing (IJCNLP 2013)*, 579-586.

Paar, C., Pelzl, J., & Preneel, B. (2010). *Understanding Cryptography: A Textbook for Students and Practitioners*. Springer. doi:10.1007/978-3-642-04101-3

Ponte, J. M., & Croft, W. B. (1998). *A Language Modeling Approach to Information Retrieval*. Research and Development in Information Retrieval. doi:10.1145/290941.291008

Potts, C. & Schwarz, F. (2008). *Exclamatives and heightened emotion: Extracting pragmatic generalizations from large corpora*. Ms., UMass Amherst.

Ptaszynski, M., Dybala, P., Matsuba, T., Masui, F., Rzepka, R., Araki, K., & Momouchi, Y. (2010). In the Service of Online Order: Tackling Cyber-Bullying with Machine Learning and Affect Analysis. *International Journal of Computational Linguistics Research*, *1*(3), 135–154.

Ptaszynski, M., Maciejewski, J., Dybala, P., Rzepka, R., & Araki, K. (2010). CAO: A fully automatic emoticon analysis system based on theory of kinesics. *IEEE Transactions on Affective Computing*, *1*(1), 46–59. doi:10.1109/T-AFFC.2010.3

Ptaszynski, M., Masui, F., Nitta, T., Hatakeyama, S., Kimura, Y., Rzepka, R., & Araki, K. (2016). Sustainable cyberbullying detection with category-maximized relevance of harmful phrases and double-filtered automatic optimization. *International Journal of Child-Computer Interaction*, *8*, 15–30. doi:10.1016/j.ijcci.2016.07.002

Ptaszynski, M., Rzepka, R., Araki, K., & Momouchi, Y. (2011). Language combinatorics: A sentence pattern extraction architecture based on combinatorial explosion. *International Journal of Computational Linguistics*, *2*(1), 24–36.

Sahlgren, M., & Cöster, R. (2004, August). Using bag-of-concepts to improve the performance of support vector machines in text categorization. In *Proceedings of the 20th international conference on Computational Linguistics* (p. 487). Association for Computational Linguistics. 10.3115/1220355.1220425

Sasai, K. (2006). The Structure of Modern Japanese Exclamatory Sentences: On the Structure of the Nanto-Type Sentence. *Studies in the Japanese Language*, *2*(1), 16–31.

Siu, M., & Ostendorf, M. (2000). Variable n-grams and extensions for conversational speech language modeling. *IEEE Transactions on Speech and Audio Processing*, *8*(1), 63–75. doi:10.1109/89.817454

Ure, J. (1971). Lexical density and register differentiation. In G. Perren & J. L. M. Trim (Eds.), *Applications of Linguistics* (pp. 443–452). London: Cambridge University Press.

Zellig, H. (1954). Distributional Structure. *Word*, *10*(2/3), 146–162.

ENDNOTES

1. By ambiguous patterns we refer to those patterns which appear on both the harmful side as well as in the non-harmful side. If a pattern appears on both sides it is ambiguous whether it is harmful or non-harmful, and its normalized weight is in the range from 0.99(9) to -0.99(9). Moreover, if an ambiguous pattern appears on both sides in the same occurrence, then its weight is equal 0, thus zero-patterns.
2. http://taku910.github.io/mecab/
3. https://taku910.github.io/cabocha/

Chapter 6
Traditional Classifiers vs. Deep Learning for Cyberbullying Detection

ABSTRACT

In this chapter, the authors present their approach to cyberbullying detection with the use of various traditional classifiers, including a deep learning approach. Research has tackled the problem of cyberbullying detection during recent years. However, due to complexity of language used in cyberbullying, the results obtained with traditional classifiers has remained only mildly satisfying. In this chapter, the authors apply a number of traditional classifiers, used also in previous research, to obtain an objective view on to what extent each of them is suitable to the task. They also propose a novel method to automatic cyberbullying detection based on convolutional neural networks and increased feature density. The experiments performed on actual cyberbullying data showed a major advantage of the presented approach to all previous methods, including the two best performing methods so far based on SO-PMI-IR and brute-force search algorithm, presented in previous two chapters.

DOI: 10.4018/978-1-5225-5249-9.ch006

INTRODUCTION

Along with Ptaszynski et al.'s (2010) first attempt, there have been a number of research attempting to develop methods for automatic detection of cyberbullying (Dinakar et al., 2012; Basave et al., 2013; Ptaszynski et al., 2010, 2016). Unfortunately, even with multiple improvements, the results remained only partially satisfying. This has been caused by a multitude of language ambiguities and styles used in CB.

To improve the effectiveness of automatic cyberbullying detection, in this chapter we perform an in-depth analysis of the performance of all classifiers previously used in CB detection, and above that, propose a novel, Deep Learning approach based on Convolutional Neural Networks (CNN). Moreover, based on the analysis of the characteristics of CNN and the initial results, we propose an optimization of CNN by increasing Feature Density of training data.

The rest of the chapter is organized in the following way. We describe all applied methods, including traditional classifiers as well as methods described in previous Chapters, and the final proposed method based on Convolutional Neural Networks. We also present the ways of dataset preprocessing used in this research, which to some extent overlap with previous Chapter. We explain the evaluation settings for the experiment and present a thorough analysis of experiment results and discussion.

PROPOSED METHODS

Below we describe the details of the applied methods. Firstly, we describe basics of data preprocessing and feature extraction. Next, we shortly explain all classifiers with their settings and modification applied in the experiments, including the proposed model based on CNN.

Data Preprocessing

The sentences from the original dataset used in this (Ptaszynski et al., 2010, 2015a, 2015b, 2016; Nitta et al., 2013) were preprocessed in the following ways:

- **Tokenization:** All words, punctuation marks, etc. are separated by spaces (later: TOK).
- **Lemmatization:** Like the above but the words are represented in their generic (dictionary) forms, or "lemmas" (later: LEM).
- **Parts of Speech**: Words are replaced with their representative parts of speech (later: POS).
- **Tokens With POS**: Both words and POS information is included in one element (later: TOK+POS).
- **Lemmas With POS**: Like the above but with lemmas instead of words (later: LEM+POS).
- **Tokens With Named Entity Recognition**: Words encoded together with with information on what named entities (private name of a person, organization, numericals, etc.) appear in the sentence. The NER information is annotated by CaboCha (later: TOK+NER).
- **Lemmas With NER**: Like the above but with lemmas (later: LEM+NER).
- **Chunking**: Larger sub-parts of sentences separated syntactically, such as noun phrase, verb phrase, predicates, etc., but without dependency relations (later: CHNK).
- **Dependency Structure**: Same as above, but with information regarding syntactical relations between chunks (later: DEP).
- **Chunking With NER:** Information on named entities is encoded in chunks (later: CHNK+NER).
- **Dependency Structure With Named Entities**: Both dependency relations and named entities are included in each element (later: DEP+NER).

Five examples of preprocessing were represented in Table 2 in Chapter 5. Theoretically, the more generalized a sentence is, the less unique and frequent patterns it will contain, but the produced patterns will be more frequent. For example, in the sentence from Table 2 in Chapter 5 we can see that a simple phrase *kimochi_ii hi* ("pleasant day") is represented by a POS pattern as ADJ N. We can easily assume that there will be more ADJ N patterns than *kimochi_ii hi*, because many word combinations can be represented by this pattern. We compared the results of classification for each classifier using different preprocessing methods to find out whether it is better to represent sentences as more generalized or as more specific. The generalization is also closely related to the notion of Feature Density we propose to optimize the proposed method.

Feature Extraction

From each of the eleven dataset versions preprocessed according to the description above, a Bag-of- Word language model was generated, producing eleven different models (Bag-of-Words/Tokens, Bag-of-Lemmas, Bag-of-POS, Bag-of-Chunks, etc.).

We also applied traditional weight calculation scheme, namely term frequency with inverse document frequency (tf*idf).

Term frequency *tf(t,d)* refers here to the traditional raw frequency, meaning the number of times a term *t* (word, token) occurs in a document *d*. Inverse document frequency *idf(t,D)* is the logarithm of the total number of documents |D| in the corpus divided by the number of documents containing the term n_t, as in equation 1. Finally, *tf*idf* refers to term frequency multiplied by inverse document frequency.

$$\mathrm{idf}\left(\mathrm{t},\mathrm{D}\right)=\log\frac{|D|}{n_t} \tag{1}$$

Classification Methods

In classification we applied all of the classifiers used in previous research on cyberbullying detection with some additional modifications. We also propose a new CNN-based classifier.

SVM or Support-vector machines (Cortes & Vapnik, 1995) are a set of classifiers well established in fields of AI and NLP. SVM represent data, belonging to specified categories, as points in space, and find an optimal hyperplane to separate the examples from each category.

SVM are also the first classifier used in cyberbullying detection (Ptaszynski et al., 2010), and have been used in other attempts extensively (see the Chapter describing previous research on CB detection). We used four types of SVM functions, namely, linear - the original function which finds the maximum-margin hyperplane dividing the samples; plynomial kernel, in which training samples are represented in a feature space over polynomials of the original variables, which allows non-linear model learning (also used in Dinakar et al., 2012); radial basis function (RBF) kernel, which approximates multivariate functions with a single univariate function, further radialised to be used in higher dimensions; and sigmoid, i.e., hyperbolic tangent function, when applied in SVM is equivalent to a simple two-layer perceptron neural network (Lin & Lin, 2003).

Naïve Bayes classifier is a supervised learning algorithm applying Bayes' theorem with the assumption of a strong (naive) independence between pairs of features, traditionally used as a baseline in text classification tasks.

kNN or the k-Nearest Neighbors classifier takes as input k-closest training samples with assigned classes and classifies input sample to a class by a majority vote. It is often applied as a baseline, next to Naïve Bayes. Here, we used k=1 setting in which the input sample is assigned to the class of the first nearest neighbor.

JRip also known as Repeated Incremental Pruning to Produce Error Reduction (RIPPER) (Cohen, 1995). It learns rules incrementally to further optimize them. It is efficient in classification of noisy text (Sasaki & Kita, 1998) and for this purpose was used in cyberbullying detection previously (Dinakar et al., 2012).

J48 is an implementation of the C4.5 decision tree algorithm (Quinlan, 1993), which firstly builds decision trees from a labeled dataset and each tree node selects the optimal splitting criterion further chosen to make the decision.

Random Forest in training phase creates multiple decision trees to output the optimal class (mode of classes) in classification phase (Breiman, 2001). An improvement of RF to standard decision trees is their ability to correct over-fitting to the training set common in decision trees (Hastie, Tibshirani & Friedman, 2009).

SPEC or Sentence Pattern Extraction arChitecture (Ptaszynski et al., 2015) is the custom feature extraction and classification system, upon which we based the cyberbullying detection method described in previous Chapter. Here, for convenience, we will abbreviate the method from previous Chapter to "SPEC". To recall, the features in SPEC are defined as ordered combinations of sentence elements and contain patterns of tokens with disjointed elements. Pattern occurrences for each side of binary class dataset are used to calculate normalized weight of patterns. Next, the score of a sentence is calculated as a sum of weights of patterns found in input sentence. With multiple modifications, such as deletion of ambiguous patterns, or various dataset preprocessing we were able to optimize the method to achieve somewhat high results (see Ptaszynski et al., 2015 and previous Chapter).

In comparison we used the results of that method optimized either for F1 or BEP (break-even point of Precision and Recall).

CNN or Convolutional Neural Networks, a type of feed-forward artificial neural networks, are an improved neural network model, i.e., multilayer perceptron. Although originally, CNN were designed for image recognition, their performance has been confirmed in many tasks, including NLP (Collobert & Weston, 2008) and sentence classification (Kim, 2014).

We applied a Convolutional Neural Network implementation with Rectified Linear Units (ReLU) as a neuron activation function (Nair & Hinton, 2010), and max pooling (Scherer, Müller & Behnke, 2010), which applies a max filter to non-overlying sub-parts of the input to reduce its dimensionality and in effect correct over-fitting by down-sampling input representation. We also applied dropout regularization on penultimate layer, which prevents co-adaptation of hidden units by randomly omitting (dropping out) some of the hidden units during training (Hinton et al., 2012).

We applied two versions of CNN. First, with one hidden convolutional layer containing 100 units was applied as a proposed baseline. Second, the final proposed method consisted of two hidden convolutional layers, containing 20 and 100 feature maps, respectively, both layers with 5x5 size of patch and 2x2 max-pooling, and Stochastic Gradient Descent (LeCun et al., 2012).

EVALUATION EXPERIMENTS

Experiment Setup

The preprocessed original dataset provides eleven separate datasets for the experiment (TOK, LEM, POS, TOK+POS, TOK+NER, LEM+POS, LEM+NER, CHNK, DEP, CHNK+NER, DEP+NER). Thus the experiment was performed eleven times, one time for each kind of preprocessing. Each of the classifiers was tested on each version of the dataset in a 10-fold cross validation procedure (which gives overall number of 1,430 experiment runs). The results were calculated using standard Precision (P), Recall (R), balanced F-score (F1) and Accuracy (A). As for the winning condition, we looked at which classifier achieved highest balanced F-score, and highest Accuracy.

Next, we apply the notion of Feature Density, introduced in previous Chapter, to analyze the correlation of number and density of features with final results, which could inform about possible ways of further improvement.

Finally, we checked the statistical significance of the results. We used paired t-test because the classification results could represent only one of two classes (harmful/cyberbullying or non-harmful/ normal).

Feature Density

To get a better grasp on the results we also analyzed the influence of how a dataset was preprocessed on the results.

To achieve this we applied the notion of Feature Density, introduced in previous Chapter. Here, we briefly explain the notion again. A dataset is the more generalized, the fewer number of frequently appearing unique features it produces. Therefore to estimate dataset generalization level we decided to calculate feature sophistication level. We achieved this by applying the Lexical Density (LD) score (Ure, 1971). It is a score representing an estimated measure of content per lexical units for a given corpus, and is calculated as the number of all unique words from the corpus divided by the number of all words in the corpus. However, since in our research we use a variety of different features, not only words (tokens), and the LD score can vary depending on which features or feature combinations were used, we called this measure Feature-based Lexical Density, or shortly, *Feature Density* (FD).

After calculating FD for all used datasets we calculated Pearson's correlation coefficient (ρ- value) to see if there is any correlation between dataset generalization (FD) and the results. Pearson's coefficient can achieve scores from 1.0 (perfect positive correlation), through 0.0 (no correlation) to -1.0 (perfect negative correlation). As the results we used the F-scores achieved by the classifiers.

Results and Discussion

All results were summarized in Table 1. The results of the baselines (kNN, Naïve Bayes) were low, as assumed. Although these classifiers can be tuned to high scores in typical sentiment analysis (Pang & Lee, 2004), they were not able to grasp the noisy, deceptive and often sarcastic language used in cyberbullying. However, it must be noticed that, especially with the help of named entities (NER), NB performed rather well, comparably to J48 and often better than JRip.

When it comes to decision trees-based classifiers, J48 scored low, similarly as it was reported in other research (Dinekar et al., 2012). However, its improved version, Random Forest usually scored better even than the best performing so far – SPEC. Unfortunately, RF is highly time-inefficient, especially compared to SVM, and thus impractical.

In many previous research on CB detection, including the first by Ptaszynski et al. (2010), SVM were the most commonly used classifier. Although later Ptaszynski et al. abandoned SVM for their inability to effectively handle larger CB sets, their research was based mostly on words (BoW). As we can observe, choice of appropriate function with good preprocessing makes SVM comparable even to the proposed CNN. The best setting was linear-SVM trained on lemmatized dataset (F1=.825). Moreover, although not scoring the highest, when the ratio of time-performance to the results is considered, SVM, which take only several minutes to train (computer with specs.: 32-cores, 256 GB RAM, high speed SSD), can be considered as the most efficient classifier.

As for the method of preprocessing, most often TOK+NER and LEM+NER scored highest. This can be explained by the fact that the data, which was annotated by expert annotators following official governmental definition of cyberbullying, often contained revealing of private information such as names, addresses, or phone numbers. As named entity recognition covered most of these cases, it is reasonable that it helped extracting meaningful features.

The best method so far, SPEC, was in fact scoring high most often, besides the proposed here CNN. Moreover, SPEC was better than SVM on every dataset, except one (LEM). Although SPEC is highly time inefficient in the training phase (generation of all combinatorial patterns), it is easy to apply and even in its fresh-trained form can be applied without any additional packages to any external media. This could be an advantage when including it in CB detection software, such as smartphone application, etc., proposed previously in the literature (Dinekar et al., 2012; Ptaszynski et al., 2016).

Interestingly, SPEC was better than CNN for datasets of the highest and the lowest Feature Density levels, meaning, the method has a "high bottom," or for the worst settings it scores high. This, along with the fact that the initial version of SPEC only included basic custom classifier, could indicate that it is possible that its performance could be further improved when applied to more advance classifiers, such as SVM, or even Neural Networks.

When it comes to the proposed method, the initial baseline-CNN with only one hidden layer did not perform well, although still was better than the baselines and comparable to most of the classifiers.

However, the final proposed method, namely, the CNN with two hidden layers, 5x5 patch size, max-pooling and Stochastic Gradient Descent, outperformed all of the classifiers in practically all settings. The only situation where SPEC scored higher (only POS features) reveals well known characteristics of Neural Nets, which perform poorly on a small number of unique features. As for the second situation, using only dependency features (DEP), which on the other hand contained the largest number of features, generation of the model was not feasible on the applied computer, and thus the results were not calculated. In the near future we plan to repeat the experiment in a more effective environment, such as a cloud computing service (Google Cloud Platform[1], Microsoft Azure[2], or Amazon EC2[3]).

As for the top three best performing settings, 2-layer CNN trained on chunks alone scored high, close to 90% of F-score. Dependency features with NER was second best with F1=92.7%. However, the optimal setting was the 2-layer CNN trained on chunks with named entities and reached F-score equal 93.5%, which is a result far more satisfying than expected, and exceeds second non-NN classifier (SVM on lemmas) over 10-percentage points.

Next, we analyzed the correlation of data preprocessing with Feature Density (FD). The results were represented in Table 2. The results clearly divided the classifiers into three groups. First group of the lowest performing classifiers (kNN, NB, J48, JRip, CNN-1L) was strongly negatively correlated with FD, which means these classifiers lose their general performance the more feature-dense is the model. This suggests that such classifiers should be fed with a feature set of limited density.

Second group contained the classifiers (all SVMs, Random Forest and both SPEC) that performed somewhat high. Their correlation with FD was negative from weak (-0.431) to somewhat high (-0.639). This, supported by the lack of statistical significance, means that FD does not correlate well with such classifiers and some other characteristics should be used for optimization of dataset preprocessing used in those classifiers.

Finally, we made an interesting discovery about the correlation between FD and our proposed method (2-layer CNN). The classifier correlated positively nearly strongly with FD. This suggests that the performance could be improved by increasing the feature density of the applied dataset. We plan to follow this path in the nearest future.

Table 1. Results of all applied classifiers (Scores averaged for positive and negative prediction calculated separately; best classifier for each dataset in **bold type fond***; best dataset generalization for each classifier – underlined)*

			LEM +POS	TOK +POS	LEM	TOK	CHUNK +NER	POS	DEP +NER	DEP	CHUNK	LEM+ NER	TOK+ NER
SVM	linear	Prec	.777	.768	**.827**	.777	.679	.563	.651	.639	.606	.820	.781
		Rec	.777	.766	**.825**	.776	.645	.563	.615	.577	.603	.818	.781
		F1	.776	.766	**.825**	.775	.623	.563	.586	.531	.597	.818	.780
		Acc	.777	.766	**.825**	.776	.645	.563	.615	.577	.603	.818	.781
	plynomial	Prec	.262	.499	.262	.263	.260	.553	.260	.260	.260	.260	.260
		Rec	.512	.499	.512	.513	.510	.545	.510	.510	.510	.510	.510
		F1	.346	.450	.347	.348	.344	.528	.344	.344	.344	.344	.344
		Acc	.512	.499	.512	.513	.510	.545	.510	.510	.510	.510	.510
	radial	Prec	.797	.753	.262	.793	.260	.565	.260	.260	.260	.752	.779
		Rec	.771	.747	.512	.756	.510	.565	.510	.510	.510	.516	.778
		F1	.765	.746	.347	.746	.344	.565	.344	.344	.344	.358	.778
		Acc	.771	.747	.512	.756	.510	.565	.510	.510	.510	.516	.778
	sigmoid	Prec	.757	.746	.262	.752	.260	.562	.260	.260	.260	.260	.771
		Rec	.549	.736	.512	.538	.510	.562	.510	.510	.510	.510	.606
		F1	.425	.733	.347	.403	.344	.561	.344	.344	.344	.344	.530
		Acc	.549	.736	.512	.538	.510	.562	.510	.510	.510	.510	.606
Naïve Bayes		Prec	.678	.671	.686	.682	.666	.570	.652	.672	.685	.708	.703
		Rec	.674	.669	.682	.678	.627	.569	.578	.555	.598	.705	.701
		F1	.673	.668	.681	.677	.599	.568	.511	.453	.539	.705	.701
		Acc	.674	.669	.682	.678	.627	.569	.578	.555	.598	.705	.701

continued on following page

Table 1. Continued

		LEM +POS	TOK +POS	LEM	TOK	CHUNK +NER	POS	DEP +NER	DEP	CHUNK	LEM+ NER	TOK+ NER
JRip	**Prec**	.606	.614	.604	.603	.628	.553	.643	.505	.685	.699	.700
	Rec	.606	.613	.603	.603	.555	.553	.533	.510	.598	.675	.672
	F1	.606	.613	.603	.603	.469	.553	.408	.345	.539	.663	.658
	Acc	.606	.613	.603	.603	.555	.553	.533	.510	.598	.675	.712
J48	**Prec**	.672	.671	.683	.675	.615	.566	.652	.260	.645	.711	.707
	Rec	.671	.666	.681	.672	.548	.566	.533	.510	.517	.708	.704
	F1	.670	.663	.680	.669	.458	.566	.408	.344	.365	.706	.707
	Acc	.671	.666	.681	.672	.548	.566	.533	.510	.517	.708	.663
kNN (k=1)	**Prec**	.639	.630	.644	.630	.578	.544	.593	.628	.576	.668	.663
	Rec	.636	.627	.640	.628	.546	.543	.529	.528	.550	.663	.659
	F1	.633	.625	.637	.626	.505	.542	.446	.427	.494	.658	.656
	Acc	.636	.627	.640	.628	.546	.543	.529	.528	.550	.663	.659
Random Forest	**Prec**	.816	.803	.818	.809	.662	.547	.623	.619	.639	.818	.809
	Rec	.809	.795	.809	.801	.632	.546	.607	.582	.580	.809	.802
	F1	.808	.794	.808	.799	.610	.544	.590	.540	.522	.807	.800
	Acc	.809	.795	.809	.801	.632	.546	.607	.582	.580	.809	.802
SPEC (highest F1)	**Prec**	.807	.756	.713	.724	.563	**.528**	.500	**.491**	.490	N/A	N/A
	Rec	.798	.839	.885	.842	.879	**.946**	.982	**1.000**	1.000	N/A	N/A
	F1	.803	.796	.790	.778	.686	**.677**	.663	**.658**	.658	N/A	N/A
	Acc	.808	.784	.770	.766	.603	**.550**	.510	**.491**	.490	N/A	N/A

continued on following page

Table 1. Continued

		LEM +POS	TOK +POS	LEM	TOK	CHUNK +NER	POS	DEP +NER	DEP	CHUNK	LEM+ NER	TOK+ NER
SPEC-optimized (highest BEP)	**Prec**	.802	.786	.784	.770	.655	.614	.548	.591	.633	N/A	N/A
	Rec	.802	.786	.784	.770	.655	.614	.548	.591	.633	N/A	N/A
	F1	.802	.786	.784	.770	.655	.614	.548	.591	.633	N/A	N/A
	Acc	.775	.780	.600	.765	.790	.635	.525	.640	.548	N/A	N/A
CNN (1 hidden layer)	**Prec**	.700	.678	.724	.704	.506	.544	.616	.499	.496	.720	.739
	Rec	.700	.678	.724	.704	.510	.544	.525	.505	.509	.716	.738
	F1	.700	.677	.724	.704	.433	.544	.393	.461	.374	.714	.738
	Acc	.700	.678	.724	.704	.510	.544	.525	.505	.509	.716	.738
CNN (2 hidden layers)	**Prec**	**.867**	**.824**	.820	**.833**	**.936**	.500	**.929**	N/A	**.899**	**.847**	**.849**
	Rec	**.866**	**.821**	.819	**.831**	**.935**	.500	**.927**	N/A	**.893**	**.847**	**.849**
	F1	**.866**	**.821**	.819	**.830**	**.935**	.495	**.927**	N/A	**.892**	**.847**	**.849**
	Acc	**.866**	**.821**	.819	**.831**	**.935**	.500	**.927**	N/A	**.893**	**.847**	**.849**

Table 2. Left part: Information on features (unique features, Feature Density) for each dataset. Right part: Pearson Correlation Coefficient (ρ-value) of Feature Density and all classifier results, with statistical significance (2-sided p-value)

Feature sophistication (←low high→)	Dataset Preprocessing	# unique 1grams	# all 1grams	Feature Density	Classifier	ρ-value	2-sided p-value
	DEP	12802	13957	0.9172	CNN-2L	**0.638**	***p=0.035**
	DEP+NER	12160	13956	0.8713	SVM-pol	-0.431	p=0.185
	CHUNK	11389	13960	0.8158	SVM-sig	-0.534	p=0.091
	CHUNK+NER	10657	13872	0.7682	SPEC(BEP)	-0.550	p=0.133
	TOK+POS	6565	34874	0.1882	RF	-0.560	p=0.073
	TOK	6464	36234	0.1784	SVM-lin	-0.564	p=0.076
	LEM+POS	6227	36426	0.1709	SPEC(F1)	-0.636	p=0.066
	LEM	6103	36412	0.1676	SVM-rad	-0.639	*p=0.034
	TOK+NER	5967	38672	0.1543	CNN-1L	-0.709	*p=0.019
	LEM+NER	5581	38672	0.1443	JRip	-0.729	*p=0.011
	POS	13	26650	0.0005	NB	-0.736	*p=0.013
					J48	-0.791	**p=0.006
				*p≦0.05, **p≦0.01 →	kNN	-0.809	**p=0.004

CONCLUSION AND FUTURE WORK

To help quickly respond to ever-growing CB problem, automatic cyberbullying detection research has started to sprout. A number of classifiers has been applied in previous research, unfortunately, with only partially satisfying results. In this chapter we compared the performance of all previously applied classifiers on our gold standard dataset. We also proposed a novel Deep Learning approach to the problem, based on Convolutional Neural Networks (CNN).

The proposed optimized CNN model not only outperformed other classifiers by over 11-percentage-points, scoring a close to ideal F-score (93.5%), but also revealed an unusual characteristics, by nearly strongly positively correlating with Feature Density. This provides an informative hint on how to improve further not only the proposed method (by increasing FD of a dataset), but also other classifiers (decreasing FD, etc.).

In the near future we plan to test the limits of potential optimization, also by applying different dataset preprocessing methods.

REFERENCES

Breiman, L. (2001). Random forests. *Machine Learning*, *45*(1), 5–32. doi:10.1023/A:1010933404324

Basave, A. M. C., He, Y., Liu, K., & Zhao, J. (2013). *A weakly supervised bayesian model for violence detection in social media*. Retrieved from: http://www.aclweb.org/anthology/I13-1013

Cohen, W. W. (1995). Fast effective rule induction. *Proceedings of the twelfth international conference on machine learning*, 115–123.

Collobert, R., & Weston, J. (2008). A unified architecture for natural language processing: Deep neural networks with multitask learning. In *Proceedings of the 25th international conference on Machine learning* (pp. 160–167). ACM. 10.1145/1390156.1390177

Cortes, C., & Vapnik, V. (1995). Support-vector networks. *Machine Learning*, *20*(3), 273–297. doi:10.1007/BF00994018

Cross, D., Shaw, T., Hearn, L., Epstein, M., Monks, H., Lester, L., & Thomas, L. (2009). *Australian covert bullying prevalence study. Child Health Promotion Research Centre*. Perth: Edith Cowan University. Retrieved from https://docs.education.gov.au/system/files/doc/other/australian_covert_bullying_prevalence_study_executive_summary.pdf

Dinakar, K., Jones, B., Havasi, C., Lieberman, H., & Picard, R. (2012). Common sense reasoning for detection, prevention, and mitigation of cyberbullying. *ACM Transactions on Interactive Intelligent Systems*, *2*(3), 18. doi:10.1145/2362394.2362400

Hasebrink, U., Livingstone, S. & Haddon, L. (2008). *Comparing children's online opportunities and risks across Europe: Cross-national comparisons for EU kids online*. Academic Press.

Hastie, T., Tibshirani, R., & Friedman, J. (2009). *The Elements of Statistical Learning: Data Mining, Inference, and Prediction.* Springer.

Hinduja, S., & Patchin, J. W. (2010). Bullying, cyberbullying, and suicide. *Archives of Suicide Research*, *14*(3), 206–221. doi:10.1080/13811118.2010.494133 PMID:20658375

Hinduja, S., & Patchin, J. W. (2014). *Bullying beyond the schoolyard: Preventing and responding to cyberbullying*. Corwin Press.

Hinton, G.E., Srivastava, N., Krizhevsky, A., Sutskever, I. & Salakhutdinov, R. (2012). *Improving neural networks by preventing co-adaptation of feature detectors*. CoRR, abs/1207.0580.

Kim, Y. (2014). Convolutional neural networks for sentence classification. *Proceedings of the 2014 Conference on Empirical Methods in Natural Language Processing (EMNLP)*, 1746-1751. 10.3115/v1/D14-1181

Kowalski, R. M., & Limber, S. P. (2007). Electronic bullying among middle school students. *The Journal of Adolescent Health*, *41*(6), S22–S30. doi:10.1016/j.jadohealth.2007.08.017 PMID:18047942

Lazuras, L., Pyżalski, J., Barkoukis, V., & Tsorbatzoudis, H. (2012). *Empathy and moral disengagement in adolescent cyberbullying: Implications for educational intervention and pedagogical practice*. Academic Press.

LeCun, Y. A., Bottou, L., Orr, G. B., & Müller, K. R. (2012). Efficient backprop. In *Neural networks: Tricks of the trade* (pp. 9–48). Springer. doi:10.1007/978-3-642-35289-8_3

Li, Q. (2007). Bullying in the new playground: Research into cyberbullying and cyber victimisation. *Australasian Journal of Educational Technology*, *23*(4). doi:10.14742/ajet.1245

Lin, H.-T., & Lin, C.-J. (2003). A study on sigmoid kernels for svm and the training of non-psd kernels by smo-type methods. *Neural Computation*, 1–32.

MEXT. (2008). *'Netto-jō no ijime' ni kansuru taiō manyuaru jirei shū (gakkō, kyōin muke)* ["Bullying on the net" manual for handling and collection of cases (for schools and teachers)] (in Japanese). MEXT.

Nair, V., & Hinton, G. E. (2010). Rectified linear units improve restricted boltzmann machines. *Proceedings of the 27th international conference on machine learning (ICML-10)*, 807–814.

Nitta, T., Masui, F., Ptaszynski, M., Kimura, Y., Rzepka, R., & Araki, K. (2013). Detecting cyberbullying entries on informal school websites based on category relevance maximization. IJCNLP, 579–586.

Pang, B., & Lee, L. (2004) A sentimental education: Sentiment analysis using subjectivity summarization based on minimum cuts. In *Proceedings of the 42nd annual meeting on Association for Computational Linguistics* (p. 271). Association for Computational Linguistics. 10.3115/1218955.1218990

Patchin, J. W., & Hinduja, S. (2006). Bullies move beyond the schoolyard a preliminary look at cyberbullying. *Youth Violence and Juvenile Justice*, *4*(2), 148–169. doi:10.1177/1541204006286288

Ptaszynski, M., Dybala, P., Matsuba, T., Masui, F., Rzepka, R., Araki, K., & Momouchi, Y. (2010). In the service of online order: Tackling cyber-bullying with machine learning and affect analysis. *International Journal of Computational Linguistics Research*, *1*(3), 135–154.

Ptaszynski, M., Masui, F., Nitta, T., Hatakeyama, S., Kimura, Y., Rzepka, R., & Araki, K. (2016). Sustainable cyberbullying detection with category-maximized relevance of harmful phrases and double-filtered automatic optimization. *International Journal of Child-Computer Interaction*, *8*, 15–30. doi:10.1016/j.ijcci.2016.07.002

Ptaszynski, M., Masui, F., Kimura, Y., Rzepka, R., & Araki, K. (2015a). Brute force works best against bullying. *IJCAI 2015 Workshop on Intelligent Personalization (IP 2015)*, 28–29.

Ptaszynski, M., Masui, F., Kimura, Y., Rzepka, R., & Araki, K. (2015b). Extracting patterns of harmful expressions for cyberbullying detection. *Proceedings of 7th Language and Technology Conference (LTC'15)*, 370–375.

Pyżalski, J. (2012). From cyberbullying to electronic aggression: Typology of the phenomenon. *Emotional & Behavioural Difficulties*, *17*(3-4), 305–317. doi:10.1080/13632752.2012.704319

Quinlan, J. R. (1993). *C4.5: Programs for Machine Learning. Morgan Kaufmann series in machine learning*. Morgan Kaufmann Publishers.

Rutter, D. R. (1987). *Communicating by Telephone. International Series in Experimental Social Psychology* (Vol. 15). Elsevier Science Limited.

Sarna, G., & Bhatia, M. P. S. (2015). Content based approach to find the credibility of user in social networks: An application of cyberbullying. *International Journal of Machine Learning and Cybernetics*, 1–13.

Sasaki, M., & Kita, K. (1998). Rule-based text categorization using hierarchical categories. In *Systems, Man, and Cybernetics, 1998. 1998 IEEE International Conference on* (vol. 3, pp. 2827–2830). IEEE. 10.1109/ICSMC.1998.725090

Scherer, D., Müller, A., & Behnke, S. (2010). Evaluation of pooling operations in convolutional architectures for object recognition. In *International Conference on Artificial Neural Networks* (pp. 92–101). Springer. 10.1007/978-3-642-15825-4_10

Sood, S. O., Churchill, E. F., & Antin, J. (2012). Automatic identification of personal insults on social news sites. *Journal of the American Society for Information Science and Technology*, *63*(2), 270–285. doi:10.1002/asi.21690

Sourander, A., Klomek, A. B., Ikonen, M., Lindroos, J., Luntamo, T., Koskelainen, M., ... Helenius, H. (2010). Psychosocial risk factors associated with cyberbullying among adolescents: A population-based study. *Archives of General Psychiatry*, *67*(7), 720–728. doi:10.1001/archgenpsychiatry.2010.79 PMID:20603453

Turney, P. D. (2002) Thumbs up or thumbs down? semantic orientation applied to unsupervised classification of reviews. In *Proceedings of ACL 2002* (pp. 417–424). Association for Computational Linguistics.

Ure, J. (1971). Lexical density and register differentiation. *Applied Linguistics*, 443–452.

ENDNOTES

1 https://cloud.google.com/
2 https://azure.microsoft.com
3 https://aws.amazon.com/ec2/

Chapter 7
Cyberbullying Blocker Test Application for Android Devices

ABSTRACT

In this chapter, the authors present an application for Android smartphones to automatically detect possible harmful content in input text. The developed application is aimed to test in practice the performance of the developed cyberbullying detection methods described in previous chapters. The final goal of the developed application will be to help mitigate the problem of cyberbullying by quickly detecting possibly harmful contents in user's entry and warning the user of the possible negative influence. The test application was prepared to use one of two methods for detection of harmful messages: a method inspired by a brute force search algorithm applied to language modelling and a method which uses seed words from three categories to calculate semantic orientation score SO-PMI-IR and then maximize the relevance of categories to specify harmfulness of a message (both methods were described in previous chapters). First tests showed that both methods are working properly under the Android environment.

DOI: 10.4018/978-1-5225-5249-9.ch007

INTRODUCTION

Although humiliating and slandering people through the Internet has existed almost as long as the Internet became a tool for casual communication between people, the appearance of new devices, such as smartphones and tablet computers, which allow using this medium not only at home, work or school but also in motion, sometimes with different access points with simplified anonymity, has further exacerbated that problem. That motivated us to try preventing the problem of cyberbullying with the use of mobile devices. We decided to apply existing methods of detecting harmful contents on the Internet and focused on transferring them to a mobile device.

The first step to fulfil this goal was developing an Android application which we describe in this Chapter. We created the application to test whether it is possible to apply the detection algorithms previously developed on much more powerful machines also on mobile devices such as smartphones and tablets, and find out which algorithm will work best. The result of this experiment and its possible implications are described in this chapter.

The outline of this chapter is as follows. Firstly, we describe other available solutions and explain how our software differs from other cyberbullying detection software. Next, we describe our application, starting from the description of its functions and elements it contains, followed by the description of interface. Further, we describe the two methods used for detecting cyberbullying applied in the software at the moment. Finally, we describe the preliminary testing meant to verify the performance of the developed application and discuss the results of those tests.

RELATED WORK IN DEVELOPMENT OF PRACTICAL APPLICATIONS FOR CYBERBULLYING DETECTION

With the popularization of mobile devices, the problem of cyberbullying has become more noticeable. Apart from the research in cyberbullying detection described in previous chapters, a number of research teams around the world have attempted to develop practical solutions for detection and mitigation of this problem. However, most of the research is still in a developmental phase and is yet to be fully applied in practice. On the other hand, there have been developed market solutions for the detection and mitigation of online bullying, having a capacity to deal with the problem to some extent. Unfortunately, such solutions are usually based on the simplest methods, which narrows the scope of their applicability. Below we present some of such solutions.

FearNot!

One of the examples of a software with a novel approach is FearNot! (http://sourceforge.net/projects/fearnot/). The authors describe it as "an interactive drama/video game that teaches children strategies to prevent bullying and social exclusion." The development of this software, which uses psychology-inspired character AI, was supported by EU funded research projects Victec and eCircus. The approach taken by the developers, namely, not to detect and stigmatize cyberbullying behavior, but rather to educate children not to become bullies, does indicate a deep insight in the problem. Unfortunately, the development of the software has stopped in early 2013.

BullyGuardPro

An example of a potentially effective software could be BullyGuardPro (http://www.bullyguardpro.com, recently restarted as BullyGuard https://www.bullyguard.com/). It is a software aimed at detecting cyberbullying activity around a user allowing her to "effectively respond, diffuse and halt cyberbullying and cyberpredation attacks". The software was developed by Lynne Edwards and April Kontostathis, who lead a team which as some of the first began the research on cyberbullying detection (Kontostathis et al., 2013). Unfortunately, at the time of writing, no details on the technology used in the software, nor its release date is yet known.

Samaritans Radar

On 29th October 2014, "Samaritans" (http://www.samaritans.org/), an organization focused on suicide prevention, launched an application called Samaritans Radar. It was a free Internet application for Twitter, which helped users monitors their friends' Tweets. Main function of the application was alerting a user when it spotted anyone in the user's online surroundings, who could be either bullied, depressed or sending disturbing suicidal signals. Unfortunately, due to serious data protection and privacy issues, which were noticed by the users soon after the time of launch, the application was closed permanently on 10 March 2015, six months after its release.

Uonevu

An interesting approach to the detection of cyberbullying in messages was developed by researchers from Trinity College Dublin and National Anti-Bullying Research and Support Centre, under the codename Uonevu (meaning "bullying" in Swahili language). The software is meant to detect particularly non-literal forms of bullying and negative stereotyping. The software works by applying a semantic knowledge base to associate concepts with each other. An example is associating the concept of "fat/obese people" with the word "pizza", which in a sentence such as "Hey, Jane, are you going to eat a whole pizza tonight?" would indicate an instance of cyberbullying. The major problem here becomes creating a large enough knowledge base of stereotypes. Unfortunately, at the moment of writing the database contains only 57 stereotypes, which is not sufficient for effective functioning of the software. However, the project is still in its developmental phase and could be an interesting solution when finished.

Twitter New Policy

On February 26, 2015, Twitter independently released its new policy regarding safety and misbehavior among its users (Twitter, 2015). Twitter allowed users to report particular tweets as harassment incidents. This provided the users who became victims of online bullying a tool for personally reacting to the bullying attacks. An account of a confirmed bully becomes locked and can be reopened only under the condition that the bully deletes her harmful tweets. This way of dealing with cyberbullying is not yet a software *per se*, but Twitter claims to be aiming at developing a method for detecting bullying messages automatically in the future. For the time being however, they declared increasing the number of staff in their support team focused on handling abuse reports.

ReThink

An example of a recent popular solution which still works, could be ReThink (http://www.rethinkwords.com/). It is an application for smartphones, which shows a pop-up warning message when user tries to send a message containing harmful contents. The idea of informing a user about possible harmfulness of a message has been noticed even earlier as an effective mean to make user re-evaluate her message before making it publicly available (Masui, Ptaszynski & Nitta, 2013). Unfortunately, though ReThink is a good example of a quick and ad hoc response to the cyberbullying problem, its algorithm for the detection of harmful contents is based on simple keystroke logging and detecting vulgar and harmful words within the string of characters. This makes it inapplicable for more sophisticated contents, not including vulgar expressions. It also fails when user makes a mistake during writing and e.g., uses a backspace, since the "backspace" character is also recorded and hinders detection of harmful words.

PocketGuardian

PocketGuardian is a newly released (September 2015) software for parental monitoring, that "detects cyberbullying, sexting, and explicit images on children's mobile devices" (https://gopocketguardian.com/). By using machine learning techniques the software provides a statistical probability that the content (sentence, tweet, e-mail, or image) is inappropriate. An advantage of this software is that it focuses not only on textual content, but includes in its monitoring range the ability to detect explicit images (nudity, etc.). Its disadvantage could be its price ($12.99 per month). The exact technology behind the software (e.g., applied machine learning algorithms, size of the training lexicon or corpus) is yet unknown. Moreover, as the software is aimed at parents trying to monitor their children's mobile devices, the developers will need to address the questions regarding the ethics of using such software and its possible influence on parent-child trust relationship.

In comparison with the software described above, the application presented in this Chapter distinguishes itself in the following ways. Similarly to ReThink it provides a tool for the user to reflect on their own written messages. However, differently to ReThink, it shows the user which exactly words or sentence patterns were considered as inappropriate. Moreover, it does not only use simple keystroke logs, but uses various Artificial Intelligence methods (at present two) to spot any undesirable contents. It focuses only on textual contents, however, differently to the PocketGuardian we do not plan to make profit of the application. Moreover, since the application is aimed to be used by the user directly, all ethical issues and any influence on parent-child trust relations, as well as any privacy issues, like in the Samaritans

Radar application, do not apply. The methods applied so far have been in development for over six years, thus the problem of insufficient data, such as in the Uonevu project is also resolved.

CYBERBULLYING BLOCKER TEST APPLICATION FOR ANDROID DEVICES

In this section we present the mobile device application we developed to implement the proposed cyberbullying detection methods.

The application was created for devices supporting Android 4.2.2 (API level 17, codename Jelly Bean) or higher. In the development process we used Java 8 and Android Studio. The application contains one activity responsible for the interaction with the user. For the process of checking the text for possible harmful content it starts a background thread. Thanks to that the user still can use his device even if checking process takes a while.

For comparison, we implemented in the application two of the methods for cyberbullying detection, described in previous Chapters. We did this to test how the method proposed here would perform when compared with other methods. In the test phase the user can use both of the methods, to compare their overall performance, which refers to not only Precision and Recall of detection, but also processing time and other features which could be used for further improvement of the proposed method.

Figure 1 represents an activity diagram of the detection process. Depending on the choice of the method of detection, application may require an Internet connection.

The application is created so that removing or adding a new method for detecting of cyberbullying was possible, and did not affect operation of the application itself.

Description of Application Interface

Application interface is designed in accordance with the standards for Android operating system (Android Developers, n.d.). Interaction with a user is intuitive and all important information is accessible in main window. Figure 2 represents the interface with description of each important element.

Below we describe the interface of the application. The numbers correspond to the numbers in red from Figure 2.

Figure 1. Activity diagram of the application

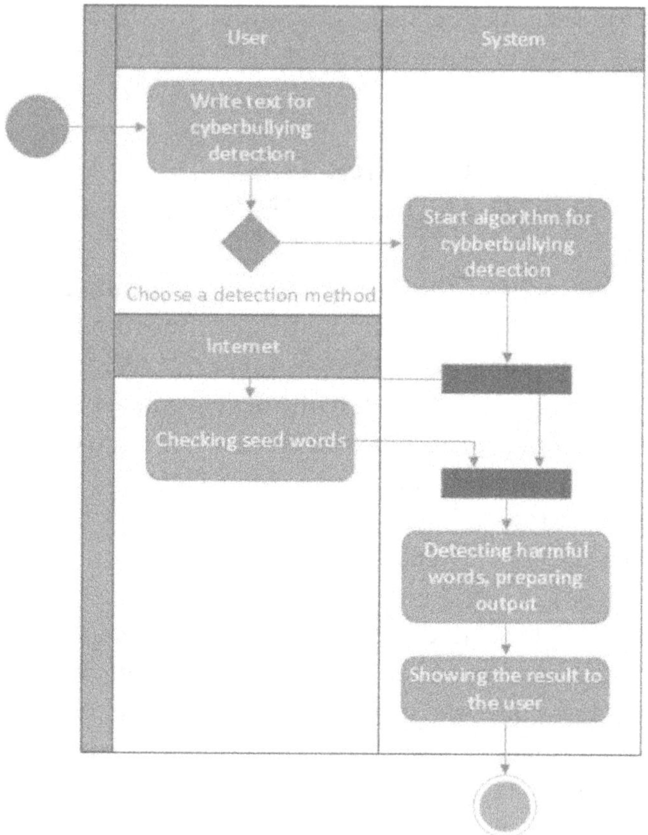

1. Name of the application,
2. Settings (contains information about the application, and short description of used methods for cyberbullying detection),
3. Input for text to classify,
4. Choice of a method for cyberbullying classification,
5. Button "Check" - Clicking on it starts the process of checking the entered text,
6. Button "Clear" - Clears the input and feedback fields,
7. Field showing the feedback of used method for analyzing the text.

Harmful Content Detection Process

Below we describe the process of detecting possible harmful contents.

Figure 2. Interface of the developed application with numbers (in red) marking each element of the interface

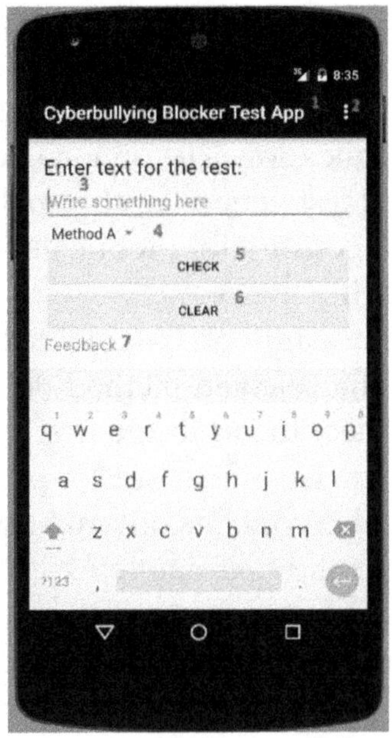

Figure 3. Text input and choice of processing method (left); harmful text output (center); non-harmful text output (right)

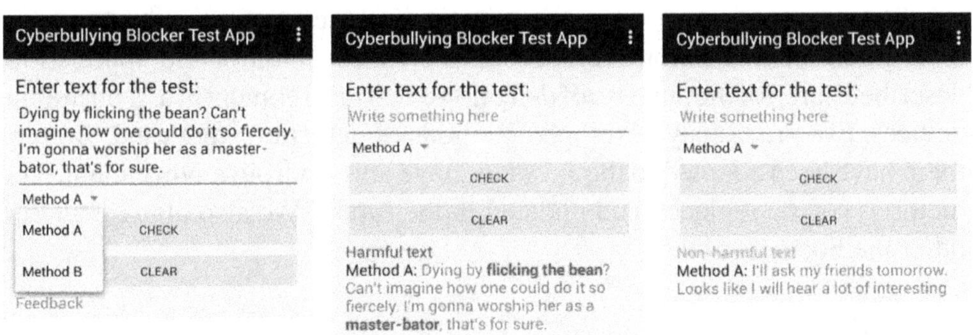

1. **Sentence Input**: Firstly, user inputs a sentence she wants to check. There is no limits of how long it can be. User can write several sentences at once. The only limitation is phone memory for the TextView control class, which is usually set to 9,000 characters. Due to limitations of smartphone screen size, the application allows the maximum of five visible lines of input, for more the user needs to scroll down. However,

larger amount of words to check will slow down the detection process for both methods. User can input any contents she wants, in which the system will detect words and patterns recognizable by the used algorithm.

2. **Selection of Detection Method**: A user should choose one method from a list of all algorithms. Short description of methods can be found in the Settings tab of the application. The option to choose the method is only available in the initial test version of the application and is intended to help select the best algorithm for mobile devices.
3. **Launch of the checking process**.
4. **Feedback:** The processing of entered text results in one of two possibilities. Either the selected method does not detect any harmful patterns or it does detect them. In the first case the returned feedback informs the user that no harmful words or patterns were detected in the input. The feedback also contains, information on which classification method was used and the text entered by the user (see right part of Figure 3). In the second case the feedback contains information about the detected harmful words and patterns, which method was used, the entered text and the detected harmful patterns represented in bold and red-colored font (see center part of Figure 3).

Methods Description

For test purposes in the developed application we plan to apply a number of different classification methods. In the first version of the application, described here, for the purpose of detection of harmful content in text on mobile devices, two previously developed methods of detection were used. Both of them have been adapted to the Java language and Android environment. The methods can be replaced and updated in the future. We also plan on adding other methods.

Method A

As the first method, further called 'Method A', we used the one presented in Chapter 5. The method classifies messages as harmful or not by using a classifier trained with a language modeling method based on a brute force search algorithm applied to language modeling. Below we shortly recollect how the method works.

The method uses sophisticated sentence patterns with disjointed elements automatically extracted with a novel language modeling method developed by

Ptaszynski et al. (2011). The method defines "sentence patterns" as *ordered combinations of sentence elements*, and uses them for brute-force searching within input sentences.

In the training of this method, at first, ordered non-repeated combinations were generated from all elements of training sentences. In every n-element sentence there is k-number of combination clusters, such as that $1 \leqq k \leqq n$, where k represents all k-element combinations being a subset of n. In this procedure all combinations for all values of k are generated. The number of all possible combinations is equal to the sum of all k-element combination clusters (see Equation 1).

$$\sum_{k=1}^{n} \binom{n}{k} = \frac{n!}{1!(n-1)!} + \frac{n!}{2!(n-2)!} + \ldots + \frac{n!}{n!(n-n)!} = 2^n - 1 \qquad (1)$$

Next, all non-subsequent elements were separated with an asterisk ("*"). Occurrences O of patterns from each side of the dataset were used to calculate their weight w_j (Equation 2). Finally, the score of a new input sentence is calculated as a sum of weights of patterns found in the sentence (Equation 3).

$$w_j = \left(\frac{O_{pos}}{O_{pos} + O_{neg}} - 0.5 \right) * 2 \qquad (2)$$

$$\text{score} = \sum w_j, \ \left(1 \geq w_j \geq -1\right) \qquad (3)$$

Method B

The second method, further called 'Method B', described in more detail in Chapter 4, uses a list of seed words from three categories to calculate semantic orientation score SO-PMI-IR and then maximizes the relevance of categories with the input sentence. Below we shortly recollect the details of the method.

There are three steps in the classification of the harmfulness of input:

1. Phrase extraction,

2. Categorization and harmful word detection together with harmfulness polarity determination,
3. Relevance maximization.

This method is an extension of the method proposed by Turney (2002) to calculate the relevance of words with specified categories according to the Equation 4, where p_i is a phrase extracted from the input, w_j are the words that are registered in one category of harmfulness polarity words, $hits(p_i)$ and $hits(w_j)$ are Web search hits for each category for p_i and w_j respectively, $hits(p_i \& w_j)$ is a number of hits when p_i and w_j appear on the same Web page. Finally, $PMI\text{–}IR(p_i, w_j)$ is the relevance of p_i and w_j.

$$\mathrm{PMI} - \mathrm{IR}\left(p_i, w_j\right) = log_2 \left\{ \frac{hits\left(p_i \ \& \ w_j\right)}{hits\left(p_i\right) hits\left(w_j\right)} \right\} \tag{4}$$

Turney's method was extended to work not only on words, but on phrases. The phrases are automatically extracted from input sentences using dependency relations. Next, for all of the phrases the relevance is calculated with seed words from multiple categories of harmful words. The degree of association for each category –PMI-IR score – is maximized so that the maximum value achieved within all categories is considered as the harmfulness *score* representative for the input sentence, and is calculated according to the Equation 5.

$$score_{entry} = max_{all\_phrases}\left(max_{all\_categories}\left(PMI - IR\left(p_i, w_j\right)\right)\right) \tag{5}$$

This method does not require excessive computer power, and works on a small list of seed words, which can be further refined and optimized as showed by Ptaszynski et al. (2016). On the other hand, this method requires a stable Internet connection for calculating PMI-IR score of the phrases with each group of seed words.

Preliminary Tests

We performed preliminary tests with the developed application. The tests were not meant to check the validity of the implemented methods, as this was already confirmed in previous research (see previous Chapters). We verified

Table 1. Comparison of different features for two methods

	Method A	Method B
Avg. # of words / patterns used in classification	11,832,430	9
Internet connection required	NO	YES
Avg. time for one sentence (in seconds and minutes)	88.46 s	8.41 s
	(1.47 m)	(0.14 m)
Best Precision	89%	91%
Recall at Best Precision	34%	9%
F-score for Best Precission	49%	16%

only whether the applied classification methods performed correctly under the new environment, and if they returned a proper feedback.

For the purpose of testing the application we prepared a set of sentences, contents of the dataset applied in previous research, from which some contained harmful words and some did not. The sentences were entered one by one to the application input field and tested by both methods. Examples of outputs for harmful and non-harmful sentences, were represented in the center and right part of Fig. 3, respectively. As our final goal, we plan to release the application for multiple languages. However, as both of the applied cyberbullying detection methods work presently for the Japanese language, at the moment the application is mainly developed for this language. However, for the description purposes in this chapter we present both the application interface and the sentence examples translated in English.

Tests were performed on virtual devices emulated by Genymotion engine (Sony Xperia with Android 4.2.2 and Google Nexus 10 with Android 5.0) and on Smartphone LG G2 with Android 5.0.2. The tests were focused on the general performance of used algorithms on mobile devices, not on usability of the application because present version of the application was created purely for verification if detection algorithms would work correctly on mobile devices and which of them is the best to use in the full version of the application. Depending on the classification method, the detected harmful words could differ. Moreover the processing speed of detection is associated with the type of device used (virtual smartphone, budget smartphone or high-end smartphone) and the length of text.

There was no clear winner. Method A achieved much better results and could be advantageous due to its lack of need for Internet connection. However, due to its use of massive numbers of patterns it takes about ten times longer to process one sentence. On the other hand, Method B works faster, but needs constant Internet connection and achieves worse results. However, if the method itself is improved enough to match Method A, it could be advantageous, since Internet connection has become less a problem these days. Results of the experiments were summarized in Table 1.

CONCLUSION AND FUTURE WORK

In this Chapter we presented an Android application for detection of entries that contain humiliating and slandering other users, to mitigate the problem of cyberbullying – a growing problem especially in Internet environment, mostly due to the rapid development of mobile devices based on a connection with the Internet.

In the proposed application we applied two methods for cyberbullying detection. Both of them have proven themselves in their role, as described in previous Chapters. Main difference between them from the point of view of software development, was that Method B to work required an access to the Internet, while retaining a low need for computing power, while Method A, did not require Internet connection, although, needed a sufficient computing power. However, since future use of this application is inextricably linked with communication via the Internet, and each new generation of smartphones represents a major technological leap, both differences do not affect the usefulness of the methods and in result – for our application.

In the near future we have three main goals for further development of the proposed application. First is to check how we can improve the performance of cyberbullying detection by using another methods or by optimizing the existing ones – in particular for mobile devices. The second goal is to find the best way to implement our software to communication applications used via Internet, such as Facebook or Twitter, whilst retaining all safety and privacy policies. For this problem for now we have two possible solutions. One is to prepare a plugin for existing applications or create our own virtual keyboard for mobile devices. Finally, the last issue is expanding the scope of our potential users by creating versions of the application for other dominant mobile systems, e.g., iOS or Windows Phone.

REFERENCES

Android Developers. (n.d.). *Android*. Retrieved from: http://developer.android.com/

Kontostathis, A., Reynolds, K., Garron, A., & Edwards, L. (2013). Detecting Cyberbullying: Query Terms and Techniques. *Proceedings of the 5th ACM Web Science Conference (WEBSCI2013)*, 195-204. 10.1145/2464464.2464499

Masui, F., Ptaszynski, M., & Nitta, T. (2013). *Intānetto-jō no yūgai kakikomi kenshutsu sōchi oyobi kenshutsu hōhō* [Device and method for detection of harmful entries on the Internet] (in Japanese). Patent Application Number: 2013-245813, Patent Publication Number: 2015-103210, Patent Registration Number: 6301119. https://astamuse.com/ja/granted/JP/No/6301119.

Ptaszynski, M., Masui, F., Nitta, T., Hatakeyama, S., Kimura, Y., Rzepka, R., & Araki, K. (2016). Sustainable cyberbullying detection with category-maximized relevance of harmful phrases and double-filtered automatic optimization. *International Journal of Child-Computer Interaction*, *8*, 15–30. doi:10.1016/j.ijcci.2016.07.002

Ptaszynski, M., Rzepka, R., Araki, K., & Momouchi, Y. (2011). Language combinatorics: A sentence pattern extraction architecture based on combinatorial explosion. *International Journal of Computational Linguistics*, *2*(1), 24–36.

Turney, P. D. (2002). Thumbs Up or Thumbs Down? Semantic Orientation Applied to Unsupervised Classification of Reviews. *Proc. of the 40th Annual Meeting of the Association for Computational Linguistics*, 417-424.

Twitter. (2015). *Update on user safety features*. Retrieved from: https://blog.twitter.com/2015/update-on-user-safety-features

Chapter 8
Conclusion and Future Directions

ABSTRACT

In this chapter, the authors summarize the research performed so far on automatic cyberbullying detection, which was the topic of this book. They summarize all chapters of the book. Next, they propose a general discussion of the potential and limitations of technology-based methods for detecting and preventing cyberbullying. They also ask what the ethical boundaries are for such technology to operate in everyday life. Should we allow constant surveillance for the sake of safety? Should we limit the technology, thus taking away its true problem-solving potential to match our freedom of speech? Or is there a third way in which both the technology is used to meet its potential, while not taking away the feeling of freedom? Let questions which arise during this last chapter become guidelines for future research on automatic detection and mitigation of cyberbullying.

SUMMARY OF PREVIOUS CHAPTERS

In Chapter 1, we presented an introduction to this book. We explained the motivations that drove us in the research and described the outline of the whole book.

In Chapter 2, we presented the background for the research described in this book. We described the problem of cyberbullying in general, with specific references to its status quo in Japan. We also described some of the

DOI: 10.4018/978-1-5225-5249-9.ch008

most relevant previous research done in the field of automatic cyberbullying detection, and pointed out research gaps that we aimed to fill in by the introduction of this book.

In Chapter 3, we focused on datasets used in cyberbullying detection research. We described and compared several datasets applied in previous research and described in detail the dataset which we decided to apply in our research. We also performed an initial analysis of the dataset to find its various characteristics. We preprocessed the dataset in several ways for further use and performed affect analysis to find out whether emotion related features tend to be characteristic for cyberbullying. Based on the results of affect analysis we also performed an initial attempt to classify cyberbullying data using a simple machine learning approach, considered as one of the baselines in later chapters.

In Chapter 4, we presented a method for automatic detection of cyberbullying entries and sorting the detected entries according to their harmfulness. The method was based on a Web mining technique, in particular, on an extended SO-PMI-IR method calculating relevance of new input documents with training documents. The method used a small number of seed words from three categories to calculate semantic orientation score and then maximized the relevance of categories. The method outperformed previously proposed Web-mining-based methods in both laboratory and real world conditions. The developed system was further deployed and tested in practice. After a year of testing we noticed a major, drop (over 30 percent-points) in its performance. We hypothesized on the reasons for the drop. To regain the lost performance and sustain it in the future we proposed additional improvements including automatic acquisition and filtering of seed words. Experimentally selected optimal improvements regained large amount of the lost performance, although not all of it. This drove us to explore new methods independent of previous limitations.

In Chapter 5, we presented a novel method for automatic detection of cyberbullying, based on a combinatorial approach resembling brute force search algorithms, with application to language classification. The method automatically extracted sophisticated patterns from sentences and applied them in classification. The experiments performed on our cyberbullying dataset showed advantage of this method to previous methods, including the ones described in Chapter 4. We also discussed pros and cons of this novel method when compared to previous ones.

In Chapter 6, we presented our study in cyberbullying detection with the use of various traditional classifiers, including a Deep Learning approach. A number of research has tackled the problem of cyberbullying detection during recent years. However, due to complexity of language used in cyberbullying, the results obtained with traditional classifiers has remained only mildly satisfying. In this chapter we applied a number of traditional classifiers, used also in previous research, to obtain an objective view on to what extent each of them is suitable for the task. We also proposed an optimal novel classifier for automatic cyberbullying detection based on Convolutional Neural Networks and increased Feature Density. The experiments performed on our cyberbullying dataset showed a major advantage of the presented approach to all previous methods, including the two best performing methods so far: based on SO-PMI-IR and Brute-Force Search algorithm, presented in previous two Chapters.

In Chapter 7, we presented an application for Android smartphones to automatically detect possible harmful content in input text. The developed application was aimed to test in practice the performance of the developed cyberbullying detection methods, described in previous chapters. The final goal of the developed application is to help mitigate the problem of cyberbullying by quickly detecting possibly harmful contents in user's entry and warning the user of the possible negative influence. The test application was prepared to use one of two methods for detection of harmful messages: a method inspired by a brute force search algorithm applied to language modelling (Chapter 5), and a method using seed words from three categories to calculate semantic orientation score SO-PMI-IR and then maximizing the relevance of categories to specify harmfulness of a message (Chapter 4). First tests showed that both methods are working properly under the Android environment.

GENERAL DISCUSSION ON AUTOMATIC CYBERBULLYING DETECTION TOOLS

In this section we address some practical issues, regarding actual implementations of the developed methods presented in this book in a larger cyberbullying prevention environment. This includes not only the potential of such methods, but also limitations, as well as ethical issues regarding the use of such detection methods.

Potential and Limitations

Apart from the attempt to automatize the Internet Patrol process presented in this book, there have been a number of attempts to deal with cyberbullying with the use of Artificial Intelligence, Machine Learning, or Natural Language Processing techniques before. Some of the developed methods have been described in "Chapter 2: Background." Additionally, some of widely available software was described in "Chapter 7" (describing the cyberbullying blocker application). However, most of the presented research is still in a developmental phase and is yet to be applied in practice. Although there are differences in details how each of those methods work, the main function of such methods, including the one proposed in this book, is detecting cyberbullying entries in written text. Even assuming, that such a method would be able to detect cyberbullying entries with a perfect accuracy, which, as we could see in this book is not a trivial problem, this simple function alone would not be of any use if not applied in practice, in a wider milieu of solutions. Several examples of such possible practical applications have been listed below.

1. Automated Internet crawler for the use of Internet Patrol members to minimize their workload, and psychological burden.
2. Software for monitoring of one's own and other people's (friends, one's children) accounts to search for bullying-related contents.
3. Gamification-based solution, in which users are engaged in a simple social game, such as conversation with a group of peers and a non-playable character avatar, during which the users are made to deal with cyberbullying situations.
4. Policy-based implementation, where an Internet portal or SNS applies the method to automatically spot and inform the user that harmful contents were found in their online post.
5. Local solution for computers or mobile devices to detect and warn a user that the contents they have just typed contains harmful words or word patterns.

When it comes to the most straight-forward application, we develop our method for the use in solution I. However, potentially the method could be applied to any of the above-mentioned possible applications. As for the examples of the above solutions, we found the following software either in development or available for use already.

Application type 2. is realized by such software as **Samaritans Radar**. It was launched on 29th October 2014, by an organization focused on suicide prevention, called "Samaritans" (http://www.samaritans.org/). It was a free Internet application for Twitter, which helped users monitor their friends' Tweets. Main function of the application was alerting a user when the application spotted anyone in the user's online surroundings, who could be either bullied, depressed or sending disturbing suicidal signals. Unfortunately, due to serious data protection and privacy issues, which were noticed by the users, soon after the time of launch, the application was closed permanently on 10 March 2015, six months after its release.

Another example of this kind of software is **PocketGuardian**. It is a newly released (September 2015) software for parental monitoring, that "detects cyberbullying, sexting, and explicit images on children's mobile devices" (https://gopocketguardian.com/). By using machine learning techniques the software provides a statistical probability that the content (sentence, tweet, e-mail, or image) is inappropriate. An advantage of this software is that it focuses not only on textual content, but includes in its monitoring range the ability to detect explicit images. As for the disadvantage, the software is aimed at parents trying to monitor their children's mobile devices, which makes it important to address the questions regarding ethics of using such software and its influence on parent-child trust relationship.

Application type 3. is realized by such software as **FearNot!** (http://sourceforge.net/projects/fearnot/) (Hall et al. 2009). Its developers describe it as "an interactive drama/video game that teaches children strategies to prevent bullying and social exclusion." The software uses psychology-inspired character AI which engages with users and teaches them how to deal with cyberbullying situations in real life. Unfortunately, the development of the software has stopped in early 2013.

Another example of gamification-based approach to the problem is represented by the recently presented **StopBully** (http://www.di.fc.ul.pt/napc/StopBULLY/), a serious game developed by the Department of Informatics at the Faculty of Sciences of the University of Lisbon (Raminhos et al., 2015). The main goal of the game is to engage users in various real-life-like situations to teach them empathetic behaviors and through such positive behaviors prevent bullying in real life.

Application type 4. is represented by, for example, **the New Twitter Policy**. On February 26, 2015, Twitter changed its policy regarding safety and misbehavior among its users (https://blog.twitter.com/2015/update-on-user-safety-features), in which they allowed users to report particular tweets as harassment incidents. An account of a confirmed bully becomes locked and can be reopened only under the condition that the bully deletes her harmful tweets. This is not yet a software per se, and for the time being Twitter simply declared increasing the number of staff in their support team focused on handling abuse reports. However, they claim to plan applying automatic approaches in the future as well.

Application type 5. is realized by such software as **ReThink** (http://www.rethinkwords.com/). It is an application for smartphones, which shows a pop-up warning message when user tries to send a message containing harmful contents. Unfortunately, the algorithm for the detection of harmful contents in ReThink is based on simple keystroke logging and detecting vulgar and harmful words within the string of characters. This makes it inapplicable for more sophisticated contents, not including vulgar expressions. It also fails when user makes a mistake during writing and e.g., uses a backspace, since the "backspace" character is also recorded and hinders the detection of harmful words. Moreover using the keylogger function is also questionable. This way the software can track any kind of contents the user inputs on the keyboard, including personal information such as account names or passwords.

Another example of the software realizing application type 5. was some time ago patented by Masui et al. (2013, Patent Application No. 2013-245813, Patent Publication No. 2015-103210). In their approach the user is also informed about possible harmfulness of a message he or she has typed. However, differently to ReThink, Masui et al. (2013) do not use keylogger function, but rather allow the user to consciously type a message in a prepared user interface to verify its possible level of harmfulness. This patented approach was applied in the Android application described in Chapter 7 of this book.

The disadvantage of most of the above software is that in most cases the applications are based on the simplest methods (keylogging, simple pattern matching on words). Therefore, although being a good examples of a quick and ad-hoc response to the cyberbullying problem, their accuracy would be limited to simple, explicit cyberbullying examples. Therefore future research will need to combine the simplicity of the ad-hoc solutions with the depth of computational models, such as the ones proposed in this book.

Finally, the limitations of all of the software mentioned above and methods described in Chapters 2 to 7 is the fact that text classification approaches would not be able to deal with other typical features of cyberbullying, such as online ostracism, impersonation (personality theft by taking over one's account) or "outing" (revealing a person's private information and secrets). Dealing with those features will require an analysis of a much wider context, than one input sentence, or even a set of text entries. For example, the system would need to have access to user's secrets to distinguish whether the "outed" information would be in fact harmful for the user. It would also need to have a constant access to the user's contacts and monitor all online behavior. It is possible that dealing with all those issues would be difficult, or even impossible from the point of view of actual real-life application, as it would be too dangerous for one software to be granted that large set of privileges.

Ethical Issues

Regardless of the technological side of the developed system, when it comes to a problem of such a weight as cyberbullying, one must always take into account ethical implications resulting from the proposed solution. Below we briefly summarize potential ethical issues which could appear for each of the types of applications described in the above section.

Type 1 application implies that the software will be used by an expert, such as an Internet Patrol member. This makes it a safe approach because the final decision on whether the detected contents is malicious or not will be made by a trained human.

Presumably, the most dubious kind of application is type 2.), where the system is allowed to monitor the user's behavior and their online environment in the search for cyberbullying-related contents. Privacy issues which result from such an approach have been serious enough to make one of the applications (Samaritans Radar) close shortly after its launch.

Gamification (type 3.), when realized in its basic form also does not indicate much ethical issues. Some issues, apart from those like user account management, could arise when the game in which the user participates is not monitored by an expert, but the user is rather left alone with the game contents.

Policy based applications are presumably the most difficult to estimate. On the one hand, when the service in question (such as Twitter) introduces a new policy top down, the users are always informed about the changes and are (or at least should be) given the choice to either continue using the service, or disagree with the new policy and stop using it. On the other hand, when a large corporation, such as Facebook or Twitter, introduces a new policy with which the users do not agree, such as forced advertisements which exploit the user account information for providing directed ads, the users, who have been using Facebook for several years and have a developed friend network, would in practice most probably be forced to tolerate the new policy.

Finally, when it comes to local solutions, it seems that ethical issues emerge depending on the way of application. For example, using a keylogger function, which in practice keeps record of all of the user's behavior, including various account names and passwords, could be considered equally or even more malicious than the second approach. However, when the analysis of the input is performed after the user's agreement, such a solution could become a useful one. Moreover, the application can be programmed to ignore fields tagged as "password" or "user ID," etc.

OVERALL CONCLUSION

In this book we presented our nearly ten year-long research on automatic detection of cyberbullying, a social problem that, although existed on the Internet for a long time, only recently has started to be considered a serious social problem. The problem of cyberbullying has also recently became more visible, together with the rapid development of social networking services, such as Facebook, Twitter, etc.

Activities described as cyberbullying consist of sending messages which contain slanderous expressions harmful for other people, or verbally bullying other people in front of the rest of online community. Cyberbullying influences mental health of Internet users, and might lead to self-mutilation and even suicide of its victims.

In Japanese society, on which we focused in particular, this problem is particularly vivid on unofficial school Web sites. To handle the problem, school teachers and members of Parent-Teacher Associations (PTA) perform voluntarily Internet Patrol to spot and delete online entries harmful for other people. Unfortunately, there is already an enormous number of cyberbullying cases and the number keeps growing, which makes the Internet Patrol an uphill task when performed manually.

One of the main goals of this study was to create a tool for the support of Internet Patrol members, with a final application in the form of an artificial Internet Patrol agent. To fulfill this task, at first we obtained a dataset of Internet entries containing cyberbullying, collected by actual Internet Patrol members, and provided to us by one of the Human Right Centers in Japan.

While looking for clues to select linguistic features to be used in machine learning algorithm, we analyzed the dataset with the use of affect analysis techniques. We noticed that **harmful entries were less emotively emphasized than non-harmful**, presumably due to the fact that harmful entries are typically written with premeditation and aim not in expressing one's own emotions, but in evoking in other users negative emotions. Moreover, **expressions of positive emotions were often used in sarcastic meaning**. For the first step of the research, we were able to specify that **the most distinctive linguistic feature for cyberbullying were vulgar expressions**. We used this feature in the creation of machine learning classifier for cyberbullying detection.

The initial machine learning-based method for cyberbullying detection faced a series of problems, such as jargonization, or different spelling used to transcribe many words, including vulgar expressions. We found out that **to deal with various spelling variations, calculating word similarity with Levenshtein distance with a few heuristic rules was greatly effective**. Unfortunately, since new vulgar words appear frequently, there is a constant **need to automatically obtain new vulgarities from the Internet to keep the lexicon up to date**. Next, to rank online entries according to their harmfulness at first we used T-score, which unfortunately, occurred biased and not ideal.

To improve the method for ranking Internet entries according to their harmfulness, we proposed a method of maximization of category relevance of an Internet entry with typical cyberbullying entries found on the Internet. Since the experiments showed encouraging results (over 90% of Precision), we deployed and tested the system for over a year in practice. **Re-evaluation of this Web-mining based method after a year revealed a sudden drop in performance (over 30% points)**. The loss could be caused by several factors, including tightening of usage policies by many Internet services. To deal with this problem we tried to obtain harmful seed words automatically. The results clearly showed that **simply adding more harmful words to the original method was not effective**. The proposed **seed word filtering method was significantly effective, although did not reach the original performance**.

In an attempt to retrieve the lost performance we applied a combinatorial algorithm, resembling brute force search algorithms, to extract sophisticated sentence patterns and used those patterns in classification of cyberbullying entries. We found out that features consisting of word **lemmas with part-of-speech information were the most successful**. Apart from achieving much better performance, the proposed method, based on **combinatorial approach to language modeling was also more efficient as it required minimal human effort**.

We also proposed a Deep Learning approach to the problem, based on Convolutional Neural Networks (CNN). **The proposed CNN model successfully outperformed other classifiers, but also revealed an unusual characteristics, by positively correlating with Feature Density**. Moreover,

Named Entity Recognition always improved CNN performance for cyberbullying detection.

As the final step of the research presented in this book, we presented an Android application for testing cyberbullying detection methods. In the initial experiments with the application we successfully tested two previously developed methods (Web-ming-based and combinatorics-based). Both methods showed satisfying performance under the Android environment.

The technology-backed computational methods, and software for detection and mitigation of cyberbullying have sprouted in recent years. It has been nearly ten years since the first paper in English on cyberbullying detection with the use of AI methods has been published (see Ptaszynski et al., 2010a). Since that we have gathered substantial knowledge about both the problem of cyberbullying, as well as ways to deal with it. The problem cannot be fully mitigated with only technological developments. As many indicate the best way to sufficiently deal with the problem is through emotional education of young people–technology users, usually digital natives, and promotion of positive and healthy behaviors while online (Pyzalski, 2012; Lazuras et al., 2012). We understand the limitations of technology in the mitigation of the problem of cyberbullying. We also recognize its potential. The uphill task done by Internet Patrol members can be sufficiently reduced with the support of automatic detection of the most potentially harmful messages. Many harmful messages can be prevented just by alerting a user of the negative character of their message, and messages already sent can be automatically detected, flagged, and deleted after an effective reaction of other users. Reporting must also be effectively introduced and executed based on an appropriate policy of Internet services.

Only all these measures, when working together in one healthy environment can effectively contribute to significant decrease or perhaps even eradication of cyberbullying from online life. Much of our life today is spent on the Internet. We cannot live without it, therefore we have the obligation to make it more comfortable for ourselves and other users. This book does not provide all, neither perhaps the best answers to how to do that. But we, the authors, believe it is a step in a good direction and hope our findings will become useful to other researchers.

FUTURE DIRECTIONS

Development of technology is never a fully finished process. There is always room for improvement and one problem solved usually brings up a few new problems more to solve. In our ten-year-long journey of developing the technology for the detection and mitigation of cyberbullying we have come across and solved or contributed to solving a number problems. A good example is the Web mining method for ranking Internet entries according to their harmfulness (Chapter 4), which, although improved the original T-score based ranking (Chapter 3), eventually lost much of its performance due to external factors. This then lead us to turning to more stable and robust solutions (Chapters 5 and 6).

The research described in this book also urges a number of steps to be taken in the near future. Firstly, we plan to improve the method for automatic extraction and updating of harmful phrase dictionary. We plan to expand the dictionary and include in it not only single words, or two-word phrases, but also more sophisticated combinatorial patterns.

Furthermore, by continuous testing of the proposed methods in practice we plan to semiautomatically collect additional datasets, and determine the optimal harmful threshold automatically by using other machine learning methods than applied so far.

We also plan to repeat the experiments by Ishisaka et al. (2011) to eliminate any potential ambiguities in human judgments about the harmfulness of words. We will also apply the proposed optimization method (Chapter 4) to other Web-mining based tasks and verify its potential and limitations in improving such methods in general.

As the general performance of the method for automatic cyberbullying detection has reached its plateau, we will implement the proposed method (or methods) as a part of a working solution for cyberbullying prevention. Technology alone cannot deal with the whole spectrum of cyberbullying, such as ostracism, impersonation or outing. And even if it was able to detect those by sacrificing user's privacy, it would not be able to solve the problem. A thorough solution would necessarily need to include human experts, such as psychologists and educators to help both cyberbullying victims and those who become bullies by choice or by chance. Only then, a software program combined with a well-planned social program would bring the desirable effects and contribute to solving the problem of cyberbullying.

For the nearest future we have two paths of further development. Firstly, to improve the detection method itself, we plan to apply different ways of dataset preprocessing to find out whether the performance can be further improved and to what extent. We have found out that too few highly generalized features (such as parts-of-speech alone) resulting in very low Feature Density (FD), cause similarly low results. However, although too much of over-specific features (sentence chunks with dependency relations, or chunks with applied named entity recognition) resulting in very high Feature Density, cause low results for most of the classifiers, they seem to improve the performance of Deep Convolutional Neural Networks. On the other hand, most classifiers achieve their highest scores with feature sets that are to some extent generalized but also plentiful (e.g., lemmas with POS) resulting in not-too-high and not-too-low FD. It could be useful to pursue this path to find out optimal FD for the applied dataset, for the proposed methods in general, but also for other datasets, both cyberbullying-related and other – to find out whether Feature Density can predict and to what extent the performance of each applied classifier.

As for the second path for further development, we have three main goals for the improvement of the developed smartphone application. First is to check how we can improve the performance of detection of harmful words by using another methods or by optimizing the existing ones – in particular for mobile devices. The second goal is to find the best way to implement our software to communication applications used via Internet, such as Facebook or Twitter, whilst retaining all safety and privacy policies. For this problem for now we have two possible solutions: to prepare a plugin for existing applications or create a virtual keyboard for mobile devices. Finally, the last issue is expanding the scope of our potential users by creating version of the application for other dominant mobile systems, e.g., iOS or WindowsPhone.

The problems related to online security have been escalating ever since the birth of the Internet. Some of them are widely known to the society, such as spam e-mails or hacking, however more and more of such problems, including cyberbullying, appear by the day and social awareness about them is not yet sufficient. There have been developed solutions for some of these problems (e.g., automatic spam e-mail detection, firewall protection, etc.), while others, like cyberbullying, only keep escalating. Recognizing such problems and developing the remedy is an urgent matter and is desirable to come into focus of Artificial Intelligence research in the near future.

REFERENCES

Hall, L., Jones, S., Paiva, A., & Aylett, R. (2009). FearNot! providing children with strategies to cope with bullying. In *Proceedings of the 8th International Conference on Interaction Design and Children (IDC '09)*. ACM. 10.1145/1551788.1551854

Ishisaka, T., & Yamamoto, K. (2011). Automatic detection of sentences representing slandering on the Web. *The 17th Annual Meeting of the Association for Natural Language Processing*, 131-134. (in Japanese)

Lazuras, L., Pyżalski, J., Barkoukis, V., & Tsorbazoudis, H. (2012). Empathy and Moral Disengagement in Adolescent Cyberbullying: Implications for Educational Intervention and Pedagogical Practice. *Studia Edukacyjne, 23*, 57-69.

Masui, F., Ptaszynski, M., & Nitta, T. (2013). *Intānetto-jō no yūgai kakikomi kenshutsu sōchi oyobi kenshutsu hōhō* [Device and method for detection of harmful entries on the Internet]. Patent Application Number: 2013-245813.

Ptaszynski, M., Dybala, P., Matsuba, T., Masui, F., Rzepka, R., & Araki, K. (2010a). Machine Learning and Affect Analysis Against Cyber-Bullying. In *Proceedings of The Thirty Sixth Annual Convention of the Society for the Study of Artificial Intelligence and Simulation of Behaviour (AISB-10)*. De Montfort University.

Ptaszynski, M., Dybala, P., Matsuba, T., Masui, F., Rzepka, R., Araki, K., & Momouchi, Y. (2010b). In the Service of Online Order: Tackling Cyber-Bullying with Machine Learning and Affect Analysis. *International Journal of Computational Linguistics Research, 1*(3), 135–154.

Pyżalski, J. (2012). From cyberbullying to electronic aggression: Typology of the phenomenon. *Emotional & Behavioural Difficulties, 17*(3-4), 305–317. doi:10.1080/13632752.2012.704319

Raminhos, C., Cláudio, A. P., Carmo, M. B., Carvalhosa, S., de Jesus Candeias, M., & Gaspar, M. (2015). A serious game based solution to prevent bullying. *Proceedings of the 13th International Conference on Advances in Mobile Computing and Multimedia*. 10.1145/2837126.2837135

About the Authors

Michal E. Ptaszynski was born in Wroclaw, Poland in 1981. He received the MA from the University of Adam Mickiewicz, Poznan, Poland, in 2006 in Japanese Studies / Linguistics. In year 2007 he joined Graduate School of Information Science and Technology, Hokkaido University, Japan, for his Ph.D. course, which he finished and earned his Ph.D. degree in 2010. In years 2010-2012 he was a JSPS Post-doctoral Research Fellow at the High-Tech Research Center, Hokkai-Gakuen University, Japan. Since 2013 to march 2018, Michal Ptaszynski was an Assistant Professor at Kitami Institute of Technology. Currently he is an Associate Professor at Kitami Institute of Technology. His research interests cross over linguistics, AI and psychology, and include such fields as natural language processing, information retrieval, human-computer interaction, science of emotions, affective computing, affect analysis, sentiment analysis, or science of emoticons. He is an author of over a hundred refereed scientific publications, with over one third of them being published in world class scientific journals. Some of the most important contributions of Michal Ptaszynski to the scientific community include: founding the field of science of emoticons, developing the first open-source affect analysis software for Japanese language, or creating a method for verification of contextual appropriateness of emotions. Together with Fumito Masui he also made the historically first attempt to tackle cyberbullying with the use of artificial intelligence, machine learning and natural language processing, which started a long-term study, concluding in the presented book. Michal E. Ptaszynski is a member of the following academic societies: The Association for Computational Linguistics (ACL), The Association for the Advancement of Artificial Intelligence (AAAI), The Institute of Electrical and Electronics Engineers (IEEE), The Association for Natural Language Processing (ANLP), The Information Processing Society of Japan (IPSJ), and The Japanese Society for Artificial Intelligence (JSAI).

Fumito Masui graduated Okayama University Faculty of Science in 1990. Later, worked at Oki Electric Industry Co., was an Assistant at Mie University Faculty of Engineering, and a Visiting Researcher at Graduate School of Information Science and Technology, Hokkaido University, in 2004. Since 2009 he has been an Associate Professor at Kitami Institute of Technology, Faculty of Engineering. He owns a Ph.D. in Engineering. He is an author of over three hundred publications and owns sixteen patents. His main contributions to the scientific community include creating a first named entity extraction tool for Japanese, founding the fields of automatic cyberbullying detection, and curling informatics. His research interests include natural language processing, tourism informatics, and curling informatics. Fumito Masui is a member of the following academic societies: The Association for the Advancement of Artificial Intelligence (AAAI); The Institute of Electrical and Electronics Engineers (IEEE); The Association for Natural Language Processing (ANLP); The Information Processing Society of Japan (IPSJ); The Japanese Society for Artificial Intelligence (JSAI); Institute of Electronics, Information, and Communication Engineers; Society for Fuzzy Theory and Intelligent Informatics (SOFT); Hokkaido Regional Tourism Society; and Japan Curling Association.

Index

I

K

L

M

N

O

P

R

S

T

U

V

W

Y

www.ingramcontent.com/pod-product-compliance
Lightning Source LLC
LaVergne TN
LVHW062124200926
848484LV00007B/1761